To Ari

S_{3a}^{3-}

5/32.

THE FUTURE OF THE LAW

By the same author

INTRODUCTION TO BRITISH CONSTITUTIONAL LAW

A SOURCE BOOK OF ENGLISH ADMINISTRATIVE LAW

THE
FUTURE OF
THE LAW

BY

D. C. M. YARDLEY

LONDON: THE CRESSET PRESS

!ade and printed in Great Britain by
The Garden City Press Limited
Letchworth, Hertfordshire

To those sturdy representatives of the generation of the future,
Adrian, Heather, Briony and Alistair.

Preface

In this book I have attempted to sketch a general view of possible future developments in English law. I have tried to avoid the great technical areas of law, such as company law, patents, copyright and taxation, mainly because they are very complicated and unlikely to be of interest to the general reader. As a matter of policy I have decided to restrict the subjects discussed to those matters which, in the main, are likely to affect ordinary citizens. Accordingly, as a single example, little is said, beyond a short passage in Chapter One, about the highly complicated and uncertain problems concerning any possible future entry of the United Kingdom to the Common Market, an event which may (though by no means necessarily will) affect the practice of the present supreme legislative authority of Parliament, if it should ever come about. Instead I have concentrated upon such central subjects as criminal law and punishment, the basic topics of civil law, contracts and torts, family law, constitutional and administrative law, planning law, and the system of courts and the legal profession. These are fundamental subjects, and of interest to a great many laymen, as well as to lawyers, but it would be impossible to be comprehensive in a book of this kind. The reader must forgive me, therefore, if I dwell upon the problems which interest *me*, to the exclusion of some others which may well be of equal importance.

Although the book is mainly about English law, I have attempted where it seems appropriate to draw parallels from and analogies with the systems of other countries, for comparative study is of particular value when thinking in terms of law reform. It is always a mistake to assume that our own system must be better than others, and if this book disabuses some people of the notion that English law must automatically be the best system of law in the world it will have served at least some purpose. In many ways English law is healthy, and ahead of its cousins elsewhere, but complacency is the enemy of progress. Some of my forecasts of future changes in the law may in the course of time prove to be incorrect, but that is a fate which must to some extent befall anyone who attempts to look into the as yet unknown. Other developments, as for example those discussed in the chapter on punishment, may in broad principle be inevitable.

Many sources have been tapped in compiling the material for this book, and I have benefited from conversations with several colleagues. But as the volume is intended primarily for the general reader I have purposely not quoted any detailed references in footnotes. In any event, the book is intended neither as a textbook upon the law as it stands nor as a compendium of the views of other people upon it. It is essentially a statement of my own assessment of the likely developments within the framework of law, and it is presented in the hope that it will provide stimulus for further thought. It is on this basis that the volume must stand or fall. A few of my ideas, as for example on planning law, have already been expressed elsewhere in various published articles, though their presentation is rather different and less technical here. On capital punishment my views have undergone a change since I published an essay on the subject in 1961. But most of my views put forward here have not previously been printed.

D.C.M.Y.

St. Edmund Hall, Oxford.
November 21st, 1963.

Table of Contents

Table of Contents

THE FUTURE OF THE LAW

CHAPTER ONE

The Background

THE GROWTH OF DIFFERENT LEGAL SYSTEMS

IT is very difficult to conceive of any nation which is without its system of law. Anarchy may be favoured by a few always, and by influential groups, even occasionally by the majority, in a single country for a limited period of time; but the fact remains that no society can continue to exist as such without some form of rules and regulations to govern the everyday activities of, and relations between, the members of that society. 'Jungle law' provides an antithesis to nationhood, and so, from the earliest beginnings of organised societies in the world, genuine law, however individually defective it may have been, has existed. It might be tempting to suppose that with the historical progress towards our modern form of civilisation separate national laws would have become unified, but human nature and the proud, even insular, habits of the citizens of different countries have prevented this from taking place. The laws of different nations have, however, influenced each other, sometimes to a very marked extent, and it is proposed to consider here briefly the kinds of influences which have been at work.

Most national laws grew, as one would have expected, out of tribal customs, and the customs of one tribe would probably bear no relation at all to those of another tribe, save that they would be bound to have to cover in some way the same sort of problems. For example, each tribe would doubtless have to settle for itself in some way its marriage customs and its rules as to ownership of property. Tribe A might decide to favour monogamy, Tribe B polygamy, and Tribe C perhaps free love! Tribe A might also decide that each man should be entitled to own two cows, Tribe B that each man might own a certain area of land, while Tribe C would perhaps prescribe some form of community of property. In any of these events it must also follow that some kind of rules would have to be evolved to cover the possibilities of wife-stealing, trespass on land, and so forth, though sometimes such rules might prove in practice to be largely ineffective. In such ways different laws, when they grew up, were bound to differ in content and effectiveness, and countries which found their own laws unsatisfactory for certain purposes would be likely to cast envious eyes upon their neighbours' more desirable laws.

English law as we know it today is descended from Germanic customs brought over to these islands by the Anglo-Saxons after the departure of the Roman invaders in the fifth century A.D. It seems that the laws of the Ancient Britons, such as they were, and of the Romans during their occupation of Britain were more or less wholly superseded by the laws implanted by the Anglo-Saxons. Though very primitive in many respects this Germanic law has enjoyed a period of some fifteen hundred years' continuous development in England. The various localities of England, the shires, hundreds and vills (to take a descending order of size) possessed their own individual variations of this law, and it was not until the middle ages that the law of England was welded into a single body of rules. This latter result was achieved largely through the work of King Henry II, who reigned from 1154 to 1189, and who was a man of considerable legal talent, and of the growing body of judges and jurists who supported the efforts of the Plantagenet kings to obtain a coherent system of law running throughout the whole kingdom, thus enforcing the 'king's peace' and cementing the power of the throne over the great nobles of the land. The customary laws of most of the other countries of Europe, however, were either supplanted or at least rationalised by the spread of Roman law in the period of the Renaissance. It has been said that 'Rome conquered the world three times—by her arms, by her religion and by her law'. It is perhaps necessary, therefore, to say a few words about this infiltration of Roman law.

Like all other systems of law, Roman law originated from ancient customs. But it was the first national system of law ever to be rationalised and codified. Rome was founded, traditionally, in the year 753 B.C., and Roman society soon resolved itself into an organised group of interrelated families. At first a monarchy, and then, from 509 B.C., a republic, the state became an empire in the year 27 B.C. The first code of Roman law, known as The Twelve Tables, appeared in about 450 B.C., though this was supplemented by direct legislation. But the classical codification of Roman law was undertaken by the Emperor Justinian, who reigned from A.D. 527 to 565, a thousand years later, and it is the Roman law as laid down in Justinian's time which has to this day been regarded as the classical Roman law. After the reign of Justinian, the study of Roman law declined, partly because of the turbulent times which succeeded him, and the eventual final break-up of the Roman empire in any real sense of the phrase, and partly because many jurists were permitted to provide glosses, often loose and inaccurate, or even contradictory, upon the rules which had been so highly organised under Justinian. With the coming of the middle ages, however, the time was ripe for a revival of systematic law study. Many countries were growing out of their long periods of chaos, and in their efforts to systematise their laws they turned to the one great code of the Roman law of Justinian as a means of guiding their reforms. Thus it was that as the Renaissance spread through Europe it carried with it the study of classical Roman law. In many countries, including Germany, which had been the source of English law, Roman law largely replaced the indigenous systems of law; in others, such as France, it was combined with customary law to provide a more modern and all-embracing system. It has been said that with the single exception of Christianity nothing has had a greater influence in moulding or determining our Western civilisation than Roman law. Scotland, which was a traditional enemy of England until James VI of Scotland became James I of England in 1603, and which even then was not unified with England for another hundred years, received the study of Roman law, along with the other aspects of the Renaissance,

3

which do not concern us here. This development in Scotland was natural enough, as she was politically very closely allied with France. But Roman law never gained a real foothold south of the border.

It is difficult to understand why England, though as much affected by other aspects of the Renaissance as other European countries, never received Roman law, but several possible reasons can be put forward. In the first place, as will be seen presently, the English lawyers had early established a method of comprehensive education in the English legal system for intending English lawyers. This, combined with the work of such jurists as Henry II in seeking to provide a law which would be uniform throughout the whole country, had tended to give English law a homogeneity which none of the more primitive laws of the other European countries could rival before the Renaissance. Secondly, the king, once he had established a national law, had a vested interest in maintaining it more or less as it stood, because it provided for the pre-eminence of the Crown. Thirdly, at the time when it seemed most likely historically that Roman law should gain a grip upon England, namely the fourteenth and fifteenth centuries, the Hundred Years War was taking place. This naturally engendered a national feeling of enmity for things French or continental, and as Roman law had come to be firmly embedded in Europe generally, and France in particular, and even in England's old enemy Scotland, it is possible that the doors of England were closed to Roman law at that time for purely political reasons. At all events it can now be said that Roman law, which had swept through Europe, and which is still the basis of most of the legal systems of European countries, except for those in Scandinavia, passed England by.

The result has been that the countries of the world today can mostly be split into those which have legal systems based upon Roman law, and those which have systems based upon English law, or, as it is more generally called, 'common law'. Broadly speaking, most of Europe, Latin America, and even certain Asian countries, such as Japan, have systems based upon Roman law, and these systems are generally known as 'civil law' systems. On the other hand common law, which has remained in England itself, has also spread to most of the countries of the Commonwealth, as well as to the United States of America and such other countries outside the Commonwealth as had previously a firm link with this country, such as the Republic of Ireland and the Sudan. Generalisation is, however, dangerous, and the variations in actual legal rules between the countries with laws based upon similar systems may well be great. Furthermore, there are a number of countries which have mixed or hybrid systems of law, in that their modern rules are derived partly from common law and partly from civil law. Such countries include Malta, the Channel Islands, South Africa, Southern Rhodesia, Ceylon, the province of Quebec in Canada, the state of Louisiana in the U.S.A., Mauritius and the Seychelles, but again it is difficult to know where to draw the line. In one sense Scotland has laws based upon Roman law, but in another it has a hybrid system in that there has been undoubted influence upon Scots law, particularly in the present century, from England. There have even been some influences the other way, such as where Parliament introduced into England the defence of diminished responsibility to a charge of murder by borrowing it from the Scots law and imposing it in England by means of the Homicide Act, 1957.

Today nothing really hangs upon whether a legal system is derived historically from Roman law or English law. But what is significant is that the codifying habits of the Romans have been bequeathed to their successors in countries possessing civil law systems, and here lies the practical distinction between the two main bodies of law. Countries which received Roman law have also usually later codified their law. This was probably inevitable, because the importation of a new system of law to replace or to cleanse the old must involve a great deal of legislation, and if this legislation can be accomplished by means of a single comprehensive document then so much the better. In England and in those countries which, by colonisation or by close relationship, possess a common law system there has never been the urgent need to codify the law in a similar way. Thus English law today is still basically the law found from the decisions of the judges through the ages in individual cases resulting from litigation or prosecution. This law is supplemented by Acts of Parliament which have the power to alter the original case law, and in countries like the United States of America it has been found necessary to enact written constitutional documents, but the body of the law is still basically provided by the decisions of the judges upon issues which have happened to arise before them. In a codified system the courts are bound to apply the provisions of the code, and the code alone binds the courts in every individual case; but in the English system the decisions of the judges themselves provide the precedents upon which later decisions will be based. More will be said presently about this system of precedent in the common law.

COMPARATIVE LAW

From the above sketch it can be seen that the relationships between many of the legal systems of the world may be quite close. It is not surprising, therefore, to find that they may still today influence each other in their development. In a number of Commonwealth countries it is common practice for the courts to rely upon English precedents if their own are lacking, and it is becoming increasingly common for Commonwealth precedents to be quoted in the English courts, either as persuasive precedents in cases of doubt, or else, less commonly, where no English precedents exist. It is obvious, of course, that a lack of precedents upon any particular point will be less likely in England than in any of the younger Commonwealth countries. In the past centuries it was practically unknown for an English court to consider the decisions of what were then colonial courts, but the growth of the two-way traffic in precedents in the present century has been a striking feature of legal development. To quote but one example of a quite common type of precedent considered in the English courts, it might not be unfair to single out the decisions of the High Court of Australia, which are regarded with the greatest possible respect throughout the common law world. The influence of civil law systems upon each other can also be seen by studying legal developments upon the continent, and the interaction of civil and common law systems has taken place through the agency of the mixed systems of law. Nor is the influence of one system upon another merely by way of imitation, for the lawyers and law reformers of various countries are not infrequently studying the laws of other countries with a view to finding advantages in the systems studied which can be consciously imported into their own systems. It is significant that early in 1963 the Wolfson Foundation made a grant of £5,000 for two years to meet the initial expenses of a Commonwealth Legal Advisory Service, initiated in 1962, which seeks to keep Commonwealth countries informed as to developments in other parts of the Commonwealth which may be of interest to them in their plans for law reform, and to send experts to territories which may request their services.

In recent years conscious efforts have been made by English lawyers to gain an insight into the laws of the Common Market countries, for it was felt that if the United Kingdom should enter the Common Market it would probably be necessary to alter some of our laws to conform to continental practice and rules. The breakdown of the Common Market negotiations has resulted in a set-back to such study, though some efforts are being made to see whether our laws tally reasonably with those of the other members of the European Free Trade Association, of which the United Kingdom is a member. If the United Kingdom does in the course of time become more closely associated with other European countries, it is almost inevitable that some changes in our laws will come about, particularly upon such subjects as restrictive trade practices and monopolies, and it can equally be stated that the continental countries involved will have to make a careful study of the common law system. Other common law countries are also actively interested in the laws of civil law countries, and it may be speculated that the influence upon each other of the civil law in Quebec and the common law throughout the rest of Canada, or of the civil law in Louisiana and the common law in the remainder of the United States, has already been profound. An interesting development in New Zealand in 1962 was the creation by an Act of the New Zealand Parliament of the office of a Parliamentary Commissioner, whose powers and duties (in connection with the investigation of grievances against the administration) are directly modelled upon a similar official in Denmark, although Denmark is a country with a legal system which is basically neither common nor civil law. As will be seen in Chapter Six of this book, a number of lawyers in England have also been pressing for the institution of such an office here. At all events it seems that the legal systems of the world continue to grow closer together in a number of ways.

This trend is bound to be more pronounced in some fields of law than in others. The mercantile laws of most countries have been similar in essence since the early middle ages. When Italy was the centre of the known world, and England was on its edge, trade was, as now, the most important occupation of the inhabitants of the countries of that world, and the traders were, as now, the most important group of people in the community. In the middle ages these traders and merchants not only provided the basis for national wealth, but they also maintained their own courts in which they dealt with such disputes as should arise among themselves according to the laws which they themselves laid down. Trade was, as ever, international, and the merchants were therefore the means of introducing into the world an early form of international law. By the end of the middle ages many national courts and systems were absorbing the laws and courts of their merchants, a process which was started in England in the early seventeenth century and completed during the eighteenth. But the foundations of the mercantile laws of the European nations had been so securely laid that the national mercantile laws today are still very similar. It is perhaps not insignificant that at the time of the recent Common Market negotiations much of the study of laws that took place was concerned with settling methods of ironing out the differences which had been grafted on to the laws concerned with the national economies since the middle ages when those laws had been so similar. In sum, it may be suggested that mercantile laws have always been close, and may be expected to become closer still during this century, while certain other national laws, such as criminal law and court procedure, although covering broadly the same ground in each country, will always maintain their individual peculiarities. There can be no good reason why continental advocates should ever adopt the English wigs and gowns. Again, though the laws of England and America both provide that rape is a crime, there is no good reason why England should ever follow the example of some of the American states in providing that adultery or fornication should also be criminal offences, though there may be more point in suggesting that those same states might profit by a study of the English rules and their limits.

ENGLISH LEGAL EDUCATION

As has been seen above, the early period of the Renaissance carried with it a revival of Roman law studies, and it was natural that these studies should have been carried on particularly in the universities of Europe. A Law School was founded at Bologna about the year 1100, and in the course of the twelfth century law teaching spread to the universities at Paris, Montpellier and Oxford. Perhaps the most interesting fact about the rise of law teaching at Oxford was that it was confined, as at the other European universities, to Roman law. Thus it is necessary to qualify what has been said already about the failure of Roman law to gain a foothold in England by the exception created by university law teaching. Yet this exception never proved to be of any very great significance for a reason peculiar to England, namely the fact that university law teaching has never played any great part in the training of practising lawyers or judges. This is a remarkable fact, and it has always divided off the system of legal education prevailing in England from the various methods adopted in civil law countries, where university law training has for centuries been intimately connected with the education of men in the laws of the countries concerned to prepare them for future legal practice. The peculiarity of the English system of legal education has even separated us from the majority of other common law countries, which in other respects have inherited the principles underlying

9

English law. In countries such as the United States, Canada, and even the new African countries of the Commonwealth, the basis of preparation for law practice is a university law school education, followed by separate professional examinations which are mostly based upon the courses taken at the universities. In the case of the citizens of British dependencies legal education has in the past been provided by courses and examinations organised by the Council of Legal Education in London, which will be mentioned below, and these facilities are still used by several of the recently independent member nations of the Commonwealth. But the tendency now is for new full members of the Commonwealth to provide home-grown legal education based upon their own universities and law schools, and this process will doubtless continue in the future.

The peculiarity of the English system of legal education stems from the fact that practising lawyers and judges established their own legal university in London very early in the middle ages, at the Inns of Court. Nobody can be quite certain when the Inns originated, but they were in operation in the twelfth and thirteenth centuries. In these Inns the lawyers developed the practice of meeting to regulate their own professional affairs, including their standards of professional etiquette, and they may be said to have formed an early example of the 'closed shop' principle. It was soon established that no one might practise in any of the courts of common law unless he should be a member of one or other of the Inns (though certain special tribunals, outside the ordinary system of English law, such as the ecclesiastical courts, were open for practise to non-members); and no one could become a practising member of an Inn unless he had gone through the process of lectures, fictitious case arguments and so on, provided by the Inn, and then been admitted as a barrister to practise at the 'Bar'. Naturally the law taught at the Inns was the ordinary English common law, and, granted this rigid and emphatic system of entry to and maintenance of 'the Bar', there was no room left for the universities to play a part in preparation of future members of the Bar. For this reason there was little point in English universities even attempting to teach English law, and it is a somewhat surprising fact that, though law has always been taught at Oxford since the twelfth century, and at Cambridge since its inception as a university two or three hundred years later, that law was exclusively Roman law until as late as the middle of the eighteenth century. Some practising lawyers had previously attended either Oxford or Cambridge, but before being able to practise at the Bar they always had to go through a period of English legal education at the Inns of Court. Men trained exclusively in Roman law were only able to practise in the ecclesiastical courts and a few other exceptional tribunals.

This method of professional legal training has persisted to the present day. Though the smaller Inns of Court have died out, four large ones have remained, Lincoln's Inn, the Middle Temple, the Inner Temple and Gray's Inn. For purposes of instruction and examination of students they have formed a combined body, known as the Council of Legal Education, which has premises very near the Law Courts in the Strand, London. It is no longer compulsory for any student to attend the courses organised by the Council, though many of the students from overseas particularly do in fact do so; but no student may become a barrister without passing the examinations set by the Council. Furthermore, a relic of the old days of residential students is the requirement that each student member must fulfil an obligation to 'keep term' at his Inn by eating a certain small number of dinners there in the course of each 'dining term', such terms taking place four times a year, for about a month each. The special tribunals in which non-common lawyers were able to practise have now for the most part died out, and this has left the common lawyers with a virtual monopoly over argument in court, save that litigants are permitted to argue their own cases, if they should so wish, without legal assistance.

Over the past few centuries there has been a split in the legal profession into two gradually resolved but definite branches, the barristers, still organised through the Inns of Court, and the solicitors. In general it might be said that the difference between the two groups of lawyers is similar to the difference between general practitioners and specialists in medicine and surgery.

The solicitors are the general practitioners, and members of the public who wish to consult lawyers must in the first instance approach solicitors. Barristers, on the other hand, have become the specialists who give written opinions for solicitors, when they are called for, upon such problems as may be within their specialist fields, and who also have the right of audience in all courts. There are certain 'inferior' courts, notably magistrates' courts, in which solicitors may also represent their clients in oral argument, but as far as the rest of the English courts are concerned oral argument may only be conducted by barristers, or by litigants in person. Solicitors are permitted to enter into partnerships with each other for the furtherance of their professional business, and most solicitors do indeed operate on this partnership system. But the Inns of Court have never permitted barristers to enter into partnerships, and to this day each barrister practises separately, though they frequently co-operate with each other, and they habitually share a single clerk among several barristers all working together in offices in the same building, known as a set of chambers.

Solicitors are historically an offshoot of the Bar, and they are now organised by a body called the Law Society, with headquarters in Chancery Lane, London, which is quite separate from the Inns of Court. A man or woman who wishes to become a solicitor must undergo a period of five years as an articled clerk to a solicitor, though this period is reduced in certain circumstances. The student must also pass examinations set by the Law Society before he can be admitted as a solicitor, and the Law Society provides for instruction of students at the College of Law in London, a recently founded institution. Attendance at the College of Law, however, is not compulsory, and, as with the Inns of Court, the possession of a law degree from a university is now of benefit to a student from the practical point of view in that it enables him to avoid a portion of the professional examinations which he would otherwise have had to sit, and it also reduces his period as an articled clerk.

The universities, therefore, do now play some part at any rate in the education of practising lawyers. Students who wish to qualify as barristers or solicitors must still sit the more exacting of the professional examinations, but some of the preliminary examinations can be avoided by possession of a university law degree. Moreover, students for the Bar who are attending, or have attended, a university are excused some of the 'dinners' they would otherwise have had to eat at their Inns. English law came into the university law curricula in the mid-eighteenth century. Sir William Blackstone was the pioneer, and he became the first Vinerian Professor of English Law in the University of Oxford in 1758, thus filling the oldest Chair of English Law in the country. Since that time the growth of the teaching of English law in the universities has been quite rapid, and of all the English universities Roman law is now only taught to any great extent at Oxford. More and more students have taken up the study of law at universities, and although university law courses are still based upon the principle that the subject is studied in order to improve the mind, yet many university law students use the knowledge and understanding which they gain in this study as their first grounding in practical law. Provincial universities in particular are inclined to narrow the gap between law as a discipline and law as a vocational subject, and they receive every encouragement to do so from the attitude of the professional bodies which are prepared to make concessions to law students in their professional training and examination if they have covered suitable ground in their degree work.

One practical result of the increasingly close relationship between the professional bodies and the universities is that lawyers and judges are far more inclined today to permit quotation in court from the writings of theoretical law teachers and critics than they used to be even in the years before the Second World War. But it should not yet be thought that the professions and the universities possess the kind of close relationship which exists in so many other countries. Very few practising lawyers teach in universities, and university law teachers, though mostly barristers or solicitors, would be unable to discharge their duties efficiently if they had to pay attention to the needs of a practice. The professional examinations still cover a large number of subjects which find no place in a university law syllabus, and the law graduate who wishes to become a solicitor must still undergo a period of at least two years as an articled clerk. The future of legal education generally will be considered further in Chapter Eight of this book.

A peculiarity of the common law system as opposed to those systems based upon civil law is that judges in the courts are drawn from among the ranks of the practitioners. On the continent it is usual for lawyers to be divided into two professions—practitioners and judges, each with their separate provisions for training. But in England, and in other common law countries, the judges are chosen from the practitioners. In the other common law countries where there is no open split of the profession into barristers and solicitors (a matter to be further discussed in Chapter Eight), any practitioner may become a judge, but in England the rule is that only barristers may be elevated to the bench, except for certain stipendiary magistrates in inferior courts who may be drawn from the ranks of solicitors. In European countries young judges will progress from inferior courts to superior courts when they have proved themselves, but in England the practitioner will have proved himself before he becomes a judge at all. If all English judges were professional men, however, the system might break down for a lack of suitable experienced barristers to fill all available judicial offices. But the saving grace is found in the existence of thousands of unpaid lay magistrates, or justices of the peace, who are appointed mainly for the purpose of deciding all cases where petty crime has been alleged. The system of J.P.s goes back to the middle ages, and it results today in the hiving off from the courts in which professional judges sit of the kind of work which is both enormously time-consuming, since petty crime is so rife, particularly in the age of parking and other petty motoring offences, and also for the most part straightforward and factual. Stipendiary magistrates are appointed in the larger urban areas, particularly in London, but the vast majority of criminal trials are nevertheless conducted by laymen, assisted by professional clerks, who must be either solicitors or barristers.

THE COURTS AND THE COMMON LAW

As England progressed in the middle ages from the state of a country with a number of local laws to that of a nation with a single legal system, so it progressed from a state in which there were a large number of different local courts, unconnected with each other, to that of a country with a single group of courts, inter-connected and administering the single body of the law of the land. It is not possible to take an accurate date which would indicate the period of this transformation, as it was gradual. A few local courts have even persisted to the twentieth century, though they have now either ceased to have any real legal functions or else have become integrated into the general legal system, as for example in the case of the Salford Hundred Court. But an arbitrary and roughly accurate date would be the year 1400. From then till now there has been one organised hierarchy of courts administering English law, though the identity and functions of the various courts have changed greatly from time to time.

At this stage it becomes necessary to advert to one of the many complications of English law. The term 'common law' has already been used to describe a system of law based upon English principles, and it is also used to refer to English law as a whole. But the term became used by English lawyers towards the end of the middle ages in a more parochial sense, namely to refer to the *existing* state of the king's ordinary law, as enforced by the ordinary courts of the land. About 1400 this English law had become rigid and inflexible, possibly because the kings had ceased to sit in their own courts, and because the judges had held office purely at the pleasure of the king. As the king was clearly satisfied with the law as it stood, it became an unnecessary risk for any judge willingly to change that law. Development of the law was accordingly hampered, and disappointed litigants took to the practice of petitioning the Lord Chancellor to redress their grievances. As the Chancellor, who was the king's secretary and a very powerful political figure, was empowered by the king to do whatever he should think fit with these petitions, he not infrequently put right whatever was

15

wrong, regardless of the ordinary law upon the point. He was said to exercise this function as 'the keeper of the king's conscience', and the body of supplementary legal rules which he built up in this way became known as 'equity'. 'Common law' was the ordinary law of the land, and 'equity' was the gloss upon the common law provided by the Chancellor's decisions in his Court of Chancery. Common law and equity were fused in the latter part of the nineteenth century, but the distinct bodies of rules built up by each system can still be traced, and wherever there is a clash between the principles of common law and equity, it has been established that equity shall prevail.

It is perhaps also best at this juncture to mention the third use which lawyers are sometimes known to make of the term 'common law'; that is, to distinguish the law which is built up by decisions in cases (including even cases in equity) from the new law laid down by Acts of Parliament—'common law' as opposed to 'statute law'. In this book it will be necessary to use the term 'common law' in all three senses, but the context in which the term is used each time should make clear the sense in which it is being employed. At all events it can be said here that statute law, equity, and common law in all its senses are now administered in the same hierarchy of courts. It is not necessary for the purposes of this book to list the actual courts which exist today, but it is necessary to discuss briefly the doctrine of precedent which is the basic feature of English law.

It has already been said that the English law courts follow the decisions of other courts in earlier cases, but it is necessary to qualify this statement because the decisions of some courts carry more weight than those of others. The general structure of the courts is governed by a two-tier appeal system. Thus a case, whether it be criminal or civil in nature (and here the word 'civil' is used in its ordinary sense, rather than to denote Roman law), will be tried in a court of first instance; from which court an appeal may lie to a court of appeal; from which court a further appeal may lie in the fairly small number of cases where the law appears to be uncertain to a second and ultimate court of appeal, which is in every case the House of Lords. It follows naturally enough that decisions of the appellate courts are regarded as being of greater weight upon points of law than those of courts of first instance, and decisions of the House of Lords as having the greatest weight of all. Accordingly a doctrine of precedent has grown up whereby decisions of the House of Lords are absolutely binding upon all courts in future cases, even including the House of Lords itself; and decisions of the lower courts of appeal are absolutely binding upon all courts of first instance and also upon themselves, though not upon the House of Lords. On the other hand, decisions of courts of first instance, though highly persuasive, are not regarded as binding upon any courts in future cases. It should perhaps also be mentioned here, as a qualification of the foregoing, that the appeal courts in criminal cases are entitled to ignore the strict doctrine of precedent if to do so would protect individual liberty by favouring the accused.

It may seem at first sight that this doctrine of precedent leads to inflexibility, but it will be appreciated that many cases are unlikely to be exactly similar to cases decided previously: indeed, as far as many civil cases are concerned at any rate, if they were so similar they would be unlikely to reach the courts at all, but would be settled out of court, because it would be clear which party should win in an actual hearing. Where cases are not 'on all fours' with any previous decisions, the earlier cases can only play the part of persuasive precedent, and if found unsatisfactory in any respect they can be 'distinguished' by later judges. Furthermore, no court is bound by a previous decision of a lower court. What the system does provide, however, is certainty, and rules which have already been settled by the courts become part of a body of law which is surely laid down. The greatest certainty, of course, will be provided by decisions of the House of Lords, for no courts may ever reverse them, though it is open to Parliament, as we shall see presently, to alter such law by means of Acts of Parliament. This latter possibility prevents the certainty of the law resulting in immutability.

It should not be pretended that the working of the English doctrine of precedent gives rise to perfect law. If it were perfect there would be little point in writing this book. Many principles may be controversial in the sense that some critics feel them to be bad. Several of these points of law will be considered later in this book. Other decisions may leave the law unclear. For example, it is not unknown for a case to be decided by the House of Lords to provide a victory for one of the litigants concerned, but to leave the lawyers uncertain what the law may be because the five Lords of Appeal (or 'Law Lords') who made the decision each gave different reasons for coming to the same ultimate conclusion. Sometimes the House of Lords decides a case by a majority of three Law Lords to two, but with conflicting reasons being given by the majority, and the same thing may happen in the lower appellate courts, where a decision of the usual quorum of three judges may be reached by a majority of two to one. Yet for the most part the law is certain, though it may need to be changed from time to time. Change may take place by way of court decisions within the framework of the doctrine of precedent, either by higher courts overruling decisions of lower courts, or by way of distinguishing previous rulings in the light of the special facts of later cases, or by certain exceptional rules which allow the appellate courts to ignore their previous decisions if those earlier rulings were given in ignorance of good case precedent or of Acts of Parliament which make contrary provision. But change may also come about by statute law, and this may be enacted for a variety of reasons, either on social grounds or else on purely legal grounds, particularly where the Lord Chancellor has been advised of the need for a particular reform by the Law Reform Committee, which works under his supervision and in conjunction with his Government office.

Most cases are decided by judges alone, but a word should be said here about the jury, which also sits in certain cases. Like so many of the modern institutions of English law the jury has its roots back in the middle ages, and it became the body which decided the facts at issue in the majority of all law cases. But during the past hundred years it has declined greatly on the civil side. Nowadays, although there is a power for any court of first instance in civil cases to order a jury to sit to decide the facts, it hardly ever does so. On the criminal side the jury is still a mainstay of the English trial, but only where the crime charged is serious. Something like 95 per cent of all criminal cases are actually tried before magistrates, who sit without a jury and who decide all facts and law arising in the cases before them. Only the more serious criminal cases of all kinds, ranging from certain dangerous driving and stealing cases up to rape, murder and treason, come before a judge and jury together, either at Quarter Sessions, or else, in the most serious cases of all, at Assizes, in the Crown Courts, or at the Central Criminal Court in London. In these cases the judge is in charge of the proceedings at the trial, as in all other cases, but decisions upon fact ('Did he or did he not do it?') are for the jury alone. The judge must help the jury by formulating the correct questions for them to answer, and by summing up the evidence given, and it is his task alone to sentence prisoners who have been found guilty, but the presence or absence of guilt itself is for the jury to decide. The jury will be discussed again in Chapter Eight, but it is worth mentioning at this stage that English law is more revolutionary in its attitude to jury trial than is the case in the United States of America, where jury trial is still employed for a great many civil cases. On the whole criminal cases are more factual than civil cases, and it is submitted that the jury, who provide something like a cross-section of the ordinary populace, can therefore play a useful part in deciding such facts as may be involved upon common-sense principles. But civil cases are often very complicated in law, and thus beyond the comprehension of laymen, and the American practice frequently leads to unwonted delay and expense.

PARLIAMENT AND THE CONSTITUTION

Our present Parliament is the result of a fusion between two very different groups of people. The House of Lords is descended from the body of great nobles of the land who advised the early kings of England, a body which was once known as the 'Curia Regis', or king's court of advisors, and which existed in Anglo-Saxon times. The House of Commons is descended from the watchdog group of leading citizens set up by Simon de Montfort in the thirteenth century to guard their own special interests against those of the king, though it has been a long step from those days to the twentieth century with its universal adult suffrage. The four centuries which succeeded the time when the Commons first appeared saw a gradual accretion of power in the hands of the members of this lower House, with the king surrendering more and more of his prerogatives into their control. In the seventeenth century the civil war was fought largely upon the question of supremacy between the king and the Commons over such matters as the right to tax the people, and the final settlement, which persists today, was reached at the end of that century when the king assented to the Bill of Rights in 1689 and the Act of Settlement in 1701. From that time the monarch has declined in power to the present position where he is head of state, with many ceremonial functions to perform, but with very little real power. Parliament has become the only law-*making* body in the country, and though the monarch must assent to legislation before it can take effect it would be a most unwise monarch who would ever attempt to refuse his assent. An example of what may happen when the king is in serious disagreement with his Ministers, who are members of Parliament, can be seen from the Abdication of Edward VIII in 1936.

For the past two hundred and fifty years the Government, though titularly headed by the monarch, has consisted of Ministers drawn from the two Houses of Parliament. It is often said that they are responsible to Parliament, and it is certainly true that individual members of both Houses may question Ministers about their conduct of affairs. It is strictly possible for a Government to be defeated by an adverse vote in the House of Commons, which is the only House elected directly by the people. But such defeats, though not uncommon during the nineteenth century, are now very uncommon indeed, largely because of the strict party discipline which obtains in the House. The relationship between the Commons and the Lords will be considered later in this book, but for the moment it is sufficient to state that the Government is normally drawn from adherents in both Houses of the political party possessing a majority in the Commons, and by virtue of its majority it is usually possible for the Government to press through Parliament legislation which it favours. A major factor in law reform by Act of Parliament is thus the support of the Government, or, in the case of private members' bills, at least its acquiescence.

Today Parliament may be said to be legally all-powerful. In many countries the possession of written constitutions means that the powers of their legislatures are defined, and sometimes even that the method of legislating is laid down in black and white. Where a legislature acts in contravention of such provisions the courts are able to nullify the resulting legislation by legal decisions, an occurrence which is not infrequent in the U.S.A., and which takes place from time to time in many other Commonwealth countries. On the continent the same thing may happen if the legislature acts in defiance of some provision of the code of law which governs the whole legal system. But in England and in a very few other countries in the world no provisions can be found which so hamper Parliament. The most fundamental of all our laws would appear to be that Parliament may do anything it likes, providing it does it by means of an Act of Parliament, though there is no binding provision to be found anywhere which lays down *how* Parliament may pass such Acts. As a political fact this means that the Government has it within its power to legislate upon anything it wishes, though the courts are only concerned with what Parliament itself enacts. If the Government were able to persuade its supporters to pass through Parliament an Act granting the Prime Minister the power to imprison anyone without trial at his own whim, and for an indefinite period, this would be law, and the courts would be bound to enforce it. Anyone who challenged the validity of the Act would get little satisfaction in the courts. But the gradual growth of our constitutional practice, largely through well-understood conventions, to the present twentieth century stability has meant that no one seriously fears that enactments of such a kind will ever take place. Should such Acts be passed there would doubtless be some possibility of political revolution, and the fact that no one in England is seriously

21

worried about the possibility of internal revolution is a sufficient testimony to the stability of our institutions and practice.

As we have already seen, case law may be altered or even swept away entirely by Act of Parliament. Thus Parliament is at the pinnacle of the English doctrine of precedent. All courts are absolutely bound to give effect to the provisions of statutes, and if statutes should themselves conflict then the courts are bound to give effect to the later or latest of the statutory provisions. One difference between the precedent value of an Act and that of one of the decisions of an appellate court, therefore, is that Parliament may always repeal or alter its previous enactments whenever it likes, a power which the appellate courts do not possess.

As Parliament began to play a greater part in the affairs of the country, so naturally it played a greater part in providing the actual law of the nation. The result has been that some areas of law are now very largely covered by statutory provisions, though case law always remains the basis of English law unless and until it is superseded by statute. Much of the ordinary civil law dealing with contracts and torts (the latter being civil wrongs perpetrated outside any contractual relationship) is still common law, but land law and criminal law, for example, are now predominantly provided by statute. In some cases attempts have been made, mostly during the latter part of the nineteenth century, to codify parts of the law. A great judge and jurist of that century, Sir James Stephen, had planned to provide a composite code of the whole of the criminal law. But the desire to codify seems to have passed, and Stephen's criminal code was never enacted. We are now back in an age where case law is regarded as sufficient to cover our problems unless there is some good reason to pass an Act of Parliament to deal with a particular difficulty. There are, however, a few Acts of Parliament which provide codes upon restricted topics, mostly passed, at least in their original form, in the latter part of the nineteenth century. Such codes cover respectively the law of larceny, forgery, sale of goods, bills of exchange, partnerships and companies, together with one or two other more minor topics. Yet, even in the case of these codes, it has been found that case law is necessary to fill up the gaps left inevitably in any attempt to forecast what might happen in the future, and also to interpret the various statutory provisions. These later cases have been treated as precedents in just the same way as any other cases, and thus it might be thought that the codes have been unsuccessful. It is submitted that the codes have had a considerable value in gathering together the basic provisions upon particular subjects, but the necessity for subsequent case law is bound to show the deficiency of any codified law. It is impossible to provide adequately for all future contingencies, and thus the common law system of case precedent, for all its certainty, may in the long run prove to be more flexible in adapting itself to changed circumstances and unforeseen situations.

SUBSTANTIVE LAW

It is not necessary here to mention more than the salient changes which have taken place in English law during the past few centuries, in order to set the stage for a discussion of twentieth-century law and its possible future. But certain general developments of the immediate past ought to be related, as they give some clear indications of the pattern of legal change, especially in the case of the evolution of family law and of criminal law and punishment.

It has already been mentioned that the middle ages saw the gradual development in England of a royal common law, administered in common law courts, with a corresponding decline of the old local laws and courts. The judges in the common law courts were disposed to treat the law as inflexible, and they achieved this on the civil side partly by a process of what were called the 'forms of action'. These forms of action were specific 'writs' which started civil actions for the various heads of claim possible in the common law. Once the correct writ had been issued in a particular action, the litigation could proceed until judgment one way or the other had been obtained. But if the wrong writ was issued the plaintiff automatically lost his suit merely on the technical defect of suing by the wrong form of action. As the number and variety of writs was strictly limited, the place for the growth of equity to satisfy genuine litigants disappointed by the remedies allowed at common law was clear. But equity too became rigid and inflexible by the seventeenth and eighteenth centuries, and so, although the growth of the doctrine of binding precedent was helped by this rigidity both in the common law and in equity, litigants' requirements made it plain that more flexibility was needed. In the nineteenth century these requirements were at last met, when the forms of action were swept away by a series of Acts of Parliament, culminating in the Judicature Act of 1873, and the system was replaced by what might be called 'free litigation'. Today any plaintiff in a civil action may bring his suit by a simple common-form procedure, whereby a standard writ or petition is issued, together with a detailed statement of claim attached to it, such statement containing the particular facts, of whatever kind, upon which the plaintiff or petitioner (as he is called in matrimonial proceedings) is basing his action. The nineteenth century, therefore, saw a revolution in the methods of bringing civil actions, and today no plaintiff will lose his action merely because he brings the wrong writ, as the individual writs have been standardised—though he will of course still lose his action if the facts alleged in his statement of claim cannot be substantiated. The Act of 1873 also radically reformed the system of courts in the country, but it is not necessary to deal further with them here. As will be seen presently, the nineteenth century also saw a considerable reform of the methods of criminal punishment. The twentieth century has been a period of many different reforms of the law. Other possible future changes will be discussed later in this book, but no such changes would have been at all feasible without the great work done by the law reformers of the last century.

English lawyers have often seemed to be preoccupied with problems of land law, and this may well be explained by the fact that land has always been the most valuable commodity we have had. For a short period of a decade or so after the Second World War land values, which had been subject to stringent statutory controls, had seemed to decline, and one would have been tempted to say that land was no longer as valuable as hard cash, or as stocks and shares. But the recent boom in land, particularly for building development, has been a timely reminder of the value placed upon land throughout the ages by our forebears. As a corollary of this importance placed upon land, it is not altogether surprising that lawyers have tended to spend a lot of time and energy in developing legal rules for the protection of possession of land. Since the Norman Conquest the common law has maintained that all the land in England belonged to the king, and he allowed his subjects to enjoy possession of parts of that land, in return for certain services or payments. By what was called a system of subinfeudation, which was a corner-stone of the feudal system, it was common practice for A to hold land from B, who held from C, who held from the king, each tenant owing services or sums of money to his lord in return for the right to possess the particular parcel of land concerned. Those who held immediately from the king, known as tenants-in-chief, often possessed great estates, on which there would be several sub-tenants, each of whom might have several sub-sub-tenants, and so on. Naturally the incomes and other benefits obtained by the king and other lords were highly valued, though the tenants who owed money and services might well be anxious to escape some of the more onerous of their duties or debts. Subinfeudation was abolished in the course of the middle ages, and in its place it was enacted that each tenant should hold directly from the king, with the result that all services and money owed in return for each tenancy was due to the king. Many efforts were then made to find methods of avoiding these feudal dues. All feudal dues were abolished finally in the latter half of the seventeenth century, but before their demise the property lawyers had succeeded in developing the system of the 'trust', whereby the legal estate in land would be held by some 'man of straw' who was unable to pay the king the dues owed, or else by some corporation which therefore never died (and many of the most onerous of the dues were payable on the death or succession of each tenant). Behind this legal tenant the real beneficial interest in the land would be held by someone else who, not being the legal tenant, was not bound to pay the dues. Though the ending of feudal dues removed the reason which had led to the invention of the trust, the trust itself has nevertheless remained a very important part of English law, and it is the device whereby a great deal of money and land is held and administered by responsible people for the benefit of, for example, infants, scholars and charities.

Today the energies of property lawyers are no longer concerned with the need to avoid feudal dues, but they are perpetually concerned with the problems of avoidance of taxation. As everybody knows, estate duty is payable on the death of every person possessing capital, including land, in excess of a few thousand pounds in value. Yet our tax laws are so designed that it is possible by various complicated devices to escape much of the duty which would normally be payable on death. It is a strange commentary upon the state of our public morality that a premium should be placed upon tax avoidance. Tax evasion, that is, actual illegality, is always condemned, and, if detected, leads to criminal prosecution. But tax avoidance, that is, the use of legal means, however tortuous or artificial, in order to escape liability to tax which would otherwise exist, is regarded as highly respectable. Lawyers spend a great deal of time evolving methods of forming companies, trusts or funds, counselling the purchase of works of art which are exempt from estate duty, or advising the transfer of certain property to children, so as to escape or reduce the tax which is otherwise due upon death. The innocent upright man who takes no steps to avoid taxation on his death leaves beneficiaries who will be penalised because of his honesty or simplicity. But the man who goes to the trouble of 'beating the tax collector' will leave behind him the bulk of his property untaxed, and he will acquire a reputation for shrewdness which will be applauded by the public at large. It would be impossible in this book to deal adequately with the tax laws of England, for the subject is in any case far too complex, but it may be stated that a law which encourages this kind of activity on the part of taxpayers and lawyers is highly unsatisfactory. No Government has ever yet had the courage to attempt a wholesale sweeping revision of taxation laws, but it may be doubted whether general morality will ever be raised significantly until such a revision is ventured.

Meanwhile the lawyers will perforce continue to spend their time and talents upon tax beating, together with other more constructive pursuits, many of which are connected with land. Wills and intestacy provide considerable work, particularly where the administration of an estate and of the testator's wishes is complicated by the ambiguous wording often to be found in wills which have been drafted without the aid of solicitors. The existence of the process of compulsory purchase of land is bound to provide another field of work for the profession. In a small island like our own, which contains the greatest concentration of population in the world, the rights of the individual landowner must be balanced against the needs of the community at large, and the balance is most likely to be achieved where expert legal assistance has been employed on both sides. Compulsory acquisition is the modern method, laid down by statute, whereby schemes of development of many kinds can be carried through despite the opposition of individuals, but the law provides rightly that no such acquisition may take place without the views of the property owner concerned being heard and considered. This does not mean that the authority engaged in compulsory acquisition is bound to hear and determine the issue in the ordinary judicial way, for it must pay particular attention to the needs of Government policy. A desirable policy cannot be put in jeopardy merely because of the wishes of one person, but as far as possible the desires of that person will be met. He may in certain cases even persuade the authority that the purchase should not take place, and it is in any case laid down by statute that he must be paid, on acquisition, a full price for the land taken from him. More will be said about planning and compulsory acquisition in Chapter Seven of this book.

Perhaps the most striking individual development on the civil side of English law in the past century or so has been in the realm of family law. Until 1882 the general rule was that all property belonging to a woman became the property of her husband when she married. But by the Married Women's

Property Act of that year it was provided for the first time that any woman marrying after 1882 should be entitled to retain all property owned by her at the time of her marriage as her own separate property, and that any property subsequently acquired by a woman married even before 1883 should be held by her in the same way. As it is now virtually impossible that there can be any woman alive who was married before 1883 it can be said that the old right of a husband to take the property previously owned by his wife has vanished. This does not of course mean that a wife is debarred from giving her property or some of it to her husband, or *vice versa*, but the old automatic legal rule concerning such a passage of property has gone. Furthermore, in 1935, a limited right of action against her husband was conferred upon a wife in protection of her separate property. Further consideration of this subject will be deferred until Chapter Five.

Dissolution of marriage is a subject which to a very late date was deeply influenced by the jurisdiction wielded by the separate ecclesiastical courts, which had continued to exist after the middle ages for the purpose of dealing with church law and clergy discipline. It is perhaps curious today to remember that among the affairs of the ecclesiastical courts, and thus of church law, was not only what we should now call the judicial separation of spouses, but also such matters as the law concerning wills. Divorce as we know it today was not possible at all even in the ecclesiastical courts, though it was possible to obtain a divorce *a mensa et thoro* or judicial separation, on the grounds of adultery, cruelty or the commission of an unnatural offence. Such a decree of a church court relieved the petitioner from the duty of cohabiting with the respondent spouse without severing the marriage tie. These courts also had the power to grant decrees of nullity where, for example, one of the parties to a marriage was under age or already married at the time of the ceremony, or if there was an inability to consummate the marriage, as well as certain other special decrees, such as the decree of restitution of conjugal rights, which called on a deserting spouse to resume cohabitation with the petitioner. The only way in which a complete divorce *a vinculo matrimonii* could be obtained was by the highly expensive and cumbrous process of a private Act of Parliament, a procedure which was of necessity restricted to the means of the very rich, and which was therefore not very common.

In 1857, however, a marked change in the law took place, for by the Matrimonial Causes Act of that year a new civil Divorce Court was set up, and it took over the whole jurisdiction over matrimonial causes previously exercised by the ecclesiastical courts. This Divorce Court was itself abolished by the Judicature Act, 1873, and its successor is the Probate, Divorce and Admiralty Division of the High Court, a division of the High Court which accordingly has a wider jurisdiction than that over matrimonial causes only, though divorce cases still supply the greater part of the actual litigation taking place there. The law administered by the Divorce Court and by the Probate, Divorce and Admiralty Division has remained basically the same as that previously administered in the church courts, though the law of nullity, for example, has been altered somewhat, as when wilful refusal to consummate (as opposed to inability to consummate) a marriage was made a ground by the Matrimonial Causes Act, 1937. But there is one enormous difference between the law of matrimonial causes after the 1857 Act and that before it, namely that the 1857 Act permitted for the first time in England divorce *a vinculo matrimonii* by judicial process. The term 'divorce' has since then been reserved for this kind of decree only, and divorce *a mensa et thoro*, which may still be granted by the court, is now always known as judicial separation. At first the grounds for divorce provided in the Act maintained the distinction which the law at that time provided between the sexes, for a husband could obtain a divorce on the ground of adultery alone, whereas a wife had to prove either adultery coupled with incest, bigamy, cruelty or two years' desertion, or alternatively rape or an unnatural offence. But in 1923 a later Act provided that either party to a marriage might obtain a divorce on the ground of adultery alone.

The most recent legislation upon matrimonial causes began with an Act, sponsored as a private member's bill by Mr. (now Sir) A. P. Herbert, passed in 1937, and now brought further up to date by the Matrimonial Causes Act of 1950. Under section

1 of this latter Act a divorce petition may be presented '. . . either by the husband or the wife on the ground that the respondent (*a*) has since the celebration of the marriage committed adultery; or (*b*) has deserted the petitioner without cause for a period of at least three years immediately preceding the presentation of the petition; or (*c*) has since the celebration of the marriage treated the petitioner with cruelty; or (*d*) is incurably of unsound mind and has been continuously under care and treatment for a period of at least five years immediately preceding the presentation of the petition; and by the wife on the ground that her husband has, since the celebration of the marriage, been guilty of rape, sodomy or bestiality.' Further consideration of the future of the law as to matrimonial causes will come within Chapter Five of this book, but it is enough for the present to note that a hundred years after the passage of the 1857 Act the stability of marriage appears very different from the days before the great reforms began. Before 1857 up to some two divorces a year might be obtained by Act of Parliament. Today the number of divorces obtained in the courts per year is round about 30,000. In 1947 it was actually nearly 60,000. The churches have not altered their attitude towards divorce, but the ordinary law has come more into line with the social needs of the people, whether or not those social needs are ideal. It cannot be denied that many of the marriages existing before 1857, or even before 1937, were marriages only in name, yet there may be more encouragement today towards the breaking up of marriages which are merely irksome or boring, regardless of the best interests of any children of the marriage. But it should not be thought that divorce is yet necessarily easily obtained, for when the grounds for divorce were widened in 1937, it was provided at the same time that no petition for divorce may be presented during the first three years of the marriage, except where it is proved to the court that there is exceptional hardship suffered by the petitioner or exceptional depravity on the part of the respondent.

The codification of parts of the criminal law in the course of the nineteenth century has already been mentioned. But the most important trend in connection with the development of the criminal law in past centuries has perhaps been in the attitude of the law-makers to punishment. As with other topics, the aims and likely development of the law as to punishment will be discussed later in this book, but it is as well to note here that the kinds of punishment inflicted as a result of conviction for crime have changed most markedly over the centuries. In the middle ages, when it was a nuisance to have to feed and keep a prisoner, the common punishments were either death or maiming. Death, together with forfeiture of property, followed automatically as the punishment on conviction for felony right up to the nineteenth century, while imprisonment of various kinds had succeeded maiming as the common punishment for commission of misdemeanours. Hanging, drawing and quartering, and public executions, were common enough punishments two or three hundred years ago, and transportation to America or Australia for quite minor offences was often regarded even early in the nineteenth century as a kind and humane punishment, regardless of the hardship and heartbreak inflicted upon the convict's family, to cite only one injustice of the system. The nineteenth century was the heyday of the reform of punishment, along with other law reforms, and nearly all offences had ceased to be capital by the end of the century, just as forfeiture and transportation had also disappeared. In the present century, imprisonment with hard labour and penal servitude have been abolished, and corporal punishment is only retained in certain cases of assaults by prisoners upon warders, though even then it is hardly ever invoked. The death sentence is now only possible in four types of crime: piracy with violence, setting fire to Her Majesty's ships or dockyards, treason, and certain types of murder, the capital penalty being mandatory only on conviction of the last two of these crimes. Penal reform is probably among the most popular of all subjects for law reformers, as it is full of human interest, but we must not forget the achievements of the past century or so.

One odd thing has in part resulted from the speedy penological reform of the immediate past, namely the apparent pointlessness of the continued division of crimes into felonies and misdemeanours. The former were originally the most serious crimes, punishable by death, and the latter were the less serious, as has been mentioned above. But this distinction has become blurred. Several crimes punished for the first time by the Court of Star Chamber, which was particularly concerned with crimes against the state, and which was abolished in 1641, were later punished by the common law courts, but they were, for no very good reason, labelled misdemeanours. Such crimes include conspiracy, unlawful assembly, riot and attempts to commit any crimes, so that it can be seen that they may well include very serious crimes indeed. Since the reforms in punishment of the last century the only significance of the distinction between felonies and misdemeanours is in some of the forms of the actual trials conducted, and it may be suggested that the distinction could well be abolished.

THE NEED FOR LAW

It is tempting to assume that there is no need to argue that law is a requirement of every civilised community, but such an assumption may be too great. There seem to be a number of people in England today who are going through a phase of anti-authoritarianism. The word 'phase' is probably correct, for it is hard to imagine that any sane man can seriously continue to believe for longer than a short period of time that anarchy can work. It may be fashionable to rebel against what seem to be pointless regulations and restrictions, but the fact must in the end be appreciated that laws of all kinds are the servants of the community as a whole. Rules and regulations are designed, first and foremost, to help the various members of the community to order their society in the way which is most congenial to the majority in that community. This is not to say that all laws are perfect, for they are often the result of compromise and uncertainty among the law-makers, and the needs of society as a whole may well be changing all the time. But laws are usually created in good faith, and their authoritarian nature exists because society as a whole wishes them to be authoritarian. The rebels against law should realise that their quarrels are not really with the laws, but with the community.

In this book many laws will be criticised, and alterations will be suggested, but the criticism is really directed at what is submitted to be inadequate or inept formulation of the wishes of society, or sometimes against the apparent wishes of society itself, not against the laws in isolation.

It may be suggested that all laws can be divided into what will be termed here natural laws and arbitrary laws. By natural laws are meant the laws which appear to mirror the moral feelings of society as a whole, such as the laws of murder, assault, marriage and the protection of property. By arbitrary laws are meant those laws which are of no concern to society as a whole from any moral standpoint, but which have been brought into existence in order to fill an obvious gap in the regulations of the community. An example of such arbitrary laws would be the rules of the road or the laws concerning wireless and television licences. The rules of the road are of no concern to the community until it is realised that unless *some* rules of the road are enforced there will be a great deal of loss of life and many serious accidents on the highways. The fact that in the United Kingdom it is obligatory to drive a car on the left-hand side of the road, while in France one must drive on the right-hand side, is in itself of small consequence. The whole object of each exercise is to prevent accidents. Similarly there is nothing natural about the rule that anyone possessing a television set must have a licence for it (and pay a fee for his licence), but the law-makers have determined quite arbitrarily that such a rule is necessary in order that revenue for the broadcasting authorities should be obtained; and society as a whole has acquiesced in this decision. There is nothing intrinsically better about natural laws than arbitrary laws, for the English law of homicide is a good example of a law which is constantly criticised upon its details, while very few people criticise the law concerning television licences. Any branch of law may be defective, and both types will be criticised in this book. But natural laws are laws which any civilised community *must* possess, whereas arbitrary laws need not exist at all. If the finance for broadcasting were readily available from some other source (as it is for the commercial television companies in the United Kingdom, which obtain their revenue from advertisements paid for by industrial concerns, though not for the B.B.C. which may not permit advertising in its programmes), there is no good reason why television licences should be necessary at all. But it is unthinkable that English law should not provide in some way for the trial and punishment of murderers. If murder were not to be condemned by the community as a whole, one of the bases not only of English law but also of the civilisation of England would have been fundamentally changed.

It follows, therefore, that law should always mirror the needs of society. In the preceding pages some of the older more barbaric forms of punishment enforced in England in past centuries have been mentioned briefly. The fact that they have disappeared is an indication that society as a whole has felt that it no longer wished to countenance them. The examples of the changes in the law as regards matrimonial causes are also in point. Though the churches have maintained their opposition to divorce, society has decided that divorce is sometimes permissible or even necessary. This example may also be cited to make another point: that although law should mirror the morality favoured by society, that morality is not necessarily the morality of the church, or of any one of the various churches. In England Christian morality must always remain a powerful force in shaping the general public standards of morality, but it is only one factor in its formulation.

If law of all kinds mirrors the needs of society, and if those needs tend to change, it follows that the law of the country—any country—is almost inevitably behind the times. This is a very important fact to appreciate, because it accounts for a great deal of the apparent inadequacy of the law. In an autocracy it would be possible for the autocrat to alter the law according to his own will alone, and perhaps to make intelligent guesses as to the most desirable law reforms. But in a democracy it is not possible that reform should come about in this way. Reform can only follow the expression of opinion that the law is currently inadequate, and in a democracy that expression of opinion must usually be forceful or made by a large number of people before it would be proper for Parliament to pay much attention to it. Thus, provided law reform does take place as and when Parliament thinks that the community need is great, it is no bad thing that the law remains to some extent always behind the times. Cautious change is more likely to meet the general requirements of the nation than hasty change. If this point is realised then the critic of the law need not be regarded as a man with a chip on his shoulder: he is performing a constitutional function, mobilising the opinion necessary before law reform can take place. Again, this is not to say that criticisms of the law are always heeded, or even that they ought always to be heeded, for some may themselves be very controversial. But at least the airing of criticism of the law is an essential element of a democratic society, and it is a part of the process which may from time to time, and sometimes should, lead to law reform.

It is also important to remember that arbitrary laws, as opposed to natural laws, need not necessarily be the same as standard practice. In the age of the motor car it is obvious that the parking of vehicles in certain places ought to be prohibited by law, and in fact English law provides that anyone who parks his motor car anywhere on the public highway which is not specifically designated as a parking area is guilty of obstructing the highway. The fact that every motorist is not prosecuted every day stems from the good sense of the police, which is a fact relied upon by the law itself. But the power to prosecute is there, and every motorist who parks his car at the side of the road could be prosecuted. The parking of cars on the highway is not immoral, and in fact we all do it regularly. But such a practice must be illegal, or at least, even if the law did not provide that all such parking was illegal, there would have to be some provision for certain kinds of indiscriminate parking to be illegal. All motorists in their right mind would admit this fact. So necessary laws may nevertheless differ from the accepted practice of society. The breaking of arbitrary laws may carry no moral stigma, but the breaking of natural laws invariably does.

Law Reform

If we accept that law should mirror the needs of society as a whole, it ceases to be necessary to detail with particularity the aims of law reform. All reforms in the law should bring it more into conformity with the generally held views of society upon specific topics. Sometimes the law is merely being brought into line with these views for the first time, or is made to mirror those views more perfectly. For example, up to 1945 if A and B were involved in an accident as a result of the negligence of both, and A alone was injured, it was often the case that A would be unable to succeed in a claim for damages against B merely because he also had been at fault. Many people, including almost all lawyers, had long felt this to be unjust, and so the law may simply be regarded as having been defective. In 1945 Parliament passed an Act to provide that where any person suffers damage as the result partly of his own fault and partly of the fault of any other person, a claim in respect of that damage shall not be defeated merely because the plaintiff was to some extent at fault, but shall instead be reduced to such extent as the court thinks just having regard to the claimant's share in the responsibility for the damage. This apportionment of liability is far more in accord with what the community at large would regard as justice. But more often the reason for reform is that the views of the community have themselves changed. The abolition in the nineteenth century of transportation as a punishment for crime was a result of the changed ideas of the community, as also was the enormous reduction in the number of capital offences. The great changes in the law of matrimonial causes, already mentioned, are other good examples of this kind of law reform. On the other hand, many reforms of arbitrary laws can be regarded as nothing more than convenience. Changes in the laws concerning car licensing, or in the regulations concerning pedestrian crossings on the highway, are mostly quite arbitrary. Provided some reasonable provisions are made for pedestrian crossings, and for the rights of precedence between vehicles and pedestrians upon them, the actual regulations themselves are really immaterial, but they may well be changed from time to time as the sponsors of such legislation may think fit. Pedestrians' associations and local authorities may well urge the introduction of new devices which they believe will be more convenient for pedestrians and fairer to all concerned, but all such rules have the agreed purpose of allowing pedestrians to cross busy roads in safety, while delaying the flow of motor traffic for the minimum length of time on each occasion. All rules and devices in connection with pedestrian crossings are, therefore, in a sense experimental.

Mass media, such as radio, television and the press, have all contributed to make us more aware of the things that go on around us in the twentieth century than were our forebears. Though the press was active in the last century, it was not aided by the telephone and radio, which enable us now to know within a few hours what has been happening all over the world. Television above all has brought the affairs of everyday life to the fireside. Politics, wars, famines, sport and even law are thrown at us. Thus the more 'popular' of legal subjects will become familiar, at least in broad outlines, to a large section of the community. There may still be few laymen who are prepared to grapple with the complications of taxation or company law, but a large number will be able to form opinions upon punishment for crime, the grounds for divorce and the protection of the consumer from unfair dealing by commercial concerns. This impetus given to popular interest in law is probably more than enough to ensure that, despite the vast increase in the preoccupations of the Government over international problems, law reformers still receive a hearing and gain Parliamentary time when heeded. Indeed law reform, at least in the more racy legal subjects, has if anything gained momentum during the present century, possibly because people who feel that international affairs are beyond their control are apt to take the attitude that they might as well channel their energies into some field which is within their competence. Spurred by mass media and mass communication, law reformers have never been so active.

But the machinery of law reform is not necessarily haphazard or dependent upon the existence of mass interest in racy topics. The Lord Chancellor, who is today the senior lawyer in the Government, and effectively head of the judiciary, is entrusted, among other things, with the supervision of preparation for law reform of all kinds. Various special law reform committees are appointed by him, and entrusted with the tasks of reporting upon the desirability of reform. Much legislation by Parliament during the past two or three decades has stemmed from the reports of these committees upon both popular and esoteric legal subjects. The most solemn or formal of all the preparatory procedures for reform is the Royal Commission. Royal Commissions may be formed by the Government to investigate any subjects the Government thinks fit, and the reports of these Commissions have led to such important legislation as the Matrimonial Causes Act, 1857, which has already been discussed. It should not be thought, however, that all the reports of committees and Commissions lead to legislation. It is a criticism of the English methods of preparing for possible law reform that they all too frequently do not lead to actual reform, and the reports themselves may be pigeonholed or forgotten. The report of the Committee on Homosexual Offences and Prostitution, published in 1957, which will be discussed in the next chapter, led to legislation upon prostitution but not upon homosexuality, though it recommended some important changes in the law on this latter subject. Yet it would be dangerous to assume that because a report has been made upon any particular legal topic, recommending reforms, the substance of the report should automatically be made into law. Strictly speaking these reports should be regarded as efforts to gather all the material needed for the understanding of various subjects, together with the considered views of a representative selection of thinking people upon that material. The material and recommendations should weigh heavily with the Government and with the country as a whole, but they should certainly not be regarded as binding upon anyone. They indicate weighty opinion, but they do not necessarily show conclusively that the country is ready for any of the particular reforms suggested. Indeed the committee members are not infrequently divided in their own opinions, and express this division in their report. The committee and Commission system is sometimes said to be the British way of ensuring that nothing is done, but that is unjust. Much reform does result from these reports, but it is reform in tune with the national desire for cautious progress. The system probably ensures as well as possible that reforms are not entered into lightly, and that full consideration is given to all sides of the problems at issue. It may well be, however, that, as was suggested in the recent book *Law Reform NOW*, a small permanent body of highly-qualified advisers should be provided to assist the Lord Chancellor in the discharge of his functions in connection with law reform.

CHAPTER TWO

Criminal Law

OF all the branches of law perhaps criminal law is the most closely associated with ordinary everyday problems of fact. Many civil law rights and liabilities may affect us without ever bringing us near to court proceedings. We make wills, license our cars, and enter into agreements with each other concerning the buying and selling of houses and goods, all without even seeming to be likely to go near a court. But the commission of a crime, followed by detection, almost inevitably leads to a prosecution, unless the offence is very trivial and the police decide to take no action. If therefore problems of crime reach the actual courts far more frequently than problems of civil law, it would appear logical that the criminal law ought to be more clearly decided and certain than any branch of civil law. Yet this is a state of affairs which is not found. The reasons are probably diverse. In the first place, criminal trial, other than for minor summary offences, takes place before a judge and jury, rather than a judge alone. Where judges sit alone they are able to decide all matters of fact and law for themselves, and to adhere strictly to the doctrine of precedent. But where judge and jury sit together the judge decides all matters of pure law (such as whether there is any case to be answered by the accused at all—if he rules that there is no such case to answer, the trial ends without the jury ever having a decision to make), but he must leave decisions upon fact, and the application of law to the facts found, to the jury. In these trials for the more serious criminal offences, therefore, no judgments as such are delivered by the trial judges, and in their place we only have 'directions' to the jury: the judge concerned in each case will sum up the evidence given at the trial, and attempt to assist the jury by formulating the questions which it is their duty to answer. Precedents, at any rate from the first instance courts, can be gleaned only from these directions taken together with the juries' verdicts, and juries have a tendency to err, if at all, on the side of leniency towards the accused. Further, the appeal courts, in which judges sit without juries, have adopted a rule that they may depart from strict precedent laid down in earlier decisions of their own courts if to do so would be in the interest of the liberty of the accused, as was mentioned in the last chapter.

In the result the criminal law, while remaining earthy and in many respects more easy for laymen to understand than many branches of civil law, contains many obscurities and ambiguities or contradictions. In this chapter we shall investigate some of the more outstanding of the unsatisfactory elements of English criminal law.

HOMICIDE

Most citizens have a fair knowledge of the distinction between murder and the lesser homicides such as manslaughter. It is generally regarded as reasonable and indeed necessary that the killing by a woman of her baby child when she has not fully recovered from the effects of child-birth (infanticide), or the killing of any person when committed under extreme provocation (one of the several types of manslaughter) should be regarded as criminal, though subject to a less severe type of punishment than is the case with murder. In fact punishments suffered by persons who commit the various categories of homicide will be discussed in the next chapter, but it is impossible to discuss the English law of murder in a book of this kind without mentioning here the fact that a conviction for manslaughter carries a possible maximum penalty of life imprisonment, while a conviction for murder carries a *mandatory* sentence either of life imprisonment or of hanging. Until 1957 all murders were capital, but the Homicide Act of that year had the effect of removing the death penalty except in the case of six particular types of murder, which will be detailed presently.

The reason why it is necessary here to mention the punishments attaching to crimes of homicide is that dissatisfaction with the law of murder stems almost wholly from the continued existence of the capital penalty. Before 1957 critics were dissatisfied with the whole law of murder, and today they are still dissatisfied with the remaining capital murders. It would be hard to find anyone prepared to argue that there should be no punishment for homicide, though the alternatives to the present types of punishment will be discussed in the next chapter. But if the death penalty were to be abolished altogether there would be very few grounds for criticising the distinctions which would remain between murder and manslaughter, for most would agree that murder, which is usually intentional homicide, is one of the most serious crimes in any system of law.

Murder consists of the killing of anyone other than an enemy in time of war with the intention either to kill or to cause really serious bodily harm, or else with the intention to do an act which the accused knows, or must as a reasonable man be taken to know, is likely to kill or to cause grievous bodily harm. As has already been said, this means that murder is usually intentional in that serious harm, at the very least, is intended to some other human being. But the definition just given discloses the possibility that intention may be imputed to a man in some cases, for he may not be that somewhat mythical character, the 'reasonable man'. In a case in 1956 the accused had killed a baby in a fit of temper caused by its screaming. He alleged that he had merely intended to shake the baby in order to silence it, and that he had no intention to cause it serious harm, still less to kill the baby. The judge directed the jury that the accused would be guilty of murder if, when he did the act which killed the baby, he must have contemplated, had he been a reasonable man, that death or serious bodily harm was a likely result. In the event the jury convicted the accused of murder, though he was subsequently reprieved. Many jurists have objected to a law which replaces a subjective test of intention by an objective test, for murder may be regarded as a very personal kind of crime; and there is much force in these objections. Yet we are presented with a considerable dilemma, for the maintenance by the state of an objective test of intention does at least promote certainty in the law. It is possible to argue that the jury is often a sufficient safeguard to the accused, in that it will frequently fail to convict a man who actually did not intend to kill or cause serious bodily harm, whether or not he should have done so if he had been a reasonable man. But this safeguard was not enough to help the accused in the case just mentioned. It may be that the law would be simplified by the effective deletion of the second part of the definition of murder given above, in restricting murder to homicide committed with the intention to kill or to cause serious bodily harm. If the death penalty is retained such a change in the law may be inevitable in view of mounting criticism, but the author's belief, as will appear presently, is that the death penalty will itself be abolished before very long, in which case such a reform in the definition of murder would be otiose. The distinction between an offence carrying a mandatory life sentence and one carrying a maximum life sentence may not be worth bothering about, when the former sentence can be reduced by remission and release upon licence in suitable cases.

We come therefore to the heart of the present problem, the division into capital and non-capital murders. The Homicide Act, 1957, specifies the following types of murder as being offences following conviction for which the death penalty must be imposed:

(a) Any murder done in the course or furtherance of theft.

(b) Any murder done by shooting or by causing an explosion.

(c) Any murder done in the course or for the purpose of resisting or avoiding or preventing a lawful arrest, or for effecting or assisting an escape or rescue from legal custody.

(d) Any murder of a police officer acting in the execution of his duty, or of a person assisting a police officer so acting.

(e) In the case of a person who was a prisoner at the time when he committed or was a party to a murder, any murder of a prison officer acting in the execution of his duty or of a person assisting a prison officer so acting.

(*f*) In the case of a person who has previously been convicted of any murder committed in Great Britain on a different occasion, any second or later murder committed by that person in Great Britain.

If the death penalty is at all necessary, either as a deterrent to the commission of murder or in order to protect such persons as police officers, then there can be no basis for serious criticism of categories (*c*)–(*f*) in this list, though the merits of capital punishment itself will be discussed in the next chapter. But the major criticism of the 1957 Act is in adding to this list categories (*a*) and (*b*), which in the view of many thinking people are arbitrary. Why, for example, should murder by shooting be a capital murder, while murder by poisoning is non-capital? If the death penalty, which is the most severe penalty possible under modern English law, is to be reserved for the worst kinds of crime, can it not be said that murder by poisoning, inevitably premeditated, is more heinous an offence than murder by shooting, which may occur on the spur of the moment? It is possible to produce a justification of the distinction, though opponents of the capital penalty are never convinced by it, largely because it depends upon the acceptance of a view that the death penalty deters criminals from committing murder. It can be argued that though murder by poisoning is a horrible crime, it is one which is usually only committed by such persons as embittered spouses who have sought poison as a means of ending a long and hated relationship. Nothing will ever deter such people from the ultimate crime, and thus the death penalty would be of no use. Murder by shooting, on the other hand, need not be so long premeditated, and it may be committed in an instant when a gun is handy. Thus the presence of the death penalty for murder by shooting will deter the carrying of firearms which might be used in the heat of the moment.

Even if such a deterrent view were to be accepted by some, it is hardly surprising that it is not found to be very persuasive by many others, for it involves the fact that a lesser punishment for a greater crime is justified because the criminal is too bad to be deterred, while the extreme penalty is exacted from lesser criminals *pour encourager les autres*. Several English judges have expressed themselves as supporting total abolition of the death penalty merely because the law as to the punishment of murder has become so inconsistent, and so it is hard to escape the conclusion that abolition will indeed come before long. As has already been suggested, such abolition would be likely to remove the serious criticisms currently raised against the English law of murder, though the problem of what penalty to substitute for the present sentence must be investigated in the next chapter.

One further type of homicide which some believe to require revision is the crime of abortion, which is committed whenever a pregnant woman unlawfully administers to herself some poison or uses an instrument, intending to procure her own miscarriage, or whenever some other person, with like intent, administers poison to or uses an instrument upon her. It is a defence if the operation is performed in good faith to preserve the life of the mother, and this has been interpreted liberally in the courts. In 1939 an eminent gynaecologist was acquitted of the offence where, with the parents' consent, he had performed the operation upon a girl of fourteen who had been raped, because he was of opinion that continuance of the pregnancy would cause her serious injury and leave her a physical wreck for the rest of her life. Despite the problems of illegitimacy which beset us today (and which will be discussed in the chapter on Family Law) it seems very unlikely that the law will be altered to make abortions more generally legal, though attempts to secure such legislation have been made in recent years. Such a step would be out of keeping with the basic moral and religious views of the community, provided that the defence of *bona fide* preservation of the mother's life is treated as sufficiently wide to cover cases where, on general medical grounds, it is desirable to procure a miscarriage.

THEFT

One of the most confused branches of English criminal law is the law as to theft and related offences. The original common law offence of larceny, which is simply another word for theft or stealing, was comparatively narrow in that it involved nothing more nor less than the taking of possession of a chattel (that is, some article of goods or money) from someone who had possession of it. The present statutory definition of the felony of larceny, contained in the first section of the Larceny Act, 1916, is as follows:

> A person steals who, without the consent of the owner, fraudulently and without a claim of right made in good faith, takes and carries away anything capable of being stolen with intent, at the time of such taking, permanently to deprive the owner thereof.

The courts have made it clear that every word of this definition is important, and the result has been that certain confusions and inconsistencies have emerged, as will be explained.

In the first place, 'things capable of being stolen' is a phrase which has led to some absurdities. At common law the courts had held that no chattel was capable of being stolen unless it had a monetary or practical value, so that so-called 'base animals', such as dogs and cats, were excluded from the class of chattels which could be stolen. Statute law has cured this defect fairly simply. But a more complex problem was presented by chattels which were attached to land, for the courts had also held that only tangible movables were capable of being stolen, and by wild animals or game, for these were not considered as being within anyone's ownership at all. A somewhat clumsy solution to these latter problems was inserted in the Larceny Act, 1916, in the form of a requirement that things attached to land, such as growing crops or fixtures in houses, must have been completely detached from the land before they could be carried away, and thus stolen. It is not sufficient for the supposed thief to cut the cabbage or tear the electric fan from the wall and then run off with it: in such a case he would not be guilty of larceny. Before his guilt can be brought home to him, he must be proved to have laid the cabbage or the fan down, and then to have carried it away at a later time. Again, wild animals or game can only be stolen if they have first been 'reduced into the possession' of the owner or occupier of the land by the process of leaving their presumably dead carcases upon the land for some appreciable time before subsequent removal. To shoot a rabbit while trespassing upon land, and then immediately to pick it up and take it home for dinner, will render the taken guilty of trespass to land, but not of larceny.

Perhaps the most surprising features of the present law of larceny become apparent in relation to the requirement that the intention to deprive permanently must have existed at the time of the taking of the article. Clearly there must be quite frequent cases when articles are removed by mistake, and it seems likely that this provision in the Act was intended to exempt such innocent takers from criminal liability. We have all picked up books or pens by mistake and taken them home, probably under the belief that they are our own, and it would be nonsensical to hold us guilty of stealing when we will, it is hoped, take steps to return the articles concerned to their rightful owners as soon as the mistake is realised. But what about the less common case where the person who has gained an article by mistake nevertheless decides to appropriate it when he becomes aware of his mistake? Such a person would be just as culpable morally as one who had taken the chattel on purpose. Provision is made in the Larceny Act, 1916, that 'taking' shall be deemed to include any obtaining of possession by trick, by intimidation, by finding, if at the time of the finding the finder believes that the owner can be discovered by taking reasonable steps, or under a mistake on the part of the owner with knowledge on the part of the taker that possession has been so obtained. This provision does seem to be an attempt to cover those cases of clear criminality which would not otherwise have come under the basic definition of larceny. But a perusal of some of the cases may show how oddly the attempt has worked.

In a nineteenth-century case, decided on the principles later incorporated in the codifying Act of 1916, one Middleton had presented at a post office a warrant authorising him to withdraw ten shillings from his savings bank account. The clerk mistakenly consulted a different warrant, relating to the sum of some £8 in respect of another depositor, and he placed this latter sum on the counter. Middleton realised the mistake, but promptly picked up the money and later spent it. Though the money had been given to him, it was held that his action amounted to a taking, and he was convicted of stealing. In a case of 1958, a lorry driver named Smith had been instructed by his employer to collect forty sacks of meal and deliver them to a purchaser. Inadvertently eight sacks too many were loaded on to the lorry, and the driver did not discover the mistake until he had completed the delivery of the forty sacks ordered, when he decided to misappropriate the remaining eight sacks. Here again Smith was held guilty of larceny. On the other hand, in a case of 1956, one Moynes was charged with stealing £9 19s. 6d. from his employers. He had been paid this sum as an advance upon his week's wages, leaving only a sum of a few shillings still due to him for that week. The employers' wages clerk, who was unaware of the advance, had at the end of the week placed the usual weekly wage in Moynes' wage packet, and then had handed the packet to Moynes, who did not open the packet and discover the mistake until he reached home, when he forthwith decided to keep the full sum. On summary trial before magistrates Moynes was convicted of larceny, but on appeal this conviction was quashed.

It is hard to draw any distinction between the fraudulent activities of Middleton, Smith and Moynes, yet the courts decided that Moynes was not guilty of larceny, while the other two accused were. Lawyers are themselves sharply divided in their views as to the reasons for these decisions, but it may be suggested that if the owner of the chattel or his agent is under a misapprehension as to the identity of the person he is dealing with, as might be said to be the case as regards Middleton, or as to the identity or quantity of the chattel involved, as in Smith's case, then if the accused decides to appropriate the chattel or part of it on discovery of the error he is guilty of larceny. Whereas if the owner or his servant or agent is under no such misapprehension, but makes his mistake because of some delusion or oversight on his part to the effect that he ought to hand over the chattel to the person he is dealing with, then he must be regarded as giving the chattel away freely, and the accused, as in the case of Moynes, will not be guilty of stealing, however dishonest his later behaviour on discovery of the mistake. As has been said by a distinguished jurist in a recent number of the *Law Quarterly Review*, '(Such cases) are a public scandal both because the courts are reluctantly compelled to allow dishonesty to go unpunished, and because of the serious waste of judicial time involved in the discussion of futile legal subtleties.'

By a series of statutes, mainly in the eighteenth and nineteenth centuries, some of the gaps left by the boundaries of larceny were filled by the creation of several other related offences. For example, although the law had provided that a servant could be held guilty of stealing from his employer if he took goods or money from that employer, yet the case was different if the servant received the article on behalf of his master from someone else and appropriated it without ever passing it on to his master. Thus a bank clerk or shop assistant who helped himself out of the till would be guilty of larceny, but if he received a sum of money over the counter from a customer and put it straight into his own pocket he would not be guilty. As a result the crime of embezzlement was created by statute in 1799 to cover this latter type of behaviour.

Another criminal offence invented to fill up the gaps of the ordinary law was that of obtaining by false pretences. If the accused should obtain the loan of some article by means of a trick, but should actually intend never to give it back, this would amount to larceny. But larceny cannot be committed where the pretence is such as to persuade the innocent party to part with full ownership of the goods. Thus, if Jones tells Robinson that he represents an umbrella manufacturer (an assertion which is quite untrue), and he persuades Robinson to give him £5 for a new umbrella to be delivered next week, and then appropriates the money obtained, Robinson will have actually intended the ownership of the money to pass to Jones or his supposed employers. Accordingly Jones cannot be guilty of stealing, though he is in fact guilty of the related crime of obtaining by false pretences. Yet, to be guilty of this latter crime the pretence must be as to some matter of past or present fact, so that if Jones had made no representation about his supposed employment, but had merely promised to bring Robinson an umbrella next week in return for the £5, the offence would not have been committed, though a prosecution for another different offence, obtaining credit by fraud, might be possible. If it is added that the maximum penalty for simple larceny or for obtaining by false pretences is imprisonment for five years, there appears to be no sense in maintaining the distinction, though larceny is a felony and obtaining by false pretences happens to be a misdemeanour, a matter to be discussed further below in connection with the classification of crimes. Obtaining credit by fraud, another misdemeanour, carries a possible sentence of a year's imprisonment, and it is perhaps not unreasonable that this should be less than the maximum penalty for obtaining by false pretences, but it is really only a fifth as grave an offence? Larceny by a clerk or servant is in a special category as far as punishment is concerned, and it carries a maximum sentence of fourteen years' imprisonment, the same as the maximum penalty for embezzlement, and both are felonies. In the case of these latter two crimes it is also now provided that on a prosecution for either a conviction for the other may be obtained, though the same principle does not necessarily prevail in the case of prosecution for other offences related to larceny.

As one further illustration of the effect which may be created by the proliferation of offences related to stealing, and their interaction with the offence of larceny itself, let us pose a simple problem. Suppose that Jones sees Robinson drop a book, and while it is lying on the ground Brown, who has just arrived on the scene, asks Jones whether it is his book. Jones answers: 'Yes, and I will sell it to you for ten shillings.' Brown agrees, and he hands over the ten shillings, picks up the book and walks off. Here Jones would be guilty of obtaining ten shillings by false pretences from Brown, but he is guilty of no criminal offence as against Robinson, because he has committed no act of taking. If, on the other hand, after receiving the ten shillings Jones goes to the trouble of picking up the book and handing it to Brown, then in addition to the offence he has committed against

Brown, he is also guilty of stealing from Robinson, because here he has actually taken the book. In either event Robinson would be able to recover the book or its value from Brown, in civil law, but it is very curious that the extent of Jones' guilt in criminal law should depend upon whether a mere mechanical act should have been performed as an adjunct to the undoubtedly criminal main purpose of his deed.

A special criminal law revision committee, appointed by the Lord Chancellor, has been sitting for some years to discuss the possibilities of reform of the law of larceny and kindred offences. What is needed is some formula which would cover all types of criminal activity against property or possession. It may seem that the difficulties in settling upon such a formula are extensive, and that that is why the committee has taken so long in its deliberations so far. Yet what would seem to have been a fair effort to solve the problems presented was provided by the Criminal Code Commissioners, who drew up an abortive Draft Criminal Code in 1879. They defined theft as 'the act of fraudulently and without colour of right taking, or fraudulently and without colour of right converting to the use of any person anything capable of being stolen, with intent to deprive the owner permanently thereof, or to deprive any person having any special property or interest therein permanently of such property or interest'. This definition, had it ever been adopted by statute, would have had the beneficial effect of getting rid of the technical distinctions concerning taking, and would have placed the emphasis where it is submitted it ought to be, upon the fraudulent intent of the accused. It would then only have remained to make some provision as to the kinds of things which are capable of being stolen, and the scale of punishments to be applied in case of conviction. Granted the fraudulent intent, any taking or any dealing with the property to the detriment of the title or interest of the rightful owner or possessor would have led to a conviction.

Oddly enough, although the law of England is still in a muddled state, English lawyers have been responsible for importing into many of the countries of the Commonwealth criminal codes which contain provisions not dissimilar from the suggestions of the Criminal Code Commissioners, and these codes show that the task of the present criminal law revision committee should not be impossible. Among the countries which now possess what it is suggested are satisfactory laws concerning the definition of theft are Canada, Nigeria, Uganda, Nyasaland and Northern Rhodesia. The Canadian Criminal Code of 1954, for example, is based very much upon the draft attempt cited above, though it goes into further detail in prescribing the ways in which theft may be committed, and it attempts to make consistent provisions as regards wild animals. As a positive attempt to suggest reform of the English law, it may be worthwhile to quote the Canadian provisions. If 'conversion' is taken to mean some dealing with property inconsistent with the lawful rights of the owner or possessor, it is submitted that the provisions are otherwise self-explanatory, and that they should effectively cover all types of criminal dealing with other people's property. The provisions are contained in a single section of the Canadian Criminal Code, and run as follows:

(1) Every one commits theft who fraudulently and without colour of right takes, or fraudulently and without colour right converts to his use or to the use of another person, anything whether animate or inanimate, with intent,

    (*a*) to deprive, temporarily or absolutely, the owner of it or a person who has a special property or interest in it, of the thing or of his property or interest in it,

    (*b*) to pledge it or deposit it as security,

    (*c*) to part with it under a condition with respect to its return that the person who parts with it may be unable to perform, or

    (*d*) to deal with it in such a manner that it cannot be restored in the condition in which it was at the time it was taken or converted.

(2) A person commits theft when, with intent to steal anything, he moves it or causes it to move or to be moved, or begins to cause it to become movable.

(3) A taking or conversion of anything may be fraudulent

notwithstanding that it is effected without secrecy or attempt at concealment.

(4) For the purposes of the Act the question whether anything that is converted is taken for the purpose of conversion, or whether it is, at the time at which it is converted, in the lawful possession of the person who converts it is not material.

(5) For the purposes of this section a person who has a wild living creature in captivity shall be deemed to have a special property or interest in it while it is in captivity and after it has escaped from captivity.

HOMOSEXUALITY

The subject of homosexuality arouses considerable controversy among those who are concerned about the proper scope and function of the law. As the law stands at present there are two main criminal offences of a homosexual nature. First, the crime of buggery or sodomy, which consists of the penetration of the anus of one person by the penis of another: if this act is committed with an animal it is termed bestiality. This crime is a felony punishable with imprisonment for life. It may be noted that the offence need not necessarily be homosexual, though all prosecutions for buggery seem to concern acts committed between males only. Secondly, gross indecency between males, an offence first created in 1885, is a misdemeanour punishable with imprisonment for a maximum period of two years.

In 1957 the Committee on Homosexual Offences and Prostitution, which was presided over by Sir John Wolfenden, reported in favour of relaxing the law to provide that homosexual acts in private between consenting adult males should no longer be crimes. To see how the Wolfenden Committee reached this conclusion it is perhaps best to quote a portion of the Report:

There appears to be no unquestioned definition of what constitutes or ought to constitute a crime. To define it as 'an act which is punishable by the State' does not answer the

53

question: What acts ought to be punished by the State? We have therefore worked with our own formulation of the function of the criminal law, so far as it concerns the subjects of this inquiry. In this field, its function, as we see it, is to preserve public order and decency, to protect the citizen from what is offensive or injurious, and to provide sufficient safeguards against exploitation and corruption of others, particularly those who are specially vulnerable because they are young, weak in body or mind, inexperienced, or in a state of special physical, official or economic dependence.

It is not, in our view, the function of the law to intervene in the private lives of citizens, or to seek to enforce any particular pattern of behaviour, further than is necessary to carry out the purpose we have outlined. It follows that we do not believe it to be a function of the law to attempt to cover all the fields of sexual behaviour. Certain forms of sexual behaviour are regarded by many as sinful, morally wrong, or objectionable for reasons of conscience, or of religious or cultural tradition; and such actions may be reprobated on these grounds. But the criminal law does not cover all such actions at the present time; for instance, adultery and fornication are not offences for which a person can be punished by the criminal law. Nor indeed is prostitution as such.

We appreciate that opinions will differ as to what is offensive, injurious or inimical to the common good, and also as to what constitutes exploitation or corruption; and that these opinions will be based on moral, social or cultural standards. We have been guided by our estimate of the standards of the community in general, recognising that they will not be accepted by all citizens, and that our estimate of them may be mistaken.

It can be seen from this passage that the Committee made no attempt to assert that homosexual acts between consenting adults in private were moral. Indeed the great majority of the citizens of this country would condemn all homosexuality as clearly immoral, and our present laws concerning homosexual acts undoubtedly stem from the attempt to make the law con-

54

form with or mirror the views of society as a whole. Yet, as the Committee pointed out, there are a number of sins which are not crimes, and the Report mentions the sexual sins of adultery and fornication. If one were to seek further anomalies, it would be possible to quote the case of lesbianism, for it is a strange aspect of our law that homosexual acts between males are crimes, while homosexual acts between females are not. If therefore it is recognised that there is a diversity of sexual activities, and that the law is highly inconsistent in its attempts to provide that sexual sins should also be crimes, it may well be thought that the Committee's ideas as to the scope and function of the criminal law in this field do at least show the merit of consistency.

If it is accepted that the criminal law should content itself with the preservation of public order and decency, and the protection of the citizens from acts of an offensive nature and from corruption, it then becomes logical to accept that there is no need for homosexual acts between consenting adult males in private to remain criminal offences. This change could also cover the commission of buggery in private between consenting adults, and it is submitted that, had the matter been within the Committee's terms of reference, the recommendations might well have extended to acts of buggery committed in private between adult males and females. As the Report runs:

> We do not think that it is proper for the law to concern itself with what a man does in private unless it can be shown to be so contrary to the public good that the law ought to intervene in its function as the guardian of that public good.
>
> Unless a deliberate attempt is to be made by society, acting through the agency of the law, to equate the sphere of crime with that of sin, there must remain a realm of private morality and immorality which is, in brief and crude terms, not the law's business.

It should be noted that the Committee expressly excepted from its recommendations homosexual acts committed in public, which must of necessity be likely to give offence to other people, and homosexual acts committed with the young or with mental defectives, where there is what might be regarded as the element of seduction. The Report states:

> We believe that it is part of the function of the law to safeguard those who need protection by reason of their youth or some mental defect, and we do not wish to see any change in the law which would weaken this protection.
>
> It is also part of the function of the law to preserve public order and decency. We therefore hold that when homosexual behaviour between males takes place in public it should continue to be dealt with by the criminal law.

Although the Committee's recommendations upon prostitution, with which we are not at present concerned, were accepted by the Government, and carried into effect by the Street Offences Act, 1959, an Act which has had the effect of clearing the streets of prostitutes by means of the imposition of severe penalties for public soliciting (though it must not be thought that the Act has put an end to prostitution, or even that it was one of the purposes of the Act to do so), the recommendations upon homosexual offences were shelved. The Government took the attitude that public opinion was not ripe for such alteration of the law on this subject as had been suggested. Certainly the Government would be right in believing that opinions may well be sharply divided on this subject, but there is probably a very great body of informed opinion which would favour the Wolfenden suggestions. The logic of the Report is hard to escape, and the record of the police in prosecuting homosexual males has been one of vaccilation. In some areas such prosecutions are virtually unknown, while in others the particular views of chief constables would appear to be shown by a small but persistent stream of court cases. But perhaps the worst facet of the present law is the possibility of blackmail which arises from the discovery of homosexual activity. Few people would doubt that blackmail is a crime which betrays one of the most despicable traits to be found in humankind. Many blackmailers are never prosecuted simply because their victims cannot face up to the difficulty of confessing their secrets to the police. When the secret involves a sexual matter the reluctance is probably even greater than in other cases, because of the very personal issues involved. *A fortiori* reluctance must be at its greatest in cases where the secret involves guilt of either a very grave crime or else a sexual crime. In 1963 the Report of a Tribunal of Inquiry upon certain matters including the security of state secrets was issued, and from that Report it became clear that, as many had long thought, homosexuals were security risks. The central character of the affair in question was one Vassall, who had committed a homosexual act with a Russian agent, and had then been blackmailed into passing secrets to other Russian agents under the threat that his behaviour would be exposed to his superiors.

It is probable that most homosexuals would be reluctant anyway for their activities to become generally known, and thus they may remain subjects for the blackmailer. But at least the removal of the criminal element from the activity, where there is no public indecency or seduction of the young or the mentally deficient, might render blackmail less likely, and, on the positive side, it might even encourage many homosexuals to seek medical treatment. In the author's view the adoption by statute of the Wolfenden Committee's recommendations would be a logical step forward for the future. No harm could be done, for such a statute would hardly encourage 'normal' people to become homosexuals! And some positive good might come out of the change in the law. The Suicide Act, 1961, had the effect of abolishing suicide and attempted suicide as criminal offences, while making special provision for the punishment of those who aid or abet the commission of suicide. The result has been that mentally sick people who have attempted but failed to take their own lives are no longer tortured further by being tried for the offence which stemmed from their illness, and medical treatment can take place unimpeded. A similar Act based on the Wolfenden Committee's recommendations might have a like effect.

OTHER SEXUAL OFFENCES

It is tempting, in the light of the above discussion, to suggest that the abolition of the crime of incest would be another logical step for the law reformer to take. Incest is committed where a man has sexual intercourse with a woman whom he knows to be his granddaughter, daughter, sister or mother, or where a woman of or above the age of sixteen with consent permits her grandfather, father, brother or son to have sexual intercourse with her, provided she knows of the relationship; and it is a misdemeanour punishable with imprisonment for seven years. Again this would seem to involve interference by the state in people's private affairs, but it is submitted that the law is justified in order to protect the family, and to guard against the dangers of the birth of deformed and mentally afflicted children. No alteration in the law, therefore, is either likely or desirable.

The only other sexual offence which may require modification is the misdemeanour committed by a man in having sexual intercourse by consent with a girl between the ages of thirteen and sixteen, a crime which carries a maximum penalty of two years' imprisonment. In the light of what will be said in the later chapter in this book on Family Law, it is suggested that such consensual intercourse with a girl of fifteen should no longer be a criminal offence, though the present provisions concerning intercourse with girls under the age of fifteen should remain. (It may be noted that intercourse with a girl under the age of thirteen is a felony carrying a possibility of life imprisonment.)

Censorship

It may also be apposite at this juncture to touch upon the question of censorship. Until 1959 it had been an offence to publish any matter which would have a 'tendency to deprave and corrupt those whose minds are open to such immoral influences and into whose hands a publication of this sort may fall', a definition fraught with uncertainty. But since the passage of the Obscene Publications Act, 1959, it is probable that the main body of our law concerning obscene publications is satisfactory. Under that Act it is an offence to publish any article (which includes books, records and films) which 'is, *if taken as a whole,* such as to tend to deprave and corrupt persons who are likely, *having regard to all relevant circumstances*, to read, see or hear the matter contained or embodied in it'. It is now also for the first time a defence to prove that publication 'is justified as being for the public good on the ground that it is in the interests of science, literature, art or learning, or of other objects of general concern'. It is right in an enlightened society that as much freedom as possible should be given to disseminate personal opinions, either by the spoken word or in print, provided the reasonable limits set by the laws of defamation and sedition are observed. The Act of 1959, therefore, is a reasonable piece of legislation in a true democracy. Literature which is robust and forthright upon sexual matters ought to be seen, by those who take the trouble to read it, for what it is, and judged by the readers upon its true merits. Little good can come from preventing the publication of such literature, for an appetite for forbidden fruits will only be whetted. The majority of thinking people have always been able to discern the respective merits of Shakespeare and of the books sometimes to be found in back-street book shops, and the fact that some people of low intelligence cannot do so should not be allowed to prevent others from exercising their minds.

But is it right to allow the young to be bombarded with sex at every turn? Since the Second World War the invasion from America of the paperback book with the lurid cover (whether or not the contents of the book measure up to such an introduction) has been a factor in our life which no one can ignore. Even the most respectable book shops have to display these books, for the covers undoubtedly provide the titillation which is good for trade. The constant bombardment of us all, old and young, intelligent and gullible, by visual sex, both from these book covers and from organised advertising of commercial products, may well be a factor in the degeneration of general moral standards which has taken place in recent years. It may well be that the Government will be forced before long to take steps to regulate this exploitation of sex for commercial ends, in order to provide the kind of protection for the public which the Wolfenden Committee considered to be a function of the criminal law.

CONSPIRACY

It is a curious aspect of English criminal law that machinery exists whereby an accused person who is not clearly guilty of any specific criminal offence may nevertheless be convicted of a residuary offence, at the discretion of the court. The offence which may be charged is the common law misdemeanour of conspiracy. This offence can only be committed by two or more people acting in concert, though it is possible to charge an accused with conspiracy with some person or persons unknown. The substance of the offence is an agreement to commit any other crime (whether or not that crime is carried out), or to commit a civil wrong, such as a tort, or to do any act which is immoral or tends to the public mischief; and, as with all common law misdemeanours, it may be punished by a fine and imprisonment, or both, at the discretion of the court. Historically conspiracy was one of a group of offences punished by the court of Star Chamber, as has been mentioned in the last chapter.

There is perhaps not much to criticise in the existence of a crime which consists in agreement by two or more people to commit other crimes, or even to commit civil wrongs, for civil wrongs committed by two or more people may well be far worse than such wrongs committed individually, and without previous agreement. The real point of criticism is in the maintenance of a crime which is committed wherever there is an agreement by two or more persons to do some other act which is not an offence by itself in law of any kind at all. Although law tends to reflect morality, it is not the same as morality, as has been stressed more than once in this book already. Supposing the suggestions concerning the law as to homosexuality which have been made above were to be enacted, it would still be possible, it seems, to prosecute for the crime of conspiracy two adult males who had agreed to commit a homosexual act in private, on the ground that they had entered into an agreement to do an immoral act! For the courts to be in a position to judge morals in this way can hardly be other than dangerous.

A case of 1961 may illustrate the possibilities of the present law. It concerned one Shaw and some others who produced a magazine or pamphlet called the *Ladies' Directory*, in which prostitutes advertised their services. The production of the magazine was a direct result of the Street Offences Act, 1959, which has been mentioned above, whereby prostitutes were effectively cleared off the streets. As was said above, prostitution was not thereby brought to an end, but of course the means by which prostitutes were able to attract their clients had to be changed. Advertisements, for instance, in somewhat cryptic terms appeared in shop windows, and the *Ladies' Directory* was available in certain shops and other places for those who asked for it. Shaw was charged and convicted of a conspiracy to corrupt public morals, and his conviction was upheld on appeal both in the Court of Criminal Appeal and in the House of Lords, though the judges in the Court of Criminal Appeal were of the opinion that conduct calculated and intended to corrupt public morals was itself a substantive offence, and thus that conspiracy so to corrupt public morals was a conspiracy to commit a criminal act. The House of Lords, on the other hand, preferred to base their decision upon the view that a conspiracy to corrupt public morals was a conspiracy to commit a wrongful act calculated to cause public injury.

Whichever reason for the decision is preferred, the implications of judicial extension of the boundaries of the criminal law are clear. It would seem that an agreement between two people to do anything is in jeopardy as being a possible conspiracy, should a court be prepared to consider that the agreement offends against public morality, for the boundaries of morality are equally vague. It may even be argued that the Shaw decision was wrong within the terms adopted by the courts themselves, for the people who would ask for copies of the *Ladies' Directory* would already have had their morals corrupted, so that Shaw and his co-conspirators were only agreeing to provide an article for the use of people who could not be further corrupted. But such an argument is pointless when we are considering whether the crime of conspiracy should continue to exist in its present form or not. Few indeed would consider that Shaw's activities were praiseworthy, and many would consider that there ought to be a criminal offence of which he could be held guilty. The present writer would associate himself with this latter view, but it is a view which carries with it a wish to see the boundaries of the law on the subject properly drawn. If loopholes in statutes like the Street Offences Act appear, it is submitted that it is not the task of the courts to fill up the gaps on an *ad hoc* basis. Criminality is not the same thing as immorality. Where certain immoral acts sufficiently offend public decency, then it is the task of Parliament to provide that such acts should for the future be criminal, but it is highly dangerous to allow what is in effect retrospective legislation by the courts.

In short, Parliament should address itself to the task of providing specifically that such behaviour as that of Shaw should be a criminal offence. The Street Offences Act, being the first effective Act to deal with the vice of prostitution, may well be regarded as experimental, and likely to require periodic amendment in the light of the experience of its working. If this amendment is undertaken sufficiently speedily, a man like Shaw would escape conviction when his activities are first discovered, but he would become liable to conviction for the same acts once they were made criminal by statute, and the law would be certain. Short amending statutes upon purely legal topics are usually passed through Parliament quickly and comparatively easily, and the time-lag need not be very great. Once this kind of statute-reform is recognised as a regular process, the controversial variety of the crime of conspiracy could be abolished without loss to the law, and it is submitted that the remainder of the crime could also go with it. There can surely be little need to maintain a separate crime of an agreement to commit other crimes, and agreements to commit civil wrongs, should they ever become obtrusive, which is most unlikely, could be catered for in the same way as it has been suggested Parliament should concern itself with conspiracies to do acts which are immoral or which tend to the public mischief.

INTENTION IN CRIME

It is a basic principle of English criminal law that a man is not to be guilty of an offence unless he has a guilty mind; that is, unless his conduct is voluntary. It is, however, only the knowledge of the act which is being done that is necessary, for ignorance of the law rendering that act criminal is no excuse. This principle is applied generally, save where statute may provide otherwise, as where in some Licensing Act particular forms of behaviour are expressly made criminal whether the accused is aware of what he is doing or not, and save for the more petty summary offences where the courts have taken the attitude that the Acts which provide for the offences were concerned solely to prohibit the activity concerned. Thus, it is an offence to park a car on the highway at night without lights (except in certain recognised and specified places), whether or not the owner of the car is aware that the lights of the car are not on. Even if the owner had left his lights on, he would be guilty of the offence if they failed after he had left the car, for ignorance of the failure would not excuse him.

These provisions as to summary offences are probably justified on the grounds of preventing unnecessary difficulty in proving a case on which so little hangs anyway. But there are some offences which are not of this trivial nature where the statutes concerned do not appear to exclude the doctrine of *mens rea*, the guilty mind, and yet where the courts have adopted a kind of half-way position between enforcing the doctrine and excluding it. The uncertainty arising from such cases is undesirable, and should be resolved. The two offences which particularly involve this kind of uncertainty are abduction and bigamy.

As regards the offence of abduction two cases of the last century may be used to illustrate the difficulties. Both depend in their result upon the interpretation by the courts of a provision in an Act of 1861, which has since been substantially re-enacted in the present Sexual Offences Act, 1956, and which ran as follows:

> Whosoever shall unlawfully take . . . any unmarried girl, being under the age of sixteen years, out of the possession and against the will of her father or mother, or of any other person having lawful care or charge of her, shall be guilty of a misdemeanour.

In the first case the accused met a girl of fourteen in the street, and, under the impression that she was a prostitute, he took her to another place and seduced her, finally leaving her where he had met her. Nothing turned upon the seduction itself, as there was not then, as there is now, any crime of having intercourse with a girl under the age of sixteen, and the accused was simply charged with abduction as defined above. The girl had in fact been in the custody of her father, but as the prisoner had not been aware of this fact—for he had not concerned himself at all with whether she was in anybody's custody—his conviction before the court of first instance was quashed on appeal. In the second case the accused was aware that a girl whom he abducted was in the custody of her father, but he believed, upon reasonable grounds, that she was over sixteen. Yet his conviction was upheld on appeal. Some jurists have argued that the cases can be reconciled in that the second accused had intentionally taken a girl out of the custody of her father, whereas the first accused had had no such intention; in other words that an accused can only be convicted if he has *mens rea* as to the actual abduction, and that the matter of the girl's age may be left to chance. But this is to apply the doctrine of *mens rea* to one part of the statutory definition of the offence and not to another part. It is submitted that the law can only be rendered consistent by making the doctrine of *mens rea* apply to either the whole of the definition or none of it. Perhaps, as regards this particular offence, it may be thought desirable to exclude the doctrine altogether, as abduction of the young may be the kind of offence to be prohibited totally, regardless of intention.

In the case of the crime of bigamy, the difficulty involved in the application of the doctrine of *mens rea* may well have been created partly by the poor drafting of the definition of bigamy in the Offences Against the Person Act, 1861. Under that statute it is laid down that bigamy is committed by anyone who 'being married, shall marry any other person during the life of the former husband or wife', though it shall be a defence for the accused to show that, at the time of the second marriage, either the first marriage had been dissolved, or the first spouse had been continuously absent for the space of seven years, and was not known by the accused to have been alive during that time. An analysis of this definition will reveal that anyone who is already married cannot marry again, but can in fact only go through a second *form* of marriage. It is accordingly unnecessary to make any proviso as to a defence in case of divorce, since divorce would bring the first marriage to an end. It is also quite unnecessary to include the word 'former' in the definition, as the so-called former husband or wife is in fact the only spouse. Once more two decided cases should illustrate the muddle into which courts have been drawn.

In 1889 a Mrs. Tolson was charged with bigamy. She had been deserted by her husband in December 1881. Her father made inquiries on her behalf and received information that her husband had been drowned at sea on his way to America, and, relying on this information, Mrs. Tolson went through a second ceremony of marriage in January 1887, at the end of which year Mr. Tolson returned from America. Although Mrs. Tolson had no defence based on her husband's continuous absence, as the period had not lasted seven years, it was nevertheless held, on appeal, that her conviction must be quashed as she had no *mens rea*. On the other hand, in a later case of 1921, a man of little education had instructed his solicitors to take proceedings for divorce on his behalf. When he received a telegram from the solicitors stating that he would shortly receive some papers for signature, he assumed that his divorce must have been obtained, and he went through a second form of marriage with another woman. Although the jury found that his belief had been based upon reasonable grounds, he was convicted, and his conviction was upheld on appeal.

It would appear that the courts have taken the view that a reasonable belief in the death of the first spouse will exonerate the accused from guilt when going through a second form of marriage, while that the validity or otherwise of a divorce is to be treated as a matter about which belief is irrelevant, however reasonable. This can hardly have been the intention of the law-makers when formulating the crime of bigamy in the first place, and it is submitted that certainty and justice demand once more that the doctrine of *mens rea* should be applied totally or not at all. The author's preference is for insisting that the doctrine should be applied, as the offence is essentially one of nefarious intention carried into effect. There can be no good reason for insisting that a second form of marriage, however invalid, must be criminal in a case where the intention was as innocent as that of Mrs. Tolson. It may be added that statute law in the present century has made provision whereby a married person who has reason to believe that his or her spouse is dead may now obtain a decree of presumption of death and dissolution of marriage, so that any second marriage would in fact be valid even if the first spouse reappeared later.

Perhaps clarification of the law would be aided by simplifying and rationalising the definition of bigamy at the same time as the reform suggested above is carried into effect. As a tentative new definition of bigamy, the following might be considered:

'It shall be an offence, punishable by imprisonment for seven years [or whichever maximum penalty may be favoured for the future], for any person, being married and knowing of his married status, knowingly to go through any other form of marriage with another person, unless the first spouse shall have been continuously absent for a period of seven years immediately preceding the later ceremony and not known to the person charged to have been alive during that time.'

THE CLASSIFICATION OF CRIMES

The major classification of crimes into felonies and misdemeanours has already been mentioned in Chapter One, where it was explained that although felonies were originally the more serious and misdemeanours the less serious criminal offences, this distinction has ceased to be applied consistently. Other examples of the blurring of the distinction have been alluded to in the portion of the present chapter dealing with theft and related offences. The gradual destruction of the distinctions between the two groups of offences has now reached a stage at which the only differences still existing can hardly justify the retention of the distinction itself. Thus, a constable may arrest without warrant anyone whom he reasonably suspects of having committed a felony, even if no such felony has been committed, though he may not exercise such a power in relation to a suspected misdemeanour. It is a crime to withhold information concerning the commission of a felony, but not of a misdemeanour. After conviction for felony the accused is formally asked whether he has anything to say before sentence, though there is no similar rule in the case of conviction for misdemeanour. Conviction for felony, followed by a sentence of more than twelve months' imprisonment, involves disqualification from sitting in Parliament and from voting in any elections, whereas conviction for misdemeanour involves only disqualification from voting in local elections (though a misdemeanant may be expelled from membership of Parliament by Parliament). Finally, civil proceedings may not be taken against a felon by anyone injured by his felony until he has been prosecuted or a reasonable excuse has been shown for a failure to prosecute him, though there is no similar rule as regards civil proceedings against misdemeanants.

The wider powers of arrest without warrant might easily be applied to all cases of suspected crime, providing the suspicion is objectively reasonable. Withholding of information of the commission of a crime might, without serious hindrance to the administration of justice, cease to be itself a crime, except possibly in the case of certain specified offences of such gravity as, for example, murder and rape. There would be no harm in allowing all accused persons the right to make a statement before sentence. Conviction for any offence, followed by a sentence of imprisonment for more than twelve months might reasonably carry the greater electoral disqualification for the duration of the sentence. And the ban upon civil proceedings until after a criminal trial might, without loss, be abandoned altogether. In the rare event of civil and criminal trials concerning the same set of circumstances coming on for hearing at the same time rules of court providing for some order of precedence, probably in favour of the criminal trial, could be drawn up; the consequent delay in the civil trial need therefore only last for a few days. All the differences between felonies and misdemeanours are of a procedural nature, and they are hardly more than trifling. It would seem that the step of abolition of the present classification may well be taken before long, thus simplifying and rationalising the law.

There is, however, one rather special aspect of the classification of crimes which demands separate treatment, and that is the distinct splitting off from the main body of felonies of the crime of treason, which can only be committed by those who owe allegiance to the Crown, and which is something of a category of aggravated felony. The offence of treason has its roots deep in the political history of the country. It is a little surprising to find that the prime authority for the existence and scope of the crime today is still an Act of 1351, which was itself a statute which codified the previous common law. This Act has been supplemented by statutory provisions passed from time to time, notably at the time of the establishment of the Hanoverian succession early in the eighteenth century, and the present headings of treason are as follows:

(a) Compassing the death of the King (or, at the present time, the Queen Regnant), the Queen Consort, or their eldest son and heir.

(b) Violating the King's wife, his eldest daughter being unmarried, or the wife of his eldest son and heir.

(c) Levying war against the Monarch in his realm.

(d) Adhering to the Monarch's enemies in his realm, giving them aid or comfort in the realm, or elsewhere.

(e) Slaying the Chancellor, Treasurer or the King's Justices, when in their places discharging their offices.

(f) Attempting to hinder the succession to the Crown of the person entitled thereto under the Act relating to the Hanoverian Settlement.

(g) Maintaining in writing the invalidity of the line of succession to the Crown established by the Act of Settlement.

Of these various treasons, no harm could be done by abolishing (b), which could be treated as rape, and (e), which could be treated as murder (or, in suitable cases, manslaughter), though

68

there would equally seem to be little harm in allowing them to remain. Happily the circumstances for which they provide have been unknown in recent centuries in this country. Headings (*a*) and (*f*) are clearly necessary in their present or somewhat similar forms if preservation of the monarchical establishment of the country is to be a matter of law. (*g*) may be said to come within the same category, though there may now be no good reason for preventing such people as may want to denounce the present line of succession from doing so in writing as well as orally: under modern conditions they cannot be regarded as the threat to the Constitution that they may have been in the eighteenth century. (*c*) is a provision necessary in some form to provide for the punishment of persons who wage civil war. Heading (*d*) has been applied to cover the case of British citizens assisting enemy states in time of war, either within the United Kingdom or else outside it. It is the only type of treason which might with some justification be criticised seriously, for the courts have sometimes been prepared to stretch the meaning of allegiance in order to be able to convict someone who sided with the enemy in time of war. Perhaps the outstanding case was that of William Joyce, who had broadcast propaganda from Germany to this country during the Second World War. Although he was a United States citizen, the fact that he had been in possession of a British passport, which had been obtained fraudulently and renewed shortly before the outbreak of war, was held by the House of Lords to be sufficient to bring him into the class of people who owe temporary allegiance to the Crown—a class which is normally composed of foreign nationals who reside in this country, or who have so resided in the past and have left either their families or some of their property here behind them.

It may well be that adverse criticism of certain individual convictions for treason may be sustained in logic, and criticism of this kind is useful in helping to make us aware of the need to keep the law suitable to the requirements of society. But the offences comprised in the term treason are inevitably infected by political necessity. Arbitrary political power over and above the law should always be deplored, and it is far better that the law itself should provide for the needs of politics, but we must recognise that some political needs do exist. The offences of treason which concern the establishment of the monarchy are necessary because the establishment of the institution of the monarchy is regarded as politically more important than many other aspects of public life, and even than the personalities of the monarchs themselves. Similarly there is a need for effective provisions to guard against fermentation of civil war and treacherous activities in time of war. Although English law provides that the term 'enemy' only covers the citizens of countries with which the United Kingdom is actually at war, it is noteworthy that provision has had to be made for the similarly treacherous activities in time of peace of those who owe allegiance to the Crown, by means of the Official Secrets Acts. Though it is possible to deplore the actual decision in Joyce's case, it must be recognised that had he not been convicted of treason it might have been necessary to amend the law of treason to cover any future activities of a similar nature entered into by non-British subjects.

Treason, therefore, is a concession to political necessity, and it is far better that this concession should be made within the framework of the law itself than by recognising that political necessity may at times override the law. In days gone by there were certain differences between the procedures at trials of felonies and treasons, in the main providing for a number of barbarisms to be practised against traitors. As these differences have now disappeared, either by law reform or by common practice, there is probably no good reason for continuing to regard treasons as a separate class of crimes, save that such a treatment emphasises the difference between 'ordinary' and political crimes. At all events the abolition of the major classification of crimes will provide the only reform which can carry substantial effects with it.

CHAPTER THREE

Punishment

THE AIMS OF PUNISHMENT

THE aims of punishment after an accused person has been convicted of a crime are often said to involve four possible elements, retribution, deterrence, reform of the criminal and protection of the general public. Views as to the order of importance in which these elements should be treated vary considerably, and there are those who are prepared to argue, on one side or another, that only one of the four has any relevance to the subject. Some may think that the purpose of punishment is purely retributive, and others will be convinced that every criminal is essentially a sick person to be treated for his illness, with a view to reform of his behaviour, and that accordingly it is even incorrect to regard this treatment as being in the nature of punishment at all. Many modern penologists seem to be allied to this latter school of thought. The present writer feels that there is something to be said for the views of all those who favour one or other of the elements mentioned above, but that the aims of punishment ought to take account of all these elements, though with an emphasis upon the last two, rather than to concentrate upon one to the exclusion of all others. In order of importance the author has a slight preference for the element of protection of the public, as it appears to be more vital to see that innocent people should not be harmed than that the interests of the convicts or potential future criminals should be put first.

On the whole it is unfashionable these days to link justice and punishment with ideas of retribution. This is particularly so since many people believe that retribution means vengeance.

This is unfortunate, for the desire for vengeance, though a natural human reaction, can play no part in any civilised system of law, while the principle of retribution properly so called has at least some claims to merit, and is based upon rational ideas. Retribution really means reprobation, a concept which has played a major part in the aims of punishment in past centuries, and which indeed may even be said to be a synonym for the word 'punishment'. Lord Denning, a judge of many years' standing, said in his evidence to the Royal Commission on Capital Punishment a few years ago that the emphatic denunciation of certain gross crimes must be shown by society in the severity of the punishments applied to the criminals. Very few penologists today would agree wholeheartedly that retribution should be the primary aim of punishment, and many would take the view that it is an irrelevant consideration to be wholly ignored. But it is submitted that although other factors are more important, and that although it is better to try to seek a method of punishment which will fit the criminal rather than the actual crime committed, yet it would be a very novel system of law which did not specify the possibility of heavier sentences for serious crimes than for petty crimes. In this sense it is hard to eschew notions of retribution altogether, and for the foreseeable future it is likely that retribution will continue to play some part in forming our ideas as to desirable methods of punishment.

The deterrent theory of punishment is that the punishments prescribed for offences should be such as to deter intending criminals from committing the crimes they might otherwise have committed. It is an essential part of this theory that the threat of punishment should be such as to make the intending criminal realise that it will be carried out if the crime is committed. If the theory is workable there is obviously much that is desirable in it, and it is probable that punishment does act as an effective deterrent in the case of a number of persons convicted for the first time, for many of these first offenders do not come before the courts again on similar charges. But it may be doubted whether punishment is an effective deterrent as far as more hardened criminals are concerned. Dr. Gregory

Zilboorg, in a recent book entitled *The Psychology of the Criminal Act and Punishment* (published by The Hogarth Press and the Institute of Psycho-analysis), has said that pickpockets were reputed to have plied their trade amongst the spectators at public hangings, in the days when this type of petty theft was itself a capital offence. Many penologists believe that even the threat of capital punishment, which will be discussed presently, does not deter a hardened criminal from committing murder to anything like the extent that a more efficient system of detection would. Certainly the possibility of long terms of imprisonment does not appear to deter the organised gangs of bank and wages robbers, currently so rampant, from their evil purposes. Perhaps it is that real criminals are not very susceptible to reason, so that fear is not very efficacious as a deterrent.

These views of the doubtful value of punishment as a deterrent may be depressing, but they do not show that punishment should not be designed at least in part as a deterrent, for it very likely does deter those citizens who would not normally be classed as criminals from committing trivial and easily-detected offences like parking a car without lights or causing an obstruction. Whether the punishment acts as a deterrent even upon decent citizens as regards the commission of serious criminal offences is less clear. The usually law-abiding man acts according to his conscience, and he would avoid serious crime even if there were no penalty at all, for the commission of such crime would offend against his moral principles.

Reform and treatment of the criminal, as we suggested at the beginning of this chapter, are regarded as being of increasing importance in guiding our attitudes towards punishment. If the criminal is indeed a sick person, then there is much to be said for regarding treatment as perhaps the only valid aim of punishment. It would probably be wise, in this event, even to drop the term 'punishment' altogether. Certainly the criminal is a misfit in society, and sometimes he may turn out to be the kind of man who is mentally not capable of preventing himself from committing his crimes. But the modern law does take account of such cases. Anyone who has sat through a few sessions in a magistrates' court will be aware that efforts are made to provide forms of probation, to obtain medical and psychiatric reports, and to insist upon treatment at mental hospitals where this treatment would seem to be required. Considerable discretion is now allowed to our judges of all kinds in deciding whether to pass sentences of imprisonment, fines or many other kinds of detention and treatment, in an effort to make the punishment fit the needs of each particular criminal. The likely developments in relation to sentencing powers will be discussed later in this chapter. Very little will be said in this book about probation and the various forms of orders dealing with mental treatment, as it is submitted that the law is for the most part developing upon correct lines here. Further development will come in the light of the progress of medical science, and the means of perpetuating this progress are already with us. The punishments to be considered separately in this chapter are mainly of the more severe kind, and in particular the most severe of all, death and imprisonment. Ever since the Report of the Departmental Committee on Prisons, published in 1895, which recommended that reformation and deterrence should be treated as the primary aims of punishment, the emphasis of our various steps in penal reform has been in this direction. This trend is likely to continue, though there is no sign as yet that the word 'punishment' will be officially dropped.

But the emphasis upon reform and deterrence, particularly upon the former (in view of the doubts about the effectiveness of the latter as regards many criminals and intending criminals), should not be allowed to blind us to the needs of the general public. Though many criminals may be mentally sick, the present author finds it hard to believe that this is the case with the majority. We have all known temptation in many forms, and most of us, it is hoped, have been able to resist the temptation to do wicked things on most occasions. The human being is certainly provided with a will-power, and though some people have stronger wills than others, the majority of us are aware of what is right and what is wrong in most instances. Many of the people charged in court with the commission of theft freely admit their offences, and also add that they are sorry they committed them. Few of them add that they were unable to stop themselves from committing the acts of which they are charged. The conclusion to which the author is driven is that it is too glib to say that all criminals are sick. They are certainly misfits, but it is submitted that a majority of them are acting criminally because they have consciously determined so to do, probably out of greed. The post office mail bag thieves and the bank robbers are not sick, they are highly organised determinedly calculating and evil men. If this is so it follows that the aims of the law should embrace the object of protecting the general public from the acts of these men. In the author's view it should be recognised as a cardinal aim of punishment to make adequate provision for protecting society as a whole from the machinations of criminals. In relation to petty crimes, such as parking offences, this aim is of course irrelevant, but as far as the more serious crimes are concerned it may well be that some more consistent provision ought to be made to ensure that hardened criminals may be kept if necessary permanently in detention so as to prevent them from doing any further harm to innocent people. Provision was made in the Criminal Justice Act, 1948, for the imposition of sentences of preventive detention along these lines, but it may be that those provisions are not far-reaching enough. Further discussion of this problem will be found below in the section dealing with imprisonment and other forms of detention.

To sum up so far, it is probable that no scale of punishments is justified unless it takes into account all four of the elements which have been mentioned. Retribution is not a popular concept, though it helps us to keep in perspective the need for a scale of punishments roughly comparable with the gravity or otherwise of the crimes concerned. Deterrence is an ideal which may perhaps be more useful in relation to the more petty crimes than the more serious ones. The recent imposition of onerous fines and disqualifications for certain motoring offences does, for example, seem to have had a salutory effect upon the habits of ordinary car drivers. Reform of the criminal is another ideal, very popular among modern penologists, and it is likely to remain a vitally important element in the development of ideas about punishment for the future. Protection of the public, a concept not quite so popular (as witness the curious backwardness of the law in only recently beginning to tackle the problem of reimbursing innocent victims of crimes of violence for their injuries, a matter to be discussed later in this chapter), should probably be regarded for the future as a major purpose of punishment. In the author's view it is even more important in essence than reform of the criminal, though the two aims often go hand in hand as a matter of practice, as will be seen presently. However large the criminal population may be, the law-abiding citizens still out-number them. If we refer back to the recommendations of the Wolfenden Committee, mentioned in the last chapter, it will be remembered that that Committee considered it to be the function of the criminal law to protect the public in the area with which the Wolfenden Committee was concerned. Should not the same considerations be applied to the principles and aims of punishment?

THE DEATH PENALTY

In the last chapter it was stated that the present major criticisms of the law of murder would be demolished by the abolition of the capital penalty, and that such abolition was likely to take place before very long. It is proposed here to consider a little further the merits and demerits of this punishment, and to attempt an assessment of its value in the law.

In the first place it may be as well to remind ourselves of the extent to which this punishment still remains in English law. The death sentence is limited to four crimes, capital murder, treason, piracy on the high seas committed with violence, and intentionally setting fire to one of Her Majesty's ships or to any naval dockyard or arsenal. Where there is a conviction for either of the latter two offences of piracy or arson, the death penalty is the maximum sentence, and except in time of war it has not been passed for many years. It may therefore be concluded that it is at least obsolescent in these cases. For treason or capital murder, however, the penalty is mandatory, except that it may not be passed upon a pregnant woman or any person under the age of eighteen. Both of these latter offences have been described in the last chapter. As the only common kind of treason is that committed by adhering to the enemies of the state in time of war, it is not surprising that criticism of the death penalty has mostly been in connection with the crime of capital murder; but it should be remembered that abolition of the penalty would affect the sentences to be passed in both types of criminal trial.

The illogicalities of the present division of murders into capital and non-capital have already been discussed in the previous chapter, but there are other aspects of the capital penalty which require attention before a definite assessment of the present law can be made. On the basis of the four aims of punishment discussed above it will be appreciated that the death sentence is retributive, and it certainly protects the public from any further criminal activities of the convicted person, while it equally clearly has nothing to do with reform of the criminal. It has already been suggested that retribution alone cannot be regarded as a satisfactory reason for the imposition of any particular punishment, while there is more to be said for basing its existence upon the need to protect the general public. But could not protection of the public be achieved without the adoption of a penalty which is so final and irrevocable? The kind of long, even permanent, detention which will be discussed in the next section of this chapter would protect the public as effectively as the death penalty. True, it would be far more expensive to carry out, as it would provide a long-standing charge upon public funds, levied in the long-run from the tax-payer. But expense is hardly of comparable importance to the question of life or death for a human being.

Perhaps one's attitude to the merits or otherwise of the capital penalty may be swayed if the punishment accords with the fourth of the major aims of punishment, deterrence, about which there is a great deal of controversy. It has already been doubted above whether the hardened criminal will ever be deterred from his commission of a serious crime merely by the nature of the punishment to be suffered if he is caught. Yet the basis for the distinction imported into the Homicide Act, 1957, between those murders which are to carry the capital penalty and those which are not is the deterrent view of punishment. As was pointed out in the last chapter, it is thought by some that a potential murderer may decline to carry a firearm so as to avoid using it in the heat of the moment, thus guarding himself against the possibility of committing the capital crime of murder by shooting. There are no figures to support this view, though equally there are no figures to support those who contradict it. Criminals are obviously unlikely to disclose gratuitously their near-commissions of capital murder! But whether or not there is any real substance in this deterrent view of the capital penalty, it is certainly true to say that many ordinary people believe that the existence of the death penalty may prevent criminals from carrying firearms, and this belief has been sufficient to bolster up common confidence in an unarmed police force. It could be that if this confidence were displaced the police would have to be armed to protect both themselves and the ordinary citizens of the country. Such a step could not be viewed with much enthusiasm, for the police in most other parts of the world seem to be regarded by the citizens with suspicion and even dislike, a feeling which is fostered by the knowledge that they carry guns. It is hard to be genuinely friendly with a man who is fingering his revolver. But it is submitted that the deterrent view is too nebulous in respect of the capital penalty to justify its retention, and that it can hardly be called in aid of the other bases of the punishment mentioned above, retribution and protection of the public. Yet if the penalty is abolished it is hoped that the police will not be armed habitually. Such statistics as we have, particularly those quoted by the Royal Commission on Capital Punishment in its somewhat negative Report, issued in 1953, would appear to show that the incidence of murders has not necessarily increased in those many countries which have abolished the death penalty. If these statistics are of any value, they would seem to show also that there would be no need for our police forces to alter their present practice of only carrying firearms upon exceptional occasions.

In the absence of any convincing deterrent argument to favour the continuance of the death penalty, and in the light of all that has so far been said upon it, it has to be admitted that there are grave objections to its remaining as a punishment provided by English law. It is true that the Home Secretary has the power to reprieve a convicted murderer or traitor, and to substitute some lesser penalty (usually life imprisonment) for that which the judge had no option but to pronounce. But, even though this power is exercised with great care and upon advice, the fact remains that it must be arbitrary where the Home Secretary attempts to decide what are and what are not extenuating circumstances. Among the objections to be raised against the continuance of the capital penalty may be mentioned the attitude of the Christian churches in denying the right of human beings to take away a man's life, even after a judicial decision. It is noteworthy that all the bishops of the Church of England have made a clear concerted decision to this effect. They have decided that, however wanton the behaviour of a murderer, his acts cannot provide sufficient ground for the taking away of the gift of human life conferred upon a man by God. For those who are less concerned with religious principles two other factors are of importance, the barbarism of the actual carrying out of the penalty and its finality.

The death penalty is carried out in this country by the process of hanging, and in other countries where the penalty remains by such methods as the electric chair, the guillotine or the firing squad. It would be hard to decide which method, of any, is more humane than the others, for the fact is that each is unpleasant. Those who support the retention of the death penalty would usually be reluctant to attend an execution, and those who have to officiate at executions have been noteworthy in expressing a marked lack of enthusiasm for the process. As was mentioned in Chapter One, our law has come a long way from the days when public executions, and hanging, drawing and quartering were commonplace. We should all express revulsion today at any attempt to revive these methods of punishment, simply because our collective ideas about punishment have undergone a progressive change, and we no longer consider that vengeance, pain and degradation are the purposes of punishment. It is a fair forecast that in fifty years' time the vast majority of the population will find it hard to understand how the law in the mid-twentieth century could have countenanced the use of the capital penalty, just as it is difficult today to find anyone who can understand how the health of the nation could have been adequately safeguarded in the days before the National Health Service, which is, after all, only some fifteen years old. The fact that a number of other countries employ the death penalty is no argument in favour of its retention, as those countries are mostly nations with political ideologies which we cannot accept. The retention of the death penalty, and even its periodic extension, in Russia and Eastern Europe, can hardly commend the institution to democratic English minds. Nor can its use in some of the emergent African and Asian nations be much help in this argument, as those countries are beset with political and evolutionary difficulties which we like to think we have left behind us in history. It is true that the death penalty is still used in the United States, but then we are accustomed to believe that, though America leads us in scientific and technological matters, we lead America in ideas of toleration and social progress. In its attitude to a national health service the United States would seem to be several decades behind us, yet it is probably inevitable that such a health service will eventually come into being in America.

There is little use in belabouring the point that the death penalty is final, but it is worth reminding ourselves of the possibility that there may be a mistaken conviction of an innocent man for a capital murder. On the whole it is unlikely in an English criminal trial that an innocent accused will be convicted, as the burden of proof is such that no man may be pronounced guilty of an offence unless the guilt has been proved beyond all reasonable doubt. This is the logical culmination of the precept that every man is to be presumed innocent until he is actually proved to be guilty. In the case of trials for serious offences, where a jury sits, this guilt must be proved beyond all reasonable doubt to all twelve members of the jury, and it is the duty of the jury to state that they are unable to come to an agreement if there is one member who is not prepared to agree that guilt has been proved; in the event of disagreement among the members of the jury a new trial must take place before a fresh jury. It is more likely, therefore, that a guilty man may not be convicted than that an innocent man should be convicted. Yet occasional mistakes *may* occur, and it is probable that such mistakes, if they ever do occur, may never be known. This is a sobering thought which may cause us to wonder whether a method of punishment which can, by its retention, sow the seed of this doubt in our minds is worth maintaining, quite apart from any other unsatisfactory elements it may have. There is no point in investigating past cases of doubt here, as the doubt cannot be substantiated, but the existence of this occasional doubt may, of itself, be a strong argument for abolition of the capital penalty. One other aspect of the finality of the sentence may be touched upon, namely the fact that its execution precludes all possibility of later reform of the criminal. From a Christian point of view every man, however bad, ought to be given the chance of changing his heart for the better, and from the more general moral aspect it is unsatisfactory that a form of punishment should of necessity render impossible the attainment of the aims of punishment currently thought to be of great importance.

From a legalistic view it can be suggested that, as the law at present provides for capital punishment, the onus is upon those who support abolition to prove their case conclusively for a change of the law, and the retentionists may well feel that this proof is lacking, as the abolitionist arguments are such a mixture of doubt and conjecture. Further, abolitionists are wont to spoil their own positive arguments by hysterical outbursts attacking retentionists as sadists and wicked reactionaries. It is hoped that enough has been written above to show that there may be many retentionists who honestly and with complete integrity believe that retention of the death penalty is needed. Their views, based upon deterrence, protection of the public and the police, and upon the difficulty of finding a satisfactory substitute punishment for criminals who commit capital murder (a matter to be considered presently), can be logically sustained. Yet it is submitted that the more humanitarian arguments of the abolitionists are probably more persuasive. Just as it is possible for the appeal courts in criminal cases to ignore previous decisions, and thus break the normal rules of court precedent, where the liberty of the individual is at stake, so it may be suggested that the burden of proof is shifted on to the shoulders of the retentionists as regards the maintenance of a criminal penalty which involves the destruction of human life. Mere emotion is irrelevant in this connection, for we ought as thinking people to ignore the outbursts of those abolitionists who believe that men holding different views must be sadists, just as we ought to ignore the quite natural wish for vengeance which the relative of a murdered person may harbour. It is probable that the mass of the population are not concerned with the question of abolition, but this is mainly because they do not think about the issues. If law reform were to wait until a true majority of the population favoured it, then it would never take place. Once a majority of thinking people favour abolition, the time will have come for the change. Already a large body of M.P.s are committed to the support of abolition, and it is likely that the step will be taken within a very few years. In this way we shall be following the example of all other non-British Western European countries, with the exception of the Irish Republic, France and Spain.

One great problem will, however, remain, and this is the question of the sentence to be substituted for the death penalty. Under the Homicide Act, 1957, those murders which were for the first time made non-capital carry a mandatory life sentence. But life imprisonment is not by any means what is seems on its face. The sentence does enable the Home Office and the prison authorities to retain a man in prison for the rest of his life, if they think fit, but more usually a prisoner is entitled to earn remission of his actual period of detention for good behaviour. The result is that many men sentenced to life imprisonment may be released after only about eight or nine years in gaol.

This is not a complete release, for the prisoner is only allowed to leave on licence, which means that, on commission of some further offence, he may be detained once more and his life sentence will revive. It may be that such a system would be adequate for offenders who commit what is now capital murder (or even treason, for most traitors could hardly be thought able practically to carry on where they left off with their previous treasonable activities). But the doubt remains whether some of these prisoners would be safe if set free, and that aim of punishment to protect the public must loom large in our minds. The whole tenour of our system of imprison-ment, unlike that of the United States of America, where impossible sentences for periods of, say, ninety-nine years are not infrequently passed, is to avoid, if possible, keeping a convict in gaol for the remainder of his life. The present Lord Chief Justice has said that it is against the spirit of English law that a man should receive such a long sentence that it would appear likely that he may die while still in prison, and most humane people would agree with this principle. It is suggested that the kind of sliding scale of possible detention which will be discussed in the next section of this chapter will be the ultimate answer to the problem presented, and that therefore this difficulty created by abolition of the capital penalty is not in-surmountable.

IMPRISONMENT AND OTHER FORMS OF DETENTION

In the popular mind the term 'imprisonment' covers all varieties of detention. Imprisonment itself is in fact the common major form of punishment still practised in England, but it is as well to remember that there are several other kinds of detention. Briefly, these varieties include the indefinite deten-tion of the criminally insane in what are called Broadmoor institutions, fairly long sentences of preventive detention for 'old lags' who are at least thirty years of age, shorter more constructive periods of corrective training for younger criminals who are serious offenders but not beyond hope of reform, Borstal training for offenders who are not yet twenty-one, but are at least sixteen years old, approved schools and remand homes for younger children, and detention and attendance centres for youths who have reached the age of fourteen, but are not yet twenty-one. In the remand homes, approved schools, detention and attendance centres, Borstals and corrective training establishments attempts are made to reform the offenders who have to attend, either by means of awakening their interest in worthwhile pursuits or by the imposition of discipline, or by an admixture of both. We shall revert to consideration of these various attempts to reform criminals, and to their likely future, presently. But first, let us consider the punishment of imprisonment, properly so called. The various different types of detention other than imprisonment are mostly applied at present to young offenders, and it will be appreciated that although statistics seem to show that juvenile offenders form an important, and if anything growing, group among the criminal population, yet the majority of criminals must still be adults, even if it be for no other reason than that they have many more years in which to develop their criminal talents.

Imprisonment certainly measures up to the primary aim of punishment already mentioned, protection of the public, though only of course so long as the criminals detained are actually in prison. It has already been stated that very long sentences of imprisonment are not in practice employed in England, and so the vast majority of all imprisoned criminals are bound to be let loose upon the public again in due course. For reasons which have been discussed we can probably discount retribution and deterrence as serious aims of punishment, at any rate as far as the graver crimes are concerned, and the only other important aim is reform. The main trouble with imprisonment as a punishment would seem to be that it fails to effect more than a very few reforms among the criminals imprisoned. Some offenders imprisoned for the first time may be so chastened as a result of their experience that they never commit imprisonable offences again, but it seems to be commonly agreed now that if a man has to go to prison for a second time, then his second or later term of imprisonment is most unlikely to effect any reform in him. As the prisons are extremely full at present, and there is a distinct need to expand prison accommodation it would also seem that far too many offenders are not in fact reformed on their first visit to prison.

It is not easy to be sure why imprisonment only rarely brings about the reform of criminals. But there are many factors which seem likely to be contributory causes. Crime often seems to flourish in periods of economic difficulty when there is a greater incentive than usual to benefit materially by the use of wits and the employment of illegal means. In the aftermath of the Second World War there was an immediate shortage of houses, food and many other of the necessary or desirable accompaniments to living. Black marketeers flourished and tax evasion was rife. Even today, when society has become more affluent, the improvement has brought many attendant evils, in that there is a great temptation to profit at the expense of others by the use of several different means of speculation, while those who find that the pace of living has become too fast may descend to dishonesty in order to 'get even' with the rest. If one adds the general uncertainty added to life by the perpetual state of cold war in international affairs, with the threat of nuclear weapons constantly over us, it can be seen that there is plenty of temptation to take a purely materialistic and selfish attitude towards life, in an effort to gain as much pleasure and comfort as possible before we are all destroyed. Whatever the reasons in individual cases, the past fifteen or twenty years have seen an overcrowding of the prisons, which has resulted in the most undesirable conditions for prisoners and their warders alike.

Most prisoners, with the exception of capital murderers awaiting execution and homosexuals, are likely to have to share cells. This destroys all possibility of the privacy which every man needs from time to time, and it also means that those prisoners who might otherwise have been reformed become contaminated for good by their perpetual contact with diehard criminals. These conditions may well breed the feeling among criminals that as society has ceased to care about them, then they will no longer care at all about the other members of society, so that, on release

85

from prison, they may well be a worse danger to the ordinary members of the public than when they first went into prison. Mr. H. J. Klare, the Secretary of the Howard League for Penal Reform, in his book *Anatomy of Prison* (Penguin Books), has said that 'an authoritarian régime reduces those upon whom it presses to a state of irresponsibility. And since most prisoners ... are already irresponsible, putting them into a large maximum security prison is rather like locking a group of drunkards into a brewery.' Efforts have been made to relieve the problems of overcrowding by the building of new prisons, but the perpetually high number of prisoners has prevented the closing down of those institutions, such as the prison at Oxford, which have for years been condemned as unfit for human habitation. The effect of the unsatisfactory prison conditions has thus been cumulative.

One further obstacle in the way of the reform of prisoners is the effect of boredom. Although efforts have been made to provide prisoners with work which will keep them occupied constructively, the excessive prison population almost inevitably means that the inmates are left to their own devices for long periods. Even if the work provided is interesting it does not last for longer than the normal working day. Once a small amount of exercise has been taken in addition, this still leaves a large number of hours to be passed which can only be filled for part of the time by eating and sleeping. Not many prisoners will want to spend the whole of their spare time reading, nor indeed with present crowded conditions is reading necessarily very easy to accomplish. Boredom is bound to be felt, and this is not healthy for the minds of prisoners. There are some criminologists who believe that one contributory reason for the high incidence of crime in the United Kingdom is the boredom caused by the ever-shorter working hours brought upon us by the advance of the welfare state and by automation. Clearly general employment is infinitely preferable to partial employment, yet it is a pity that full employment can only be obtained by substantial reductions in the hours of the working week, for those without the wit to employ their spare time constructively, or at least harmlessly, may well be tempted to while it away by doing harm to others, often just for the thrill of the experience. Along with boredom it is not often realised that the interruption in the family lives of the prisoners and their dependants may have a disastrous effect upon the attitude of convicted men after their release. Many people are aware of the hardships endured by prisoners' families, and the welfare state, fortunately, does make some provision for alleviating these hardships, at least financially. But few have given any thought to the fact that imprisonment inevitably means an interruption of the normal sexual relations between husband and wife. At first sight this factor may seem insignificant, but the consequent frustration can be sufficient to embitter some men against society for good.

The whole puzzle presents us with an appallingly difficult problem. The truth is that we do not know how best to cope with the community's misfits. In fact it is as well to recognise that we probably never shall know the solution, for the minds of these men must work along very different lines from those familiar to the people who are anxious to find the solution. Individual successes will always be scored by penologists, but a general solution destroying the whole cause of crime seems beyond the range of possibility, particularly since human beings are so imperfect and are always prone to err. But the immensity of the task should not deter us from continuing the quest for a panacea. There is no doubt that some good has been done by the reforms effected periodically in different branches of the law, though it cannot be pretended that the law has been thereby rendered perfect. To ignore injustice would be to surrender a large part of the power of determination with which human beings are provided. Consequently efforts must continue to cleanse the law of its imperfections, even if true perfection is not capable of achievement. In the sphere of punishment the efforts which have so far been made to provide suitable variations of the stock penalty of imprisonment have already been mentioned. Corrective training, detention centre attendance and the like are all manifestations of the efforts that have been made in this century to discover the best methods of reforming convicts. Although protection of the public has been stressed in this chapter as a prime aim of punishment, it must go without saying that to reform a criminal truly will also automatically act as a protection for the public. As criminals who are sentenced to imprisonment or other forms of detention are, in the English system, almost certainly going to be set free again in due course, it also follows that concentration upon reform will kill the two birds with one stone. Preventive detention and, at least in theory, the sentence of life imprisonment upon an accused person convicted of non-capital murder have been designed to protect the public where reform is seen as being impossible, though both these sentences may be regarded as imperfect from this point of view. No sentence of preventive detention may be for longer than fourteen years, and with remission for good behaviour, both this sentence and the sentence of life imprisonment, as has already been mentioned, may be substantially reduced in length. It must be considered below whether, in cases where reform seems impossible, some more effective protection for the public may not be found.

The failure of the present prison system to effect substantial reform among prisoners must lead us to maintain our efforts to discover better methods of punishment. Already some experiments within the ordinary prison system have been tried, and they appear to have met with limited success. A few of the more recently-opened prisons have been styled 'open prisons', where the inmates have been put upon trust not to escape. Much more freedom within the prison itself has been afforded to the prisoners, and, although there have been some escapes and some later convictions of former inmates, there also appears to have been a fair number of prisoners who have not been convicted of any further offence after their discharge. Admittedly the scheme is young as yet, and it is not possible to make any confident predictions, but it may be that progress in penal reform is being made here. Another scheme which has met with some success has been that whereby selected prisoners who are within a year of completing their sentences, if those sentences have been of imprisonment for a period of over four years, are permitted to leave prison during the day-time to take up ordinary work outside. The fact that they are still prisoners is kept secret as far as their fellows at work are concerned, and the scheme has the advantage of easing the prisoners back into ordinary life gently, thus helping them to see things in their true perspective before being left to cope with the world on their own. There have been some failures in the scheme, as seems inevitable in any plan which depends upon human participation, and there has been one bad case of a prisoner committing murder while on parole, but prison governors are, on the whole, very enthusiastic about the successes that have been achieved by the scheme. Clearly very careful selection of the prisoners who participate is necessary, as the public are brought into contact with them, but with care the plan would seem to have great promise, though as yet only about 200 prisoners at a time take part in it.

Both the schemes outlined above throw some onus upon the shoulders of the prisoners themselves to show that they are worthy of the privileges conferred, and the supervision which still affects them must act as an encouragement to live up to what is expected of them. More effective rehabilitative measures may make greater demands upon the prisoners than some other methods of punishment or treatment, but the stimulus thus demanded may well awaken the germ of worth which resides in all but the most exceptional humans. It is likely that more and better hostels must be provided to care for the needs of ex-prisoners within the months immediately succeeding their discharge, though no after-care will do much good unless the right attitude to society has been fostered during the period of detention.

Even if open prisons and parole schemes are employed widely by the prison authorities, there must remain a large group of prisoners who are not trustworthy enough to be subjected to such methods of detention. In an ideal state it may be that imprisonment as we know it should be abolished altogether. Detention could not be totally abolished, however, for the public would then cease to be protected from the depredations of those criminals who would be bound to continue to exist merely because of the frailty of human beings and the difficulties involved in keeping the whole of society living in a state of harmony. In place of prisons, however, it may be suggested that detention communities might be built up. These communities would consist of large areas where the prisoners, together with their wives and families, if they consented to go, would be sent. There each family would have its separate house or flat, and each prisoner would be put to work which was the same as, or as sufficiently similar as possible to, that which he normally did, or wished to do, in ordinary life. The presence of family units would destroy any parallel between this type of detention and the old 'transportation'. The community would contain its own sports and recreation facilities, and possibly it might also maintain its own modification of a local authority. The only difference between this community and any ordinary township would be that each prisoner would be subject to supervision by the equivalent of our present warders, who would make regular reports upon the prisoner's progress towards a more responsible way of life. Wives and families would always be allowed to come and go between the community and the outside world as they pleased, but the prisoners would not be allowed to leave at all until they were judged by the supervising authorities to be safe as regards the general public.

Of course there would be escapes and later convictions under such a scheme, and some prisoners might even find that life in the community was more attractive than life in the wider, more cruel world. But it would be up to supervising authorities to try to remedy the causes of such failure, and to make those who are lazy, rather than mentally retarded, face up to their responsibilities. At all events it is submitted that a scheme of this kind would be more likely to produce reformatory results than many others. The detainees would not feel that the world had ceased to care for them, and normal sexual relations between spouses need not be interrupted, causing frustration. But unfortunately the idea may be nothing more than a pipe dream in a country as small as the United Kingdom and with such drains upon its financial resources. Where in this island could one find an area of land which is large enough and sufficiently well sited to lend itself to the building of such a community as has been outlined? It could not be placed on unhealthy land, such as Dartmoor or the Yorkshire Moors, and there are probably very few other spare areas which are not needed for either agricultural purposes or new towns (as to which, see Chapter Seven on Planning Law). The expense might be mitigated somewhat by applying the prisoners themselves to the task of constructing the houses and other buildings needed in the communities, but the capital expense, and the expense of maintaining the detainees, would in any case be very high. It may be, therefore, that we must turn, reluctantly, to other methods of punishment or detention.

In considering other methods it is submitted that more attention should be paid than at present to the personalities of the prisoners themselves. To some extent the judges and magistrates certainly do their best to account for this factor. Two men guilty of exactly the same offence may well receive different sentences on account of their disparate ages or their different records. But once the sentence has been passed, the only possibility of reduction or alteration of that sentence is by means of such pilot schemes as are being applied in the open prisons or by way of parole, or by obtaining remission up to one-third of the usual sentence (or by a rather different calculation in cases of life imprisonment) for good conduct. But there are pointers which suggest that alteration in the length of sentences may be more widely employed in the future. In Borstals, for instance, training is commonly specified as an indeterminate sentence with a minimum of nine months' detention and a maximum of three years. The total period of control extends to four years from the date of sentence, the remainder of which period after release from the institution being spent under the supervision of the Central After-Care Association. There is even provision whereby an offender may be released before the minimum period of nine months has been completed if the Home Secretary so directs. Such a scheme takes account of the amenability of an offender to reformatory methods. It may well be that some offenders would be effectively reformed after a very short time spent in prison, and that to keep them in prison after that short period is to run the risk that boredom and bad conditions may so infect their minds as to persuade them that reform is pointless.

It is submitted that the time is coming when it will be realised that a fixed maximum sentence for each offence might be passed

by the judge upon each offender, the period bearing a relation
to the seriousness of the crime committed. Thereafter the offender could be discharged on licence or parole at any time within
that maximum period if it is considered that his personality has
improved sufficiently to justify release. This would give the
prisoner the incentive to show that he is capable of reform, an
incentive which is so lacking in the prison system as it exists at
present. This kind of indeterminacy within the fixed maximum
sentence could well be the subject of experiments, whereby an
offender committed to prison might, after a time, be moved on
to some form of corrective training or to an attendance centre,
where he would be free to mingle with the ordinary public, provided he reported regularly to the centre and underwent specified training there.

All such ideas would involve a change in the present methods
of sentencing, for under the current law it is up to the judge or
magistrates alone to determine the actual sentence within statutory limits. It is even possible for the judge to impose only a fine
or a period of probation, or just the technical sentence of discharge, upon an accused person found guilty of quite a serious
crime (provided the lawful sentence is not mandatory), where
the judge feels that the circumstances warrant leniency. One is
loathe to remove the power to work mercy, and it is suggested
that judges should retain their power in all cases where that
power now exists, to pass any sentences they think fit less than
detention. But where a judge is satisfied that a sentence of
detention of any kind is warranted, he should simply pass a
formal sentence of the maximum length allowed by law as
regards the particular offence, while making it clear to the convicted man that his sentence will be subject to active review.
This review would be conducted by a permanent board of
prison officers, doctors, psychiatrists, probation officers, social
workers and such other members as may seem suitable to the
Home Office authorities, or as may be laid down by Act of
Parliament. Not every member of the board should have to be
present at every meeting, but a certain quorum, according to a
specific composition, would be laid down statutorily. The board
would receive regular reports upon the various detainees, and

it would determine how and when the variation of the punishment or training of particular offenders should take place. It should have the power to order the release on parole of any prisoner at any time, even within a few days of sentencing, if it thinks fit, thus in effect introducing a system of suspended sentences. It may equally make provision for the continued detention of dangerous criminals up to the maximum sentence imposed upon them. Thus, in the case of a life sentence, it would be possible for the board to see that the offender really remained in detention for life, if the requirement of protection of the public so demanded, though it would always have to keep the case under review.

Though this suggestion may seem to be radical in that it would alter considerably the functions of judges in criminal trials, it is not really so revolutionary as it may seem at first sight Similar boards already determine questions of remission for good behaviour, and they operate the Borstal scheme which has been referred to. The criminally insane, who under present law are sentenced to be detained in a Broadmoor institution for the duration of 'Her Majesty's pleasure', serve a period of detention which is wholly within the discretion of such a board. It is logical that if the aim of indeterminacy within the framework of a determined maximum sentence is to be attained, in order to make penal methods accord more nearly with the need to reform the individual offenders sentenced, then the actual duration of the sentence should lie at the discretion of a group of specialists rather than of one man. It seems probable that judges may even welcome the chance to be relieved of what must be a somewhat distasteful task. The requirement that no man should be deprived of his liberty without a decision in open court after the hearing of both sides will have been adhered to, but the actual length and nature of the detention prescribed will be in the hands of a body of men whose objectivity and skill in penal methods ought in practice to be unrivalled.

In conclusion it is submitted that, although the penal community scheme may, in the long run, provide the best method of dealing with criminals who must be detained in order to keep them from doing further harm to innocent members of the public, the most likely developments in penal reform in the future are along the lines of indeterminate and suspended sentences, with many possible variations as to their actual nature, within prescribed maximum periods. There are many who feel that really long sentences are the only answer in cases of hardened criminals, particularly those given to violence and such serious offenders as bank robbers. Even on the now largely unsatisfactory deterrent view of punishment such long sentences *might* occasionally act as a deterrent to others. But the scheme of the sliding scale of detention outlined in this chapter would make adequate provision for the actual imposition of long sentences where needed, provided that the maximum sentences allowed by the law are sufficiently long. In the case of, for example, rape, burglary and robbery with violence, the law already provides for a maximum sentence of life imprisonment, and so it seems likely that little modification of the present provisions as to maximum penalties would be needed.

CORPORAL PUNISHMENT

Corporal punishment (often referred to rather emotionally by its opponents as 'flogging') was abolished in 1948 except in cases of mutiny or personal violence against prison officers committed by male prisoners. Even these latter cases have rarely resulted since 1948 in imposition of the penalty, which requires the order of a visiting board, including magistrates, and the confirmation of the Home Secretary. It is difficult to hazard a view as to the desirability of maintaining this form of punishment in prisons in the kind of exceptional case for which it is provided. It may be that there is some point in retaining it as a possible remedy for violent conduct against a hard-pressed prison service. But public opinion has sometimes been expressed forcefully upon the question whether corporal punishment should be reintroduced as a penalty to be imposed mainly upon youths who commit offences involving violence. The kind of offence which those who favour the penalty's reintroduction usually have in mind is the wanton coshing of an elderly woman in order to snatch her handbag.

It is submitted here that there is nothing inherently wrong with a form of punishment which hurts a criminal physically, so long as it is not excessive, and provided that it is an effective punishment in the sense that it reforms the offender concerned or curbs crime. Several of the methods adopted in detention centres for youths who have reached the age of fourteen, but who are not yet twenty-one, involve discipline which the subjects may find irksome. Yet discipline properly applied never did anyone any harm, and indeed the imposition of some form of discipline would often seem to be called for as far as young offenders are concerned. The record of the detention centres seems to be fairly good in achieving some measure of reform among the attenders, though this must be read in the light of the fact that, by any standards, far too many first detainees in all kinds of penal institutions in this country come back to the courts to be convicted again. Many penologists argue that the physical pain and injury to pride which would be inflicted upon young offenders sentenced to corporal punishment would only turn them further against society, but of course these arguments cannot be substantiated as we do not practice this method of punishment anyway.

If these objections were the only ones to be advanced it would probably be worth trying the reintroduction of whipping for a trial period at least, to see whether any appreciable difference in the incidence of violent crime and repeated violence was effected. Those who favour the reintroduction believe that the shame of the penalty might cause many youths to see themselves in society in a more accurate perspective, while the idea that they should 'have a taste of their own medicine' is not wholly based upon the wish for vengeance, but, more constructively, depends upon the view that most of us dislike physical pain, and that therefore the threat of physical pain would deter youths from committing their present gross though pointless crimes. Although parents differ widely in their ideas about the methods of bringing up children, some believing that occasional spankings are salutory, while others never lay a finger upon their offspring, it does appear that there are occasions where a quick smack effects a world of difference in a child who has reached the pitch of rage or intransigence where reason cannot penetrate, and experience shows that such chastisement does nothing to destroy the mutual love and respect between parent and child.

But it is in this often-quoted parallel that the fallacy about corporal punishment is exposed. If the penalty could be inflicted on the spot after an act of violence by a youth, the relation between the offence and the punishment would be clear to the offender. A lesson would probably be effectively taught, and the chance of reform might well be high. But this prompt action is precisely what can never take place. Because English law insists, and rightly, if we are to keep at bay the merest possibility of totalitarianism and retain our basic concept of justice, that no one may be punished until he has been properly tried, convicted and sentenced, and because such trial inevitably means the passage of time before it is embarked upon, let alone concluded, the penalty when pronounced must of necessity be exacted cold-bloodedly. When the penalty is a fine, imprisonment, probation or any of the other multitude of possible sentences (with the exception of the death penalty, which has already been discussed separately), its calculated quality is an advantage, but the same cannot be said about any form of corporal punishment. By the time the penalty could be inflicted, the whole point of the analogy with parental discipline would have disappeared. It is not without relevance here that police officers have expressed themselves as non-committal upon the question of reintroduction of the penalty, but have stated that if it is reintroduced they do not wish to have the task of carrying it out. In the face of these objections it seems unlikely that the penalty will ever make a reappearance in the general penal armoury of the law of England.

Other suggestions have sometimes been made for coping with the menace of the irresponsible youth who commits acts of violence, and these suggestions are by no means the products of the minds of those who merely wish to avenge themselves upon the younger generation. The basic idea of those who wish to find some other method of punishment which will teach them a short, sharp lesson is that imprisonment, with all its concomitant dangers of criminal infection, may be avoided. Surely, they say, it is better to inflict a penalty which brings home to them the enormity of their acts, while at the same time sparing them a longer period of incarceration, and also saving the taxpayer the necessity to pay for their detention. There is much in these arguments, and a former Lord Chief Justice has recently suggested that reintroduction of the stocks might work the cure that is needed, in that public ridicule might bring about a sense of shame which would prevent a repetition of their crimes. Although this idea is attractive on all the grounds mentioned above, it seems unlikely to be followed up seriously, largely because the punishment suggested would probably smack too much of a return to the middle ages when today we are usually striving towards penal advancement. It may also be doubted whether the general British public, well-mannered as it now is in many matters, would do any more than hurry by the stocks, pretending not to look! Certainly it is hard to visualise anyone actually throwing a rotten tomato at the enstocked offender, unless the thrower were a youth from some rival gang, in which case the aim of the whole exercise would have been defeated by the encouragement in other youths of the kind of violent urges which we wish to see purged.

REPARATION

It is a very odd fact about the English criminal law that no general provision has been made in the past for compensation to be paid by criminals to persons injured by their offences. On the whole the law has left the victim to seek any civil remedy which may be open to him. There have been a few exceptions where the court may, for example, order a person convicted of malicious damage to property to pay such sum, not exceeding £20, as may appear to the court to be reasonable compensation to the person whose property was harmed. Again, where a person has been convicted of felony, the court, if it thinks fit, may award a sum not exceeding £100 to compensate the victim for loss of property suffered as a result of the felony. But these exceptions have not been consistently planned, and in particular they have not extended to any offences against the person.

In 1961 a Working Party, which had been set up by the Home Secretary, produced a Report about the possibilities for providing compensation for the victims of crimes of violence. Although it is tempting to suggest that the criminals themselves should be made to pay compensation, the difficulties involved in such a proposition are great. In the first place, many such crimes are undetected, and it would be ludicrous to provide that a victim would only be entitled to be compensated if what would be to him or her the accident of a conviction were obtained against someone. Again, even if a conviction were to be obtained, that would be no guarantee that the offender would have the means to pay. And must the innocent family of a criminal suffer privation because the father is paying compensation to some stranger? In the event the Working Party suggested that state compensation should be made available to the victims of violent crime. The Report found that the cost to the Exchequer would in fact only amount to about £1,150,000 in an average year, on the basis of previous experience of hardships caused by violent crime, so that the sum involved on the national scale is not prohibitive. It is still a trifle unsatisfactory that the state should have to shoulder the burden, though it may not be very far removed from some of the other payments that are made under the welfare state. It is submitted that efforts must be maintained to find a suitable way of recovering some portion at least of the sum involved from the offenders who are convicted of crimes of violence, and one suggestion made by the Working Party that offenders might, on release from prison, be given an adverse PAYE Code number is worthy of attention. It may be less penal upon the rest of the offender's family than other forms of attachment of wages.

Two further Reports dealing with the subject under discussion have been made in the past few years, by a Committee of JUSTICE, the British Section of the International Commission of Jurists, and by a Committee of the Conservative Party respectively. Both Reports, though differing in details, recommend, *inter alia*, that 'crimes of violence' should be defined in a schedule to some future statute, and should include sexual offences;

that compensation should be confined to direct victims, save that dependants of victims who suffer fatal injuries should be eligible for awards; that compensation should be payable for pregnancy, and for the maintenance of the child, if these result from a crime of violence; and that persons injured while assisting the police should be compensated irrespective of the nature of the offence which gave rise to the injury. It is also suggested that once the victim has received compensation from the state his right of civil action against the offender should be taken over by the state, which should seek to recover a contribution from the offender if it is economically practicable, though only to the extent that it does not impede the offender's rehabilitation.

Legislation based on the efforts of those who compiled these three Reports is currently being planned. The state has a duty to maintain law and order, and it is only one aspect of truly effective remedies for criminal offences that victims should be compensated for physical harm suffered as a result of violent crime. Efforts must also continue to make criminals pay as far as possible for the results of their crimes, but the limits here to what the law can effectively and justly provide are clear, and the advance in this sphere may well prove to be slow.

THE AGE OF CRIMINAL RESPONSIBILITY

Until 1964 any human being who had reached the age of eight could be held responsible in England for the commission of a crime. But by Act of Parliament this age of criminal responsibility has now been raised to ten. It seems reasonable that children of tender years should be protected from the full force of the criminal law, because their acts, however undesirable in their effects, can hardly be regarded as the acts of people who really know what they are doing. In the debates leading up to the passage of the recent statute, a majority in the House of Lords had favoured raising the age of responsibility for crime to twelve, and it is significant that the laws of most other European countries provide that children under ages varying from twelve to fourteen are exempt from criminal liability. Children, as well

99

as adults, may commit acts which would ordinarily be considered criminal. But we have progressed a long way from the days when children of four or five, and even dogs and cats, were hanged for criminal offences. It may be suggested that the age of criminal responsibility in England may yet be raised further than its present level, and that the burden of disciplining children below the age chosen will be placed more clearly where it ought to be, on their parents and guardians.

CHAPTER FOUR

Contracts and Torts

In Chapter One the various uses of the term 'common law' were explained, and it may be recalled that the two more parochial meanings of the term as regards English municipal law covered, first, the ordinary law of the courts as opposed to the supplementary rules provided by decisions of the Lord Chancellor, and, secondly, case law as opposed to statute law. If we take the common factor in the two meanings of the phrase we find that the case law provided by the ordinary courts of England can be described as common law by either definition. It is our purpose in this chapter to grasp a few of the problems which beset this basic body of English law, which is mostly covered by the rules concerning contracts and torts.

A contract is an agreement between two parties to perform some one or more obligations in relation to each other. It is a mutual compact between the two parties whereby one promises to do something in return for either another promise or an act performed by the other. For this agreement to be recognised as binding in law the promise or act on each side must also involve some form of sacrifice by the party concerned, though this requirement that each should provide 'consideration', as it is called, often amounts to little more than a technicality. To offer £1 for a Rolls-Royce car would amount to sufficient consideration in law, as the sacrifice of £1 is being offered! The parties to a contract are said to be in privity of contract, and the law will provide a remedy, usually by way of an award of damages, where one or other of them fails to discharge his duties under the terms of the agreement. A tort, on the other hand, is some wrong recognised by the law as giving rise to a remedy, again usually by way of damages, at the instance of another person, even though no special contractual relationship may have existed at the time between the wrongdoer and the person wronged. Broadly speaking, no one outside a particular contractual relationship is entitled to claim any recompense for breach of that contract, as this right is only enjoyed by a party to the contract itself. But anyone who is wronged according to the rules of civil law by any act of another person at all is entitled to claim a remedy for the tort committed against him. Sometimes a tort or a breach of contract will amount also to a criminal offence, but the punishment of crime is a matter for the state, rather than the individual complainant, though criminal proceedings may be set in motion through the agency of a private individual. The private suitor can only gain actual recompense as a result of litigation by succeeding in a civil action brought by himself (if we ignore the possibilities of reparation for crime which we discussed towards the end of the last chapter). Thus, when discussing contracts and torts we may ignore the possible criminal aspects of particular activities involved, for the private claimant can only be concerned with civil law.

The law of contracts and torts, therefore, provides us with the fundamental principles for civil liability to individual citizens, and it also incidentally provides the basic rules governing commercial practice. As already stated, this body of law is, in origin, case law, and it is the main body of civil law built up in the ordinary courts of the land. Equity has in the past tended to fill up some of the gaps left even in this sphere of legal development, and statutes have from time to time amended the law, or occasionally altered it radically. Today the changes which can be envisaged are bound to come from the passage of statutes, and the possible developments of the law discussed in this chapter must be considered as being likely to come about, if at all, through Acts of Parliament. Case law is still developing, and new decisions help us to distinguish the differences between the various rules of law to be applied by the courts. But the great age of really fundamental alteration of the law by the courts has passed centuries ago, its final vestiges having been found in the exercise of jurisdiction by the Chancellor in developing his equity. The mantle of law reform lies now upon Parliament.

THE RECOGNITION OF THE MODERN NEEDS OF CONSUMERS

The traditional approach of the law to contractual relationships has always been that they are purely private matters, and that no one need ever enter into a contract unless he freely wishes to do so. In days gone by this principle of freedom of contract was probably a reality in most cases. No one need accept an offer unless the terms were congenial to him, and no one need make an offer unless he was satisfied that he fully intended to enter into a binding contract if the offer should be accepted. But commercial practice in the twentieth century has given the lie to what now seems a naive approach to the making of contracts. The advance of science and technology has given rise to an age in which it is no longer a luxury to possess a car, a television set, a washing machine or a refrigerator. Such articles have rapidly become the accoutrements of all. Yet the manufacturers of, and traders in, these pieces of equipment have organised their affairs so carefully as to be able to insist that they will only sell upon certain set terms. Although the common law has been reinforced by a Sale of Goods Act of 1893, which makes specific provisions as to minimum standards of the quality, etc. of goods sold, yet there is no provision to prevent a particular merchant from insisting that he will not sell to anyone unless the purchaser agrees to waive his ordinary legal rights and to accept the less generous terms offered by the seller. Accordingly the common 'guarantee' which attaches to many articles on sale to the general public often amounts to a condition that the purchaser will accept the terms offered by the manufacturer instead of those which would normally apply if no such special provisions were made. In a seller's market, the purchaser has no option but to accept such terms or else to forego the desired article.

The law of torts has provided some alleviation for the purchaser, and indeed for all consumers, whether or not they are the actual contracting parties who purchased the goods. The principle has been developed that anyone who may objectively be thought to be the kind of person likely to consume or use goods which have been manufactured negligently, and who suffers injury from the goods, whether by way of illness or in any other physical way, on account of the negligent manufacture, is entitled to damages to recompense him for the injury incurred. Thus, a person who bought a chisel, and who was injured by a piece of the blade breaking off and entering his eye while he was using the tool, was held entitled to damages because the chisel had not been made with the care which ought to be exercised by manufacturers of such delicate tools: not enough attention had been paid to the quality of the steel used in the manufacture. Similarly, a purchaser of underclothes who contracted dermatitis, because the manufacturers had not taken enough care to see that excessive amounts of harmful chemicals were not left on the garments before despatch to the shops, was awarded damages for the injury suffered.

But this principle, valuable though it is, does not apply to the plight of the purchaser of goods who is affected, not by personal injury, but by the fact that the goods are not of an adequate quality to perform the tasks for which they were sold. All consumers have experienced new cars, lawn mowers and other articles of machinery which have either failed to work efficiently right from the start, or else have developed faults within a very short period of time. Under the ordinary law it could be said that such articles were not fit for the purposes for which they were sold, and that therefore the onus would be upon the sellers either to replace them free of charge to the customer or to pay compensation equivalent to the cost of putting the machines in working order. Many 'guarantees' do appear, on their face, to provide that the manufacturers will do just this, but they are frequently illusory, because they may well actually provide that although the manufacturers will replace defective parts free of charge within a limited period of usually six months or a year, yet the cost of labour and carriage must be paid by the customers, and this latter cost may often be substantial.

The ordinary law of contract has adapted itself as far as possible to meet the needs of the situation, and the most significant recent development within the courts has been the doctrine of fundamental breach. Under this doctrine the courts will be prepared to hold that a whole contract is void, whether or not conditions are included in the contract purporting to prevent the purchaser from obtaining redress in case of various faults in the product he is buying, if it can be held that the article sold is so defective that it in fact ceases to be an article of the kind contemplated by the contract at all. A not uncommon type of case has been where a second-hand car is sold subject to conditions exempting the seller from all liability for mechanical faults. Here the courts have sometimes been prepared to hold that the faults discovered in the car are so extensive that the vehicle cannot, in fact, be called a car at all; so the contract is set aside, and the seller is ordered by the court to pay back to the buyer the purchase price.

But it is clear that more legal protection is needed for the buyer, who may well be left with insufficient remedies if he has purchased an article, covered by a 'guarantee', which turns out to be defective, though not physically injurious, and yet not so defective that the doctrine of fundamental breach can be invoked. Private organisations have sprung up with remarkable rapidity in the past decade. The Consumers' Association, who publish the monthly magazine *Which?*, and various local consumers' associations and societies have been in the forefront of the campaign to protect purchasers from the combined expertise of trading and manufacturing interests. These associations have made it their business to warn about misleading advertisements, to compare value for money in similar articles made by different suppliers, and to try to secure fairer terms for consumers in 'guarantees' and hire-purchase agreements. Notable achievements have included the persuasion of several motor car manufacturers to reform their 'guarantees' so that they conform more nearly to the ordinary legal provisions protecting purchasers. This movement for consumer protection resulted in the setting up of an official Committee on Consumer Protection, which reported in July 1962 upon various measures desirable for the further protection of the consuming public. It would probably be out of place here to attempt any detailed technical consideration of the measures recommended by this Report, but it may be mentioned that it was recommended that most clauses in contracts excluding manufacturers' or sellers' liability should be made ineffective by law, and that an implied condition that goods shall be of merchantable quality shall apply to all consumer sales. As far as hire-purchase transactions are concerned, the Committee considered that no owner of goods subject to hire-purchase (and these owners are almost always the hire-purchase finance companies, to whom the goods are sold outright by the retailer, and who therefore take the place of the retailer in what would have been in ordinary conditions the contract of sale) should be able to obtain their repossession, on default of any payment due under the agreement, unless a court order has been obtained; and such an order would normally only be made where it is clear that the purchaser has no wish or ability to complete the transaction. The Report also recommended the establishment of a Consumer Council to collect information about consumer problems, to consider what action may be required in relation to them, and to promote that action by advising the consumers and all other parties, and by persuading manufacturers and distributors. When statutory action would appear called for, the Council would press Government departments to take the necessary initiative.

The changes in the law proposed by the Committee on Consumer Protection may take some time to effect, but most of them seem likely to be made in the long run. In the meanwhile the Consumer Council has already been set up, and though it has no powers to make regulations or enforce laws, yet it will maintain a watching brief over the needs of the consumer and upon the adequacy of the law for his protection. At all events the law in this sphere is gradually being moulded to the needs of the individual in the twentieth century world of commerce.

Related to the consumer in a sense is the purchaser of a dwelling-house. Much has been done to assist him in surmounting the difficult obstacle of the high price currently required to pay for the property being bought. Building society mortgages and local authority loans, together with various insurance and other schemes, now make it possible for anyone with a reasonably sound job, and a regular income therefrom, even if it is only small, to arrange for the purchase of a house suitable to his requirements. But the law has so far paid inadequate attention to the agents who, in the vast majority of house sales, arrange for the purchase by the buyer from the seller. These estate agents, who are remunerated by fees levied on a percentage basis from the sums paid in each sale, are in many cases highly respectable and hardworking people, who take great trouble to advertise available properties in honest, though naturally the most attractive possible, terms, and who take pains to provide prospective purchasers with properties suitable to their financial and other needs. Many of the firms of estate agents are headed by qualified surveyors with high professional standards. But unfortunately, although the surveyors' profession is well regulated by law, and maintains a recognised professional body which controls entry to the profession by means of such devices as examinations, the same does not apply to the more general occupation of the estate agent. A reputable surveyor may well carry on business as an estate agent, but an estate agent need not necessarily be a surveyor, and there is no organised or regulated body of qualified estate agents. It is perfectly possible, therefore, for anyone to set up as an estate agent, whether or not he has any previous training or experience, or even aptitude. It is not surprising that some estate agents, therefore, have been thought to be guilty of sharp practice or even worse. It has been suggested that some of the agents who advertise properties for sale at fixed prices asked, are yet prepared to sell at figures either higher or lower, according to demand, if prospective purchasers make separate financial presents to the agents. It is suspected that on some occasions a firm will buy a property on its own account from a client, without disclosing that they are the purchasers until a late stage of the transaction: the firm may then sell the house to another purchaser in a later transaction at a much higher price, thus extracting a clear profit on the second sale in addition to the usual commission on the first sale.

It cannot be healthy either for the general professional standing and repute of all estate agents or for the general public that such suspicions should be possible. Most reputable estate agents are known to favour the introduction of some form of professional organisation. The first need is a Register of Estate

Agents, and a body of such agents themselves responsible for problems of professional discipline and etiquette, in much the same form as exists for other professions. It would then be up to the professional body to determine its conditions for entry to the profession, which may well include an examination. These latter matters can be left to the profession to work out for itself, but the need for Parliament to provide by statute the basic framework for the organisation of a profession with recognised standards of conduct is clear. The step has been taken for many other professions in the past, and the time for reform to be undertaken as regards estate agents is more than ripe. In a country where land is very valuable and housing is highly priced it is extraordinary that the reform has not been undertaken before.

INSURANCE, NEGLIGENCE AND ANIMALS

In the realm of torts the most significant developments of the recent past have been the growth of the concept of negligence and the increasing influence of insurance companies upon the law. It is not intended to say more than a few words here about the latter, partly because we shall refer to it again in the chapter on Family Law. It is enough here to say that under modern conditions most awards of damages by the courts in tort cases are now in fact paid not by the nominal defendants, but by their insurance companies. A specific instance of this will be mentioned when we deal with family law, but the practice is very widespread. The point is amply illustrated if we remember that a high proportion of tort cases are 'running down' actions stemming from motor accidents, and that it is obligatory in law for all motor vehicles to be covered by an insurance policy. Add to this class of case the actions brought against large industrial concerns for negligence in their commercial activities, and it will be appreciated that no self-respecting company would omit to insure itself against possible legal liability. Today only a few private individuals will be likely to have to pay their own damages, if sued for torts. It is a matter for conjecture as to whether this reality should be reflected in the titles of the actions actually brought in court. At present insurance companies, though effectively conducting the case, sometimes on both sides, are titularly non-existent for the purposes of the litigation.

So far as the growth of the concept of negligence is concerned, it is noteworthy that the courts have shown themselves far more inclined these days to decide cases wherever possible upon the basis of what the so-called 'reasonable man' ought to have done. For every fact situation it is feasible to construct a standard of care by which to decide whether the alleged wrongdoer has in fact committed a tort or not. Thus, in one of the examples quoted earlier in this chapter, where the manufacturer of underclothing was held liable in damages for causing the wearer of one of the new garments sold by a retailer to contract dermatitis, the reason for the decision of the court was not solely that the plaintiff had suffered physical harm, but that the harm caused resulted from the manufacturer's failure to adhere to the standard of care which should have been displayed by the reasonable manufacturer of undergarments. In the past the courts have been more prepared to consider that tests of strict liability should be applied, but today there are comparatively few cases in which plaintiffs are able to recover damages merely by proving the injury suffered and tracing its cause: increasingly the courts insist that damages will only be allowed if the defendant, as well as causing the injury, has also been in breach of the particular duty of care which is deemed, by objective consideration in court, to have been upon him.

It is submitted that this spread of negligence as a test of liability is desirable, for although we can all sympathise with a man who suffers injury, yet it by no means follows in justice that someone else should automatically have to pay for that injury. There are times when an accident should be regarded as just 'bad luck'. The barriers of strict liability are being progressively broken down, but it may be worthwhile to mention one or two of these barriers which still lie in the way of what is rapidly becoming an ubiquitous test of negligence. The notable exceptions to the present trend of progress are provided by cases concerning escapes of harmful objects from land and damage of various kinds done by animals.

An occupier of land who brings on to his land anything which
would be likely to do damage if it escapes will, according to the
present law, be liable for all the direct consequences of its
escape, regardless of whether or not he has been negligent. This
is a rule which has been maintained in this form by the courts
for almost exactly one hundred years, since a famous House of
Lords decision of 1868, and it has led to the making of certain
difficult distinctions, such as the difference between things
likely to do damage and those not so dangerous, and the
distinction between things already naturally on the land and
those which have been brought there—for it is only where
things have been brought on to the land that the strict liability
rule applies in the form just described. Again, there is some
doubt whether the rule applies to cases where the injury
suffered is personal rather than to other land or inanimate
objects, and there is some authority in recent decisions for the
view that damages will only lie for personal injuries caused by
escaping objects if the defendant occupier of land was also
guilty of negligence in his custody of the article which escaped.

But perhaps one actual case, decided in 1957, will illustrate
the injustice which can be caused by the present rule. Part of a
large country house had been converted into separate flats and
dwelling-houses, two of which were occupied respectively by the
plaintiff and the defendant. A severe frost had caused water
pipes in the defendant's loft to freeze up, and so the defendant
asked a firm of builders to thaw them out. Two of the builders'
workmen, neither of whom was a plumber, set about the work
with a blow-lamp, which as a matter of fact was proved to be a
highly dangerous means of thawing these particular pipes out.
Some felt lagging caught fire, and the flames spread to the
plaintiff's premises, where they caused a great deal of damage.
Although the negligence could properly be attributed to the
workmen, the defendant was held strictly liable for the escape
of the fire, which was a dangerous object that had been brought
upon his land. If the case had had to be decided upon the basis
of negligence it is clear that the builders would have had to pay
damages, if sued, but that the actual defendant, though he
might possibly have avoided all suspicion of negligence had he

been careful to employ a registered plumber to do the work needed, was still most probably not in breach of any duty of care resting upon the 'reasonable occupier of premises which contain frozen pipes'. It is certainly a chastening thought for any occupier who cares to dwell on such matters that the defendant would not have avoided his liability even if he had employed a plumber, if the same damage, for the same reason, had taken place. It seems not unreasonable to believe that the plaintiff's claim, in circumstances such as these, ought properly to succeed against the builders, but not against the occupier. The state of the law is such that House of Lords' decisions make it impossible for the courts alone to change the present rules substantially, and it is submitted that the time is coming when the legislature will have to undertake a revision of the present law affecting the liability of occupiers for injury caused by objects escaping from their land.

The law as to liability for damage caused by animals is of ancient lineage, and it contains many fine points and distinctions which can hardly be investigated here. Broadly, however, injuries caused by animals are of two main kinds, personal injuries caused by biting, scratching and other assaults, and damage to land or goods caused by the escape of animals from fields or houses. It may be well to dwell for a moment upon these in turn.

Where personal injuries are caused by what we might term generally assaults, the liability of the person who ought to have had custody of the animal will vary according as whether the animal is classified as dangerous or tame. The distinction between dangerous and tame animals is not made upon commonsense grounds applied to each animal in question, but depends upon existing case decisions upon the species of animals involved. Tigers, gorillas and elephants have been held to be dangerous, and so a well-behaved Burmese elephant which had been worried by a dog, and had accordingly struck out with its leg and caused injury to a circus performer, was also held in 1957 to be dangerous in essence. Dogs, cats, horses and cows, on the other hand, have been held to be tame. Once an animal is classified as dangerous or wild, nothing can alter its status, and the law provides that the custodian or owner of such an animal keeps it entirely at his peril, and is strictly liable for all injury it may cause. Bertram Mills Circus, Ltd., who owned the Burmese elephant, were therefore held liable to pay damages for the injuries caused by the elephant, even though they had made strict rules prohibiting dogs in the circus area. The owner of a tame animal, on the other hand, is not liable for any injury it may cause to humans or to other living creatures which is beyond the normal results of following its natural instincts (such as where a dog chases a cat), unless he was previously acquainted with a special propensity of the animal to cause the actual kind of damage which took place—though statutory exceptions have been made to provide for the strict liability of owners of dogs which cause damage to livestock. This rule has justifiably given rise to the common belief that 'the first bite does not count'.

Where damage has been caused by the escape of an animal from land, the law is even more inflexible in its approach to the problems raised. It is well settled that the owner of cattle will be strictly liable for any damage caused by its trespass on to another person's land (though slightly less strict rules apply to cases of trespass by other types of animals). But if the escape is by any tame animal on to a highway, the occupier of the land is not liable at all for any damage done as a result of the escape, whereas he is strictly liable for any damage done by the escape of a dangerous animal. The rule concerning escapes of tame animals on to the highway stems from the principle that there is no duty upon anyone to fence his land, so that it would be unreasonable to expect an owner of unfenced or defectively fenced land to keep his animals in. Thus, if a farmer's cows stray from his land on to the garden of a next-door neighbour, without crossing a highway, the farmer will be liable for the consequent damage to the neighbour's garden. But he will not be liable at all if one of his horses jumps through a gap in his fence, of which he is well aware, and which he has neglected to repair, on to the highway and knocks down a cyclist, causing him serious injuries. The only possibility of success in an action based upon the cyclist's injuries would be if it were proved that the farmer had actually led the horse on to the road, after which it had escaped and done the damage complained of, or else (though this is disputed) possibly if it could be proved that the horse was in the habit of performing the kind of act just described, and to the knowledge of the farmer.

The unsatisfactory nature of these rules is readily apparent, and a few years ago the Lord Chancellor submitted the whole problem to his Law Reform Committee, which reported upon the matter in 1953. The main changes recommended by the Committee were the abolition of the distinction between dangerous and tame animals, and the introduction of a rule that liability for damage done by every class of animal should be based upon the test of negligence, though they also recommended that the onus of proving that there had been no negligence in any particular action should rest upon the defendant. The implementation of such a rule of proof would be contrary to the general rule in negligence actions, where the plaintiff must normally prove the negligence of the defendant, but it may well be justified in that the actual injury suffered from an animal can be said to speak for itself, and to show *prima facie* that the owner or custodian of the animal must have been negligent in allowing it to do the damage. The Committee thought that the strict liability rule might be retained as far as trespass by cattle to adjoining private land was concerned, but that liability under this head should be limited to damage done to land and crops. In every other case the ordinary principles of negligence actions should be the guiding factors.

These suggestions would seem to accord with commonsense. They would, if implemented, allow the courts to take cognizance of the fact that not all individual animals currently labelled dangerous are necessarily likely to do harm, while the present provision that knowledge of a dangerous propensity in a tame animal is necessary before liability can accrue for its assaults would be adequately covered by the new, wider rules. It might be expected that the agricultural community would oppose the recommendations so far as they affect escapes of tame animals from land on to the highway, but this opposition, motivated mainly by self-interest, can hardly be allowed to stand in the way of the good of the majority of the population. It may be argued that it is impossible and also undesirable to fence the various moors of England and areas like the New Forest, but it would not of course be necessary to do so. Owners of land in those areas would be able to discharge their duty of care quite easily by judicious placing of warning notices—a practice which to some extent is already observed.

The Law Reform Committee's recommendations have not yet been carried into law by Parliament, but it is submitted that the changes recommended are bound to come. There have been several recent cases of motorists injured by escaping animals which could have been prevented from escaping by the use of a moderate amount of care. The law must cater for the needs of the age of the internal combustion engine, and it cannot remain for ever bound by the historical shackles of the middle ages.

LIMITATION OF ACTIONS

Where a cause of action in either contract or tort has come into being, the injured party is not entitled to hold the threat of a possible action over the prospective defendant indefinitely, as such behaviour would add an undesirable state of uncertainty to living. By a series of statutes, therefore, Parliament has enacted that there shall in every case be a specific period from the date of every cause of action during which the appropriate action may be begun, and that thereafter no such action may be entertained by the courts. Generally the limitation period is six years, though in special circumstances in contract cases it may be as long as twelve years. In tort cases, on the other hand, an Act of 1954 has reduced the limitation period from six to three years in cases where damages are sought for personal injuries.

The broad result of these provisions is not strictly to oust the cause of action altogether, but to make it impossible for a slothful plaintiff to succeed in an action brought 'out of time', the net result in the end being in fact much the same. At any rate, the application of limitation periods is conducive to speedy litigation if it is to take place at all, thus ensuring that there is an end to court actions within a not too unreasonable length of time, and eventual peace between the parties. Special provisions exist to cover cases where there are continuing causes of action, in that a new period of limitation is deemed to begin to run on every fresh occasion that damage occurs, or where a cause of action has been concealed by the fraud of the prospective defendant, when the law allows the beginning of the limitation period to be delayed until the plaintiff is made aware of the fraud and of his right to sue. But a blot upon the just state of the law has for many years existed where, without fraud, and through mistake or mere ignorance, an intending plaintiff is unaware of the cause of action. In such a case the courts have always in the past held that there is no legal reason why the period of limitation should not run, as usual, from the date when the actual cause of action accrued.

This latter rule has proved itself particularly unfair in a number of cases involving miners who have contracted such diseases as pneumoconiosis, caused by inhalation of various kinds of dust, the effects of which only become apparent after several years. In some decisions the courts have, with obvious reluctance, been driven to hold that the plaintiffs have lost their right to bring their actions before the courts because the limitation period has in each case more than run since the date on which the damage from inhalation of dust took place despite the fact that the consequences of this damage could not be noticed by the plaintiffs until some years later. The result was that some plaintiffs with good causes of action for negligence against their employers were prevented from enforcing their normal legal rights simply because of delay which was no fault of their own. Fortunately a committee, sitting under the chairmanship of a High Court judge, reported recently that this defect in the law should be remedied, and the Limitation Act, 1963, gives effect to this recommendation. The Act is specifically designed to cover the cases of people who contract diseases like pneumoconiosis, which can for a long time remain dormant or quiescent, and which can do their damage to the human body insidiously and secretly. The Act provides that in such cases of personal injury, provided the leave of the court has been obtained, the normal limitation period shall not begin to run until the existence of the disease becomes known to the plaintiff. This new rule adequately covers the obvious defects in the old position, and it may be expected that the law on this subject will be satisfactory for the future.

APPORTIONMENT OF DAMAGES

Until about twenty years ago the usual result of an action in contract or tort carried to its completion was that one party to the action or the other would be financially successful, but that the court was generally powerless to award a sum of money to the plaintiff which took into account the fact that he was also partly to blame for the train of events leading to the court case. In a simple 'running down' case in tort the court would be bound either to order the defendant to pay full damages for the injuries suffered by the plaintiff or else to hold that the plaintiff had failed to prove his case at all. In actual fact, even though the defendant may well have been mostly to blame, it would be an unusual set of circumstances where the plaintiff was not himself partially negligent by, for example, failing to look both ways with sufficient care before deciding to cross the road. A similar result was obtained in cases in contract where the doctrine of frustration applied. Under this doctrine the parties to a contract are excused from the necessity of carrying out their agreed obligations if some wholly unforeseen circumstance has occurred which renders it virtually impossible to perform the contract on both sides in its original contemplated form. A common frustrating event in the past has been the outbreak of war, which obviously has rendered it impossible for English merchants engaged in international trade with merchants of the enemy country to continue to carry out contracts entered into in peacetime without being guilty of treasonable offences covered by the criminal law. The application of this doctrine of frustration to the law of contracts has been recognised by the courts for a long time, but until 1943 the legal effect of frustration was that the parties were merely excused from continuing with their contractual obligations, and it was not possible for a court to order the repayment of any money already paid under a contract for work done or goods to be supplied in the future. Nor was it possible for a party to a contract to recover any money by way of compensation for work already performed or expense already incurred under the terms of the contract.

Two statutes, one in 1943 dealing with the effects of frustration, and one in 1945 dealing with cases where both parties to an action in tort have been guilty of negligence to some appreciable extent, introduced a more rational method of dealing with such cases. The principle of apportionment is now applied to both types of case. Where a plaintiff sues a defendant for negligence, the damages to be awarded to him must now be reduced according to the proportion in which his own negligence, if any, has contributed to the cause of the accident involved. The same rule applies to any damages to be awarded to a defendant who cross-claims for injuries which he also may have suffered. Thus, if A claims £1,000 damages to recompense him for his injuries, and B counterclaims for £500 to cover the loss that he too has incurred as a result of the accident, and the court decides that each claim is valid, both sums will be reduced by the court according to the extent of the responsibility of each party for the accident. If, in the exercise of its powers, the court finds that the parties were equally to blame, then A will be awarded £500 and B £250; while if A is held to be one-tenth to blame and B nine-tenths, then A will receive £900 and B £50, leaving the balance of £850 in fact to be paid by B to A. In the result a plaintiff may still win his case even though he was partially to blame for the accident, but the defendant is enabled to reduce his financial liability according to the amount of blame in law to be attached to the plaintiff. In cases where contracts have been frustrated it is now provided that sums already paid by one party to the other under a contract so affected must be returned, though the courts may order a portion of the money to be retained to cover expenses already incurred under the contract. Similarly, if any valuable benefit has been obtained by one party by reason of some partial performance of the contract by the other, then the court may order some reasonable sum to be paid over to recompense the other party for the work done in providing this benefit.

These apportionment rules are clearly far more in accord with the just disposal of the matters in issue in the actions concerned, and it may be predicted that they are the forerunners of several other similar rules which will be introduced into other branches of the law. In particular there are two other aspects of the law of contract which it is submitted require reform of this kind.

The first of these topics is the present law dealing with mistake. Many people who enter into contracts may turn out to have been mistaken as to some matter of detail, or as to the effect the contract will ultimately have upon them. But the law will not normally relieve them of their contractual obligations unless the mistake is of a fundamental nature. Thus, in a case decided in 1932, Lever Brothers, Ltd., had given the 'golden handshake' to the chairman of one of their subsidiary companies by giving him £30,000 as compensation in return for his giving up his post. Subsequently Lever Brothers discovered that the former chairman had engaged in certain speculative dealings of an improper nature which would have entitled them to dismiss him summarily and without compensation, and they sought to have the contract declared void on the ground of this fundamental mistake on their part, so that they might recover the compensation money which had been paid. But the House of Lords held that a mistake of this kind as to the *quality* of the chairman was not sufficiently fundamental to render the contract void. The type of mistake which has, however, sometimes been held sufficiently fundamental to render the contract void is that where one party, at the time of entering into the contract, is under the belief that the other party is someone quite different. There are a number of cases where fine distinctions have been made in trying to determine whether the mistaken party really thought the other party was some other definite person, or whether he merely was unaware of the other party's true identity, in which case it has sometimes been held that he did not really care about the actual identity, and that the mistake was therefore not sufficiently fundamental to avoid the contract.

But a case decided in 1960 illustrates both the practical difficulties which face the courts in this area of law, and also the reform which is most likely to bring at least a more just solution than may be the case under the present rules.

The plaintiffs were three elderly ladies who had advertised for sale a car which they jointly owned. A prospective purchaser who called on them agreed to pay £717 for the car, but he wished to pay by cheque and to take the car away with him on the spot. The plaintiffs were hesitant about accepting a cheque rather than cash, but the man finally persuaded them to agree by saying that he was 'P. G. M. Hutchinson, of Stanstead House, Stanstead Road, Caterham'. After one of the plaintiffs had verified that this name and address appeared in the telephone directory, the ladies were sufficiently convinced of the identity and credit-worthiness of the man to accept the cheque and part with the car. The man, however, promptly sold the car to a dealer, and then disappeared, and the cheque was dishonoured. The plaintiffs therefore brought an action to recover the car from the dealer. The action was actually brought under one of the rules in the law of tort which has not been specially discussed in this book, but which enables the owner of property to recover that property from anyone else in unlawful possession of it, however unwittingly or innocently that possession may have been obtained. The basis for the plaintiffs' action, therefore, was that the car belonged to them, and not to the dealer, and they could only prove that the car belonged to them if they could prove that their contract of sale of the car was void because they had been mistaken as to the identity of the purchaser. In the event the Court of Appeal, by a majority of two judges to one, decided that the contract had been void, as the ladies had definitely intended to deal with Hutchinson and not just with the man who happened to have been negotiating with them. But this decision has been criticised on the ground that it can be argued that the plaintiffs were not really interested in the man's identity, but rather in his credit-worthiness, which was a matter of quality only.

It is no part of our purpose here to argue on one side or the other, but it will be appreciated anyway that the practical result of this decision as far as the parties were concerned was that the plaintiffs recovered their car intact, while the dealer lost the whole sum he had innocently paid to the bogus Hutchinson. As the villain of the piece had disappeared, the only parties to the civil action were both honest and, by all commonsense standards, innocent. Yet one party (or group of parties) lost nothing while the other lost all. (And this is not to mention the possible inequity arising from the fact that one party may have to bear the costs of both sides before the courts, a matter to be discussed in Chapter Eight.) It is not surprising that in this case the one dissenting judge in the court made what was in effect a plea to Parliament when he suggested that although he would have decided in the defendant's favour as the law stood, the only satisfactory method of dealing with problems of this kind would be by introducing the principle of apportionment between the two innocent parties. If such a principle were to be extended into this part of contract law, and it is submitted that such a development is a distinct possibility in the near future, then at least both innocent parties would have to bear their share of the losses involved in the transaction. This would not be perfect justice, for that could only be attained by making the rogue who had vanished bear the burdens involved, but at least a fairer solution would be reached in the dispute between the unfortunates who are left inextricably involved in the web he has woven.

The other branch of the law of contract which may well be affected in a similar way is that concerned with misrepresentations. Where a seller induces a purchaser to buy some article on the strength of his representations as to its virtues, a different result currently prevails, where these representations, though not dishonest, prove to be untrue, according to whether the statements made are incorporated as terms of the contract of sale or not. If the misrepresentation becomes a term of the contract, as where a purchaser buys a car on the express understanding that he will only buy it if it is, as the seller alleges, a four-seater, then the party misled is entitled to repudiate the contract if the term is sufficiently important to warrant this action, and in any case he may also sue for any damages which may be appropriate if he has suffered any loss on account of the misrepresentation. If, on the other hand, the misrepresentation does not become a term of the contract, his only remedy at present is to ask the court to set the contract aside, and he is not entitled to damages. In fact, in the latter type of case, he is not only unable to obtain any financial compensation for loss suffered, but also there are a number of circumstances in which the courts are at present barred from setting the contract aside, particularly where the complainant in any way indicates or affirms that he is prepared to try and make the contract work.

As an example of this latter type of situation we may take the facts of a case decided in 1958. The defendant had advertised for sale a lorry which he described as being in 'exceptional condition'. When the plaintiff called to see the lorry, the defendant told him that it was capable of 40 m.p.h., and covered eleven miles to the gallon, and the plaintiff then bought the lorry, although the representations made about it, which were untrue, though honestly made, were not incorporated as terms of the contract. The purchaser almost immediately found that the lorry consumed eight gallons of petrol over a journey of forty miles, and that it would hardly reach a speed of 25 m.p.h. The plaintiff made persistent complaints about the lorry to the defendant, but he nevertheless continued to use it for a few days, during which he discovered that there was a serious oil leak, a crack in one of the wheels, and that the dynamo had ceased to function. The plaintiff thereupon accepted an offer by the defendant to pay half the cost of a reconditioned dynamo, and the lorry was then sent on a journey to Middlesbrough, in the course of which it completely broke down, and an expert found that it was totally unroadworthy. The plaintiff sought to have the contract set aside, but the court held that he had affirmed the contract by continuing to use the lorry despite the appearance of the defects in the vehicle.

The real vice about this limitation upon the right to have a contract set aside is that it works hardship upon the kind of person who, out of ordinary feelings of decency, is not prepared to be immediately truculent about a contract which turns out not to be so much to his liking as he had at first thought. The ordinary man may well behave as the plaintiff did in the case just cited, and hesitate to take the extreme step of telling the seller that he will have nothing more to do with the vehicle. Yet by acting in a conciliatory way he may well prevent himself from ever obtaining any redress from the courts. This particular gap in the justice of the present legal rules has now been generally realised, and a few years ago the Lord Chancellor submitted the problem for the consideration of the Law Reform Committee. The Report of this Committee, recently published, contains the recommendation that the present result of affirmation of a contract by a person who was induced to enter into it by some innocent misrepresentation which does not become a term of the contract should be limited to cases where he has expressed his acceptance of goods *after examination*. Furthermore, it is suggested that in cases where the misrepresentation does not become a part of the terms of the subsequent contract, the court should have a discretion to award damages to the injured party instead of setting the contract aside. These recommendations have been warmly welcomed by lawyers, and it seems reasonable to hope that they will be carried into law quite soon. If so, it may be suggested that the general principle of apportionment will have been applied once more, though in a rather less obvious form than hitherto. To permit the plaintiff in a case similar to the above example to recover a sum of money which will enable him to put the vehicle into roadworthy condition would enable him to end up with a lorry of the kind he had originally intended to buy, at no further expense to himself, while also allowing the seller to retain such portion of the original purchase price as is not required to pay for the repair to the lorry. The seller will therefore retain the sum for which he ought perhaps to have sold the defective vehicle in the first place, and justice will have been as nearly done as possible.

SEDUCTION AND ENTICEMENT

Two of the more unusual causes of action in the law of torts are seduction and enticement. An action for seduction is not, as the layman might think, a suit brought by a distressed girl against her seducer. On the contrary, it is an action maintainable by the master of any female servant, who has been deprived of her services as a result of her seduction by the defendant. In other words, it is basically an action for loss of a servant's services, and it does not lie at the instance of the person seduced (nor should it be confused with the crime of seduction of the young mentioned in the chapter on Criminal Law). Once this point is made, it becomes clear that although there may still be some point in allowing employers to bring actions in some circumstances against people who, by their torts, deny the employers the services of their employees, yet to allow such an action to be based upon seduction alone is hardly in keeping with the needs of the age. This is all the more so since the woman or girl who is the victim of the seduction, and who as a result may bear a child, is not permitted even to be joined as a co-plaintiff in the action. But there are still greater oddities about the state of the law. A father is deemed to have an automatic right to the services of any unmarried daughter under the age of twenty-one who ordinarily lives at home, so that in this case there is not even the need for the father plaintiff to prove that he has lost any services at all. In fact practically the only seduction cases litigated these days are actions brought by fathers for the seduction of unmarried daughters who have still not attained their majority. It is also remarkable that in seduction cases the damages recoverable are not, as is the usual rule, limited to the actual injury suffered (in this case the value of services lost), but may include vindictive damages, probably because the action is in reality far more concerned with redressing the wrong done to the honour and feelings of the parent than it is with any legal fiction of loss of services.

The action for enticement lies wherever someone induces a wife to leave her husband, a child to leave home, or a servant to leave his or her employment, and it lies at the instance of the husband, the parents or guardian, or the employer, whichever is appropriate. Once more the action is based upon the fiction of the loss of services, and in modern times it has only been of importance in the field of matrimonial relations.

In a Report issued in May 1963 the Law Reform Committee

recommended the abolition of both these two causes of action, and although three members of the Committee of fifteen (the three being two judges and a solicitor) disagreed with their twelve colleagues, and submitted a minority report, it may be expected that these two outdated types of action in tort will eventually be abolished by Act of Parliament. The Committee considered that a husband whose wife has been enticed away from him already has an adequate remedy in divorce proceedings, where it is always possible for the court to award a petitioner husband a sum of damages to be paid by the correspondent who has committed adultery with the wife. The Committee was not asked to decide whether a seduced female ought to be given an independent remedy on her own account against her seducer, and this is a possible development of the law which deserves further consideration. Such an action would, if permitted, take its place alongside the present rules which permit an unmarried mother to obtain a court award of a sum of money to help with the upkeep of the child, but it is difficult to say whether there would be any great advantage in permitting it.

The Committee considered that the only causes of action of the kind under discussion here which merited any form of retention were those where an employer had genuinely suffered financial loss through a wrong committed against a servant by some third person, such a wrong being far more commonly an act of negligence than by way of seduction or enticement. Quite apart from the services lost through injury, the employer may, for example, have continued to pay wages to the injured employee. Here the majority of the Committee favoured granting the employer a direct right of action against the wrongdoer, though they recognised that difficulties would have to be faced in deciding where the employer alone should be allowed to sue, where the employee alone should be entitled to sue for his injuries, and where both should be able to recover damages. They foresaw the dangers of allowing a duplication of damages, but believed that the difficulties could be overcome by detailed work upon their proposals. It is probably too complicated a matter to pursue further here, but at least it may be hoped that we shall soon have seen the last of the actions for seduction and enticement in their present anachronistic forms.

DEFAMATION

A final word should be said here concerning the law of defamation, because it has been subjected to some criticism in recent years. The tort of defamation is committed, in general, wherever a false statement is made which would have the likely effect of bringing the subject of the statement into ridicule or contempt in the eyes of ordinary people, and that statement is communicated to anyone other than the person about whom it is made. If this 'publication' of the defamatory statement is transitory, as, for example, by word of mouth, it amounts to slander, but if on the other hand it is in some permanent form, usually in writing, it is libel. The main difference in practice between libel and slander is that the former is always actionable at the suit of the person defamed, whereas an action for slander will normally only succeed if the plaintiff can prove that he has actually suffered a financial loss as a result of being defamed. There are exceptions to this latter rule, and also certain defences based upon fair comment, etc., which we need not pursue here. But the general law of defamation, and particularly of libel, has been criticised primarily upon the grounds that the press needs more protection from possible lawsuits, and that the relatives of deceased persons have no right, as in the case of most other torts, to protect their relations' reputations by bringing actions for defamation.

As regards the first criticism, the law has already been made more fair by the Defamation Act, 1952. Under this Act, any person who has published words alleged to be defamatory of another person may, if he claims that the words were published by him innocently in relation to that other person, make an offer of amends. The actual amount of the amends to be paid may, if disputed, be decided by the court, but the fact that the offer has been made is, provided the defamation really was innocent, a complete defence to any action for defamation, and the injured party will receive no more money than is truly necessary to recompense him. It is submitted that no greater safeguard for the press is needed than this, for the law must properly protect an individual's reputation where it is put in jeopardy. It must of course be very trying for living people to hear or read statements which may be defamatory of their deceased relatives, but an action for defamation is so essentially personal, and to allow relatives a right to sue would be to give rise to the possibility of gold-digging actions. Should the law allow relatives of Earl Lloyd George or descendants of Oliver Cromwell to bring actions for defamation by way of bald criticism of those two men? A line must be drawn, and it is surely drawn properly according to the present law.

In short, with the exception of the position of the jury in defamation actions, referred to later in Chapter Eight, no significant change in the law of defamation is envisaged in the future.

CHAPTER FIVE

Family Law

EQUALITY OF THE SEXES

ONE of the results of the old common law doctrine that a married couple should be treated for legal purposes as being one person was that it was impossible for one spouse to sue the other in any civil action during the subsistence of the marriage. For obvious reasons it was necessary to puncture a hole in this rule to enable judicial separation or divorce to be obtained, and the steps taken to provide legal rules concerning matrimonial causes have already been mentioned in Chapter One. Similarly we have also alluded to the legislation concerning married women's property in the latter part of the nineteenth century, whereby a wife was entitled for the first time to retain after marriage the title to property which had belonged to her before marriage. Yet until very recently the basic rule that in general no spouse may sue the other was still in force. Neither spouse was permitted to bring an action against the other for such ordinary civil matters as, for example, breach of contract or negligence. As a result, although an Act in 1935 had given a wife the limited right to sue in the courts to protect the ownership or possession of her separate property, no such provision was made as regards her husband's own property. In a sense, therefore, the old inequality of the sexes had been partially remedied by giving to wives rights of action in the courts which their husbands could never enjoy, though it must not be thought that such actions brought by wives were common.

At first sight the general rule appeared reasonable. It might be thought to be an aid to the stability and felicity of marriage that there should usually be no possibility of legal suits brought by one partner to the marriage against the other. Certainly it is to be hoped that there are not many married couples who harbour the desire to sue each other. But unfortunately the theoretical legal position gave a false picture of the actual nature of some kinds of court action. Let us take a simple example. Suppose that a wife had been injured in a car crash, caused by the negligence of her husband, who had been driving the car at the time, while she was his passenger. In these circumstances it is to be hoped that the wife would never have wished to sue her husband, whatever the injuries. But we all know that the husband was insured against damage caused by accident under a policy taken out with an insurance company, for every driver was and is obliged by law to be covered by such an insurance policy. Under the common law rule it would have been impossible for the wife to obtain any compensation from the insurance company because it was not the company which caused the accident, but her husband. The growth of insurance has meant that many defendants in court actions do not in fact have to pay the damages awarded against them, although the actions brought are still technically against the actual wrong-doers. So if the injured person had been a stranger (and if the insurance policy was of the comprehensive variety, covering injury to passengers), he would have been able to recover compensation from the insurance company by technically suing the driver. But because, in our example, the injured party was the driver's wife, who was thereby barred from any action in court against her husband, the company would not have been bound to pay her anything at all, however comprehensive the terms of the policy. The same result would have applied if the wife had been the driver, and it had been her husband who was the injured passenger.

Another example, which actually occurred in a case of 1939, was as follows. H and W, a married couple, while motoring in their car, driven by H, were involved in a collision with X, a stranger driving his own car, and W alone was injured. It was proved that the blame for the accident lay equally upon H and X, and when W sued X for damages she was awarded full compensation for all her injuries. But, when X then claimed that H ought to contribute towards the sum recovered, he failed because H could never have been held liable to W at all. Admittedly it was X's insurance company which really paid the damages, while H's insurance company was exempt from having to contribute anything, but it is as well that justice should apply between insurance companies as between anyone else. The law was at the very least illogical.

This state of affairs was clearly undesirable in the twentieth century, when the number of possible motor car injuries to passenger wives or husbands, caused by their spouses' fault, has become great. Accordingly it was necessary to alter the general law, and the Law Reform (Husband and Wife) Act was passed in 1962. Under this statute it is provided quite simply that each of the parties to a marriage shall for the future have the same right of action against the other as if they were not married (though the court is granted the power to stay any action in which it considers that no substantial benefit can accrue to either party from its continuance, a power which may effectively prevent actions being brought out of mere marital pique or to air petty grievances).

There is no reason to believe that the Act of 1962 will further divide some spouses by breaking up the marriage through litigation. As the Law Reform Committee Report, upon which the Act was based, stated: 'It is the wrongful act or omission, not the existence of the legal remedy, which may cause unhappiness and will, if relations are already strained, tend to disrupt the marriage.' The Act of 1962 may be one step in a growing recognition that insurance companies are often the real parties to litigation. At present the parties to a civil suit will still be named as 'Smith' and 'Jones', but we may be approaching a time when the names of the two individuals involved in the accident will be forgotten, and the action will be known not as *Smith* v. *Jones*, but as *Blankshire Assurance* v. *The Accidental Cover Co.*

One other clear step in the cause of the equality of the sexes seems called for, and that is the abolition of the action for breach of promise of marriage. The basis for this action is that an agreement to marry is just as much a contract in civil law as an agreement to purchase a ton of coal. As we have stated in Chapter Four, a contract to be valid and enforceable in English law must consist of an offer by one party, followed by an acceptance by the other in the terms offered, each promise carrying with it 'consideration' for the other. Thereafter, if one party fails to carry out his side of the bargain, the other will have the right to sue him for damages to compensate him for the loss he has sustained thereby. Where, therefore, two people have agreed to marry, the offer and acceptance are clear from the state of the engagement, and the consideration for the agreement is provided in that each has agreed to forego his or her single state. Where this agreement is later broken by one party failing to honour his or her promise, there is a breach of contract, and it is this breach which may be the subject of an action for breach of promise of marriage. The logic of this would appear to require that either innocent party should be able to sue the party in breach, but it is a legacy of the days when it was felt that a man was giving up more in marrying than a woman, and that only the woman was losing a valuable benefit if the marriage never took place, that the law has always only allowed a woman to obtain financial relief in an action of this kind.

The action seems to have been much abused. There have been several occasions when a scheming woman has extracted a promise of marriage from a man, and then held the threat of a breach of promise action over his head lest he should try to escape the marriage. Equally there have been cases where the promise to marry has been denied by the man, and it was difficult to arrive at a true assessment of whether or not there was a contract at all, because it would be rare to find a witness of the actual proposal and acceptance. Again, a woman may often obtain heavier damages where she can prove that she consented to intercourse on the strength of the engagement which has now been broken, on the grounds that she has been thus devalued on the marriage market, though in the mid-twentieth century it may be doubted whether her surrender need still be measured in financial terms. And it is to say the least fallacious that a broken engagement may be a loss to a woman, but never to a man. The action for breach of promise of marriage is a hang-over from a different age, and on those occasions when breach actions are brought the vast majority of the newspaper-reading population treats them as comic interludes with a Gilbertian flavour. It cannot be healthy that the law should be brought into this kind of disrespect, for it indicates that it has outlived its purpose. The day cannot be far removed when the legislature will take the opportunity to abolish the action altogether.

Divorce

The present grounds for divorce in English law were summarised in Chapter One, and it will be remembered that divorce may only be obtained if some matrimonial offence has been committed by the other party to the marriage—adultery, desertion and cruelty being clear offences, and insanity in the nature of a constructive offence. The party at fault has no right to seek a divorce based upon his own offence. The question whether the doctrine of the matrimonial offence should continue as the basis for the English law on divorce is very controversial, though the Royal Commission on Marriage and Divorce, which reported in 1955, supported, by a majority, the continuation of the present basis for the grounds for divorce. A substantial number of the members of the Royal Commission, on the other hand, favoured the addition of a new ground for divorce founded upon the complete breakdown of the marriage.

On the whole it is probably true to say that very few people in England would favour the granting of divorce upon grounds as nebulous as 'incompatibility' has proved to be in some of the states of the U.S.A. Equally many still feel that a definite matrimonial offence by one party ought to be proved before dissolution is allowed, but there is also much force in the argument that there is no point in enforcing the perpetuation of a marriage that has totally broken down, merely because neither party is insane or has been guilty of adultery, desertion or cruelty. Early in 1963 Mr. Leo Abse, M.P., sponsored, as a private member's measure, a Matrimonial Causes Bill, under which he had proposed that divorce should be obtainable (*a*) at the suit of either the innocent or the guilty party, where a matrimonial offence has been committed, after seven years' separation, or (*b*) by consent, after seven years' separation. The difference between separation and desertion is that the former means no more than that the parties are living apart, while the latter implies that they are living apart at the instance of one and against the will of the other. For Mr. Abse's second proposed new ground for divorce, therefore, there need have been no matrimonial offence committed by either party.

The motives behind Mr. Abse's proposals were those of humanity. He quoted figures to show that about a third of all illegitimate children were born to cohabiting parents who were apparently living in permanent union though unmarried. These illicit unions, he maintained, had all the potentialities of permanent and happy marriages, but were denied the seal of legality because at least one of the parents in the relationship was already married to someone else who was not prepared to divorce the erring partner. A spokesman for the opposite viewpoint was the present President of the Probate, Divorce and Admiralty Division of the High Court, Sir Jocelyn Simon, who, in a speech to a branch of the Magistrates' Association, stated that to permit any form of divorce by consent would be tantamount to society disclaiming its concern in the endurance and stability of marriages. Marriage, he thought, was an institution of society, under which children gained legal, moral and social rights. Wives, he said, were not infrequently brought under a quite cruel and relentless pressure to divorce their husbands who wished to remarry, when they themselves desired a reconciliation and resumption of married life. Divorce by consent would increase the scope for such grievous situations. He was also of the view that consensual divorce would be a dangerous thing even in those cases where marriages had been irreparably broken. To quote Sir Jocelyn's actual words, as reported in *The Times* of April 8th, 1963:

Is it consonant with our ideas of justice that a husband who has enjoyed the services of his wife during her springtime and summer, should be able to cast her away in the autumn and claim that the marriage has irretrievably broken down because he has certainly no intention of returning to a woman who has lost all attraction for him: . . . ? The truth is that many marriages break up—irretrievably if divorce is available—for no other reason than that the wife has lost her sexual attraction before the husband has lost his.

Similar opposition to Mr. Abse's proposals were voiced by leaders of the Anglican, Roman Catholic and Free Churches, and many M.P.s of all parties felt that to open the doors to divorce by consent could lead to a major change in the whole basis of marriage which ought not currently to be permitted. Although Mr. Abse tried to substitute a clause which would take into account doctrinal or conscientious objections by the respondent, and which would prevent divorce if a decree would be harsh or oppressive to the respondent or contrary to the public interest, the House of Commons made it plain that to insist on the retention of any clause of this nature in the bill would ensure the defeat of the whole measure. So Mr. Abse reluctantly withdrew the clause altogether, and a later attempt to revive it in the House of Lords also failed. Mr. Abse stated that the result was that the law was still choked by humbug and pretence. He believed that the true significance of marriage lay not in the ceremony in church, synagogue or register office, but in cohabitation in love and affection in the home and family. Thus, he said, the position remained that where the bond had irrevocably been broken the marriage may yet have to continue in name, while a suburban housewife, married for years and with several children, would give her husband a ground for divorce immediately if in a moment of madness she had a quarter of an hour's adultery with the milkman.

It is clear that the view of Mr. Abse, and those who would agree with him, demands great respect. Yet law and society are presented by an inevitable dilemma caused by the frailty and illogicality of human behaviour. Is it better that a spouse should be able to escape from an irrevocably broken marriage, whatever the other spouse may feel about the matter, or that the wishes of the reluctant spouse should prevail? Which is best for the children, that the hollow marriage should be dissolved, thus abolishing pretences, or that a united home should still be open to them despite the disharmony between the parents? Probably no one will ever know, because each set of circumstances will react differently upon each set of parents and children. If so, then the cause of conservatism here would seem to demand adherence from the law for the time being. True, the children of illicit unions mentioned by Mr. Abse are in serious difficulty because of the underprivileged position of illegitimates in the eyes both of the law and of society at large. Yet here perhaps the solution would be best found not in trying to facilitate divorce still further, but in continuing the process of ironing out the differences which the law makes between the status of legitimate and illegitimate children. In this respect much progress has already been made. Mothers with illegitimate children are entitled to practically all the benefits under the welfare state that are available to mothers of legitimate children. Since 1959 an illegitimate child has been entitled, just like a legitimate child, to sue anyone who causes the death of his father by negligence, if he has thereby incurred financial loss. Many other examples of this equalisation within the law could be given, though it is also fair to point out that there is some way to go yet. There are still a number of far-reaching rules regarding inheritance to property which favour legitimate children as against illegitimate children. Nor should one forget the social stigma which attaches to illegitimacy, though the higher incidence of illegitimacy, which will be discussed in the next section of this chapter, may be doing something to reduce this kind of prejudice. Probably no law could compensate a child for the fact that his father does not live with his mother, and still less can it affect the situation where the child is not even aware of his father's identity. But the law *has* eased the hardships which lie upon illegitimates, and, by a series of statutes since the Report of the Royal Commission on Marriage and Divorce, it has also been made easier for illegitimates to be legitimated. We are already well on the way towards providing that all children of marriages which are later declared void, upon one of the grounds of nullity (such as a failure to conform with one of the requirements of the marriage ceremony), shall be legitimate. It could be that, except for the rules concerning such matters as succession to estates and titles, the inequalities in law between legitimate and illegitimate children will eventually be erased altogether.

If then it is accepted tentatively that no drastic alteration to the basis of our divorce law is likely in the near future, there may still be some room for improvement upon points of detail. It is commonly believed that collusion between the parties to a marriage in order to manufacture false evidence of adultery is rife, and although the presence of collusion is a discretionary bar to the granting of a divorce, its detection may be a matter of chance. It could be that some more systematic method of routine inquiry, certainly in the case of hotel adultery cases, would be feasible, though the prospect for such a modification of the law cannot be regarded as very bright: it would probably lead to much fruitless search with very little return in the form of detection of collusion.

A more likely development would be the abolition of the present requirement that a party petitioning for divorce who has himself or herself also committed adultery must submit a discretion statement, in which the adultery is confessed. If such a statement is submitted, the judge then has a discretion whether or not to allow a decree of divorce. The discretion is usually exercised in favour of granting divorce, unless the adultery disclosed is so outrageous in comparison with the offence alleged against the respondent that the judge feels it would be unjust to do so. But if the statement is found to be deficient concerning the actual instances of adultery by the petitioner, or if no statement is submitted and yet adultery is proved against the petitioner, the result will be that the discretion will almost certainly be exercised by not allowing the decree of divorce. This rule seems to be out of keeping with reality and to give rise to a great deal of chance so far as discovery of adultery is concerned. People who have committed adultery are usually reticent about their act, and it may well be that a petitioner with genuine grounds for divorce sometimes runs the risk of failing to obtain his decree merely because he cannot bring himself to confess to perhaps a single lapse from virtue of which he is now ashamed. Thus the law seems to favour the man with no sense of shame. It is submitted that it would be more just to abolish the need to make discretion statements. The argument that this would lead to an increased risk of collusion can hardly be serious. Nor would the law necessarily be brought any nearer to a system of consensual divorce. On the credit side, many unnecessary blushes would be spared, and the need which some comparatively innocent people at present feel to lie to their legal advisers would disappear.

Although Mr. Abse's Matrimonial Causes Bill became a somewhat truncated measure as a result of the opposition to one of its main clauses, as indicated above, it nevertheless retained provisions dealing with a portion of its original purpose. When the Bill became an Act in the summer of 1963, it introduced into the law rules designed to aid the healing of apparently broken marriages, and it was welcomed on all sides of the House of Commons, by all the churches, and by the community at large. The encouragements to reconciliation provided by the Act are based upon recommendations made by the Royal Commission in 1955. Under the old law a man who discovered that his wife had committed adultery virtually had to decide forthwith and irrevocably whether or not to divorce her. If he told her that he had forgiven her, or if he had sexual intercourse with her even once after knowledge of the adultery, the ground for divorce disappeared (thought it would reappear if ever the wife at some future time committed another matrimonial offence). It was most unsatisfactory that anyone should have been placed in this position without warning, for there are few people who can so uproot their lives and habits at a moment's notice as to decide to terminate the marriage relationship immediately. And many who did decide to terminate the marriage were forced into a position where they did not dare to attempt any reconciliation lest they should lose their ground for divorce if the reconciliation proved impossible. If a deserted wife persuaded her husband to return, in the hope of patching up their differences, she immediately lost her ground for divorce. If the husband had returned only for a single day, before again deserting her, the wife would then have had to wait another three years before she could petition for divorce.

The new Act provides in effect that every married couple shall have three months in which to make up their quarrel, during which time the wronged party does not lose his eventual right to a divorce. In the course of this period the parties may even have intercourse without prejudice to the grounds for dissolution. Once this law is generally known, or wherever legal advice is taken when grounds for divorce appear, it seems likely that many couples will attempt a reconciliation, secure in the knowledge that they are not committing themselves irrevocably one way or another. If unfortunately the wronged party finds that he or she cannot tolerate the past offence, then he may still petition for divorce, provided that he withdrew from cohabitation within the permitted three months. The main opposition to this reconciliation provision was voiced in the debate in the House of Lords, notably by Lord Hodson, a Lord of Appeal, and by Lady Summerskill, who pointed out that the clause was weighted against the wife. Should a wife become pregnant during the months when a reconciliation is being attempted, the husband would still be at liberty to claim that the trial period had been a failure. But this possibility is probably a defect which we must be prepared to put up with in order to reap the many benefits which the Act should bring; and a substantial majority in each House was satisfied that the benefits of the new provisions outweighed the defects. The Act applies to all grounds for divorce. So now, to take but one example, a woman who has left the matrimonial home because of the cruelty practised upon her by her husband, may return to live with him for up to three months, on receiving a promise of better conduct for the future, without barring her right to divorce on the ground of cruelty by her condonation. As a result of its eventual form Mr. Abse's bill became known as the 'kiss and make up' bill, and few would deny that it is a sound step forward towards the encouragement of the stability of marriage.

MARRIAGE AND ILLEGITIMACY

One of the most distressing aspects of modern society has been the great increase in illegitimacy. It has been suggested above that a lot may yet be done by the law to iron out the differences between illegitimates and legitimates, and even that the status of illegitimacy itself might one day be largely erased from the law. But in the meanwhile some more short-term measures to tackle the problem may be considered. Recent figures show that nearly 50,000 illegitimate children are born each year, and an *Observer* survey in May 1963 found that in England and Wales one child in every sixteen born today is illegitimate. The rate is even more alarming among children born to mothers under the age of twenty, where one in four is illegitimate.

Doubtless many of these unfortunates are born to parents in the position which moved Mr. Abse to propose acceptance of divorce by consent, or at the instance of either the guilty or the innocent party after seven years' separation. Others are born in circumstances which would prevail in any age and in any society which depends upon human participation. The occasional lapses of the many, or the habitual low standards of sexual morality of the few are found to occur anywhere and in any age. But the real reason for the startling rise in the incidence of illegitimacy in recent years is the general change which has come about in the moral standards of present-day society as a whole. It seems now to be generally accepted as a fact that pre-marital sexual relations are much more commonly indulged in than they have been in the immediate past centuries. Perhaps the only remedy for such a situation lies in the recovery by many people of a sense of the balance which should be kept between personal indulgence and social and family responsibilities. Particularly in the case of the adolescent population there may be a need for a conscious effort to replace with reason and responsibility the attitudes engendered in them by the morality of the 'pop' song and the twentieth-century novel. But this is a matter which is within the province of parents and the family, and not of the law.

Granted a state of affairs which gives rise currently to a high incidence of illegitimacy, the only aspect of the matter which we can relevantly discuss in this book is whether the law can be altered in any way to bring relief to those unfortunates who may be born into the world illegitimate. If the statistics of illegitimate births for 1961 are examined it will be found that nearly 900 of the babies were born to mothers under the age of sixteen, and over 700 of these were born to mothers aged fifteen. Now one distinction which can be drawn between these babies and all other illegitimate babies is that they alone could never under any circumstances have been born legitimate, even if their parents had done their utmost to regularise the situation, for the simple reason that in English law marriage under the age of sixteen is forbidden. Indeed it is even a criminal offence for a man to have intercourse with a girl under the age of sixteen, whether or not she consents. Here the law seems to have failed to keep in step with the requirements of the times. It is obvious that an age below which marriage should not be allowed must be fixed in law, for this is designed, if for no other reason, to protect females who cannot be regarded as physically and mentally ready for the connubial state and for child-bearing. But it has been recognised that, for a variety of reasons, children often reach the age of puberty a year or two earlier these days than they would have done in the last century; and they therefore are likely to wish to have sexual intercourse that much sooner than would otherwise have been the case. If it is also accepted that there can be little difference between the mental readiness for marriage of a girl of sixteen and girl of fifteen, then it becomes logical that the age of marriage should be lowered. Several other countries already permit marriage at the age of fifteen, and some even allow it at younger ages. It is not suggested here that the law of England should permit marriage under the age of fifteen, because it is submitted that girls of fourteen or less, however physically well-developed, will be mentally quite unfit for taking on the responsibilities of a status intended to last for life. Many will think that even sixteen-year-old girls are usually mentally too young for marriage, but here the good of the children born to mothers of such an age must be put before such considerations.

Accordingly, although little can be done as yet to relieve the underprivileged status of the hundred or so illegitimate children born each year to mothers under the age of fifteen, it is suggested that a significant step can be taken for the benefit of those born to girls who have reached the age of fifteen. By lowering the age of legal marriage to fifteen, it will become possible for the parents of babies born to mothers of that age to marry (provided the father is also at least fifteen, which will almost certainly be the case, since boys reach the age of puberty later than girls), unless one of them is already married to someone else, a contingency which seems on current figures to be remote. It will also be necessary to alter the criminal law, so that consensual intercourse with a girl aged fifteen (or even possibly fourteen) will no longer be a crime, for it will no longer be a function of the law to protect by the imposition of criminal penalties the chastity of girls who may render their babies legitimate by marriage before the birth takes place.

FAMILY PROVISIONS

In many countries the law provides that when a person dies his or her near relatives are entitled automatically to a specific proportion of his estate, whatever provisions he may have made to the contrary by will. In England it was for many years possible for a testator to leave the whole of his property away from his family if he so wished, but an Act of 1938, which has been modified by another Act of 1952, brought the English law more nearly into line with the position which prevails so often elsewhere. But there is an important difference between the present English law and that in many other countries, and that is that although it is now possible for the court to order reasonable provision to be made out of the estate for near relatives, it is nevertheless up to the relatives themselves to apply for such provision to be made. The Acts permit the court to make an order in any case, whether or not the deceased person made a will, and regardless of any provision which he may have made, but which is inadequate, in favour of the deceased's wife or husband, any daughter who has not been married, or who is, by reason of some mental or physical disability, incapable of maintaining herself, any infant son, and any other son who is, by reason of some mental or physical disability, incapable of maintaining himself. Sons and daughters, for this purpose, include both adopted and legitimated children, and indeed there is no reason to quarrel with the list of people who may receive financial help under the statutory provisions. Yet the fact remains that because the law does not make automatic provision for such people, the machinery for the financial aid is only brought into play in each case by an actual application to the court. As will be readily appreciated, there may well be many wives or other relatives who, for reasons of pride or family feeling, are unwilling to make an application to the court, and it seems that the law is, consequently, in danger of failing the very people it has so conscientiously set out to assist. Accordingly, although there is no need in a book of this kind to attempt to deal with the kind of financial proportions which widows or other relatives should receive, it is suggested that it may well be worth while in the future investigating the possibility of providing automatic and fixed rights for those persons who at present have the right to apply to the court for family provision after the death of a deceased.

CHAPTER SIX

Constitutional and Administrative Law

PARLIAMENT—COMMONS AND LORDS

As has been stated in Chapter One, the most fundamental feature of the law of England is to be found in the power of Parliament to change at will any of the detailed laws dealing with various aspects of our life. It is therefore of the highest importance that both the efficiency of and the just execution of its duty by Parliament should be maintained. When complaints of dilatoriness or complacency are raised against the legislature, they should be taken seriously. In the present section of this chapter it is proposed to consider whether Parliament is effectively doing the job it should do, and retaining its vigour in its approach to national affairs.

The job of Parliament involves two distinct functions, that of creating or changing the laws which govern the inhabitants of this kingdom, and that of debating upon a multitude of matters which affect the interests of some or all of us, but which need not necessarily have any special relationship with law as such. Critics of the present composition or functions of the Houses of Parliament have mostly been divided into those who have an objection to the present organisation of the House of Lords, and those who, on a wider front, attack the results of the fairly rigid political party system, which are mainly to be seen in the House of Commons. It is not proposed to deal with various detailed criticisms which are sometimes made of the actual procedure of Parliament, as these are rather too technical for adequate treatment in this book. We shall consider first the effects of the party system upon the Commons. In the Lords party politics are not so obtrusive, partly because of the permanent Conservative majority among those peers who do belong to political parties, and partly because a good proportion of the peers do not lend their regular support to any of the parties. The composition of the House of Lords and its relationship with the Commons will be discussed later in this section.

The basic reason for the prominence of the party system in the Commons is the accident of history. In the seventeenth century Parliament as a whole often found itself in bitter conflict with the monarch and his ministers, and this conflict even erupted into civil war in the 1640s. But by the end of the century the struggle had been won by Parliament, and the king had agreed that for the future he would only exercise his individual powers by the consent of Parliament. When the Hanoverian kings came to the throne early in the eighteenth century a number of factors tended to throw more power still into the hands of Parliament. The first two Georges were more interested in their German possessions than in England, and they were hampered by a scanty knowledge of the English language. Accordingly they tended to place more and more of their constitutional powers in the hands of their ministers alone. As these ministers found that it was essential to come to terms with the wishes of Parliament, particularly in order to obtain the money required to maintain the functions of government, it was not a very great step in our constitutional evolution to find that the ministers themselves were soon drawn exclusively from among the ranks of the most influential members of the two Houses of Parliament. With the growth of the political party system the ministers then became the leaders of the party which possessed a majority in the more important of the two Houses, the Commons; and this is the position which still prevails today.

Constitutional theory has it that because the ministers are members of the Houses of Parliament, and are dependent for their continuance in office upon continued majority support in the Commons, then they are responsible to Parliament, in the sense that they must be able at all times to justify their actions to Parliament when called upon to do so. Certainly ministers are constantly pressed by questions asked in the House about the discharge of their official functions. Certainly too the uncovering of maladministration in a Government department will lead from time to time to the resignation from office of the responsible minister. But the downfall of a modern Government has hardly ever been brought about by the disapproval of some of those members who usually support it. Governments sometimes lost the confidence of the House in the last century, when parties were wont to split up, and when the presence of uncommitted Irish members and a few independents lent some uncertainty to the probable outcome of debates and motions of censure. But today the party machines are well-oiled and efficiently maintained. A member of a party who votes against the party line on an issue of importance will often be subject to party discipline which can even result in expulsion from the party. In 1956, at the time of the Suez crisis, one Labour M.P. who disagreed with his party's official policy found that his constituency Labour Party was so hostile to his retention of his seat in the House that he had to stand down forthwith. A Conservative who had taken a line adverse to that of his party's official policy found that, although it was possible to remain in the Commons as an independent member for the duration of that Parliament, his constituency party refused to support his nomination as the party candidate, even on reinstatement within the national party, at the general election of 1959.

The truth is that in many respects the individual M.P. must subordinate himself to the wishes of the party. Although ministers are supposedly responsible to Parliament, in fact party discipline ensures that any Government measure can be pressed through Parliament, however vociferous the opposition expressed from the other side of the House. While Parliament in theory controls the Government, in fact the Government controls Parliament. It is said that this system does at least ensure that we have a strong Government, and such an assertion cannot be denied. The Government knows that it can get its own way whenever it really wants, and this does ensure that policy, whatever it may be, is carried through without being held up by the interests of minorities. In a sense we settle the broad Government policy to be followed for the next few years every time we hold a general election, and it may follow that having made our bed we ought to be prepared to lie on it. If we are discontented with Government policy, then the remedy is at the next election. But to see the dangers that may be inherent in our present constitutional system it may be well to scrutinise the events which have taken place in some newly-fledged Commonwealth countries, which have inherited a constitutional system modelled very closely upon that of the United Kingdom.

The independent Commonwealth countries have multiplied with great rapidity since the Second World War, when we have been passing through an era of decolonisation of the old British Empire. The older Dominions, as they were called twenty years ago, were joined in 1947 by India, Pakistan and Ceylon; and in 1957 began another spate of Independence Acts, which have so far brought into being the new nations of Malaysia, Ghana, Nigeria, Sierra Leone, Tanganyika, Uganda, Kenya, Zanzibar, Cyprus, Jamaica and Trinidad and Tobago. It is clear that the immediate future will bring the addition to this list of at least Nyasaland, and very probably also Malta, the remaining West Indian colonies and the Rhodesias. Although democratic institutions, as we understand them, seem at present to be secure in India, Malaysia, Jamaica, Trinidad and Sierra Leone, and in the older Commonwealth countries, Canada, Australia and New Zealand, there is some doubt about the likely constitutional futures of many of the other nations in the list. Pakistan, after one peaceful revolution, has eschewed the British model for its Constitution and adopted a form of presidential system more akin to that of the United States, where the Government is not dependent upon its close relation with the legislature for its continued existence in office. A somewhat uneasy democratic society is maintained in Cyprus and Ceylon, and it is not yet clear whether democratic institutions will be successfully preserved in countries like Nigeria, Kenya and Uganda. What is clear, however, is that in Ghana at least, and to some extent in Tanganyika (and perhaps in the coming years the same will also be true of Nyasaland), autocratic government is emerging. The great weakness of the British system is that if the Government has the actual power, should it wish to exercise it, to control the legislative and other proceedings of Parliament, then there is always the possibility that it will use its power to prevent the Opposition from playing an effective part in the political life of the country. In Ghana the Government has been able to secure the passage of Acts conferring power upon the Government itself to detain people without trial for long periods, a power which has been used on occasions to detain members of the Opposition, thus preventing them from taking part in any active political life at all. Furthermore the existence of these powers has been a considerable factor in discouraging other members of Opposition parties from playing a truly active part in opposing the Government. The step from here to real dictatorship is so short that it is hard to be sure whether there is indeed any step still to be taken. Sir Ivor Jennings, one of our most distinguished living constitutional lawyers, has said that in order to discover whether a country is democratic one should look to the status of the Opposition. The status of the Opposition in Ghana is neither high nor healthy. This is not to say that the Government of Ghana is itself necessarily unhealthy, for there is little doubt that it is supported by the vast majority of the populace. Perhaps autocracy is needed in young, growing nations, and England has in its history been through its own periods of autocracy. But developments taking place in Africa are indicative of the things which could in theory happen here, for the basic principles in the Constitutions of the African countries are the same as ours.

In theory, therefore, the Government in this country could persuade Parliament to pass Acts dealing with any matters it wishes by the simple expedient of ordering its party supporters in the Commons to vote for the measures proposed. There is no reason in law why Acts cannot be passed to confer upon the Government the power to detain anyone, including a member of the Opposition, for life without trial, or to put to death the inhabitants of any city in the kingdom it should choose by whim, or indeed to carry out any nefarious purpose it may have in mind at all. Yet we know that statutes of such a kind never will be passed, for the simple reason that constitutional convention is far stronger in the United Kingdom than the actual letter of the law. The traditions of free speech and the fair share of Parliamentary time between the Government and the Opposition have been built up over the centuries. We have had these centuries in which to establish our constitutional practice, and thus have been given, by the accident of history, an advantage which the newer countries of Africa have never had. It seems quite possible that future centuries will produce in Africa the kind of mature democratic institutions which we are fortunate enough now to enjoy. This result can hardly be achieved by the artificial implanting of foreign concepts, and this is why the British constitutional importations in Africa have been of doubtful value. So far as Africa is concerned we must be patient and wait for developments in the fullness of time. It must be recognised as a fact of life that British concepts of Government and Parliament cannot be transplanted to other countries with complete and immediate success.

The conventions of the British Constitution and the ordinary practice of political life certainly do provide us with many safeguards against the undue exercise of Governmental power. Again, despite the power which the Government can, and not infrequently does, wield, another safeguard is provided by the independence often displayed by the party members on both sides of the House of Commons who sit as 'back benchers', that is, those members who are neither ministerial members of the Government nor members of the Opposition 'Shadow' Government. This vigorous independence is displayed particularly at that part of each day's proceedings known as Question Time, when private members may ask ministers any questions they choose about their departments and the conduct of their official duties. It is quite common for back benchers of the Government party to be as hostile in their questioning, and as probing in their attacks, as members of the Opposition, and they serve the purpose, not only of keeping ministers up to the mark in the discharge of their duties, but also of reminding the Government that, although they will normally support the Government in any vote in the House, their votes are not to be taken completely for granted.

Even so it must be conceded that actual revolt among back

benchers when they are called upon by the Government to vote upon party issues is rare. Few members are ever anxious to put their seats in jeopardy by having to face a general election earlier than would normally be the case. The safeguards which already exist in our system should not be allowed to blind us to the deficiencies which will always remain to a greater or lesser extent in anything dependent for its operation upon the human element. Whichever way one looks at the problem, the fact will always remain that if the executive is persistent in its wish to press through a particular policy it can practically always succeed in accomplishing its aim. To this extent, therefore, Parliamentary control of Government activities may be rendered nugatory.

One suggestion which has been made frequently in recent years is that Parliamentary proceedings should be televised, so that the whole nation may see what the Government is proposing, and so that all members of the House will be more obviously forced to carry out their duties. So far the Government, with the support of most members on both sides of the House, has resisted this suggestion, and it is submitted that in broad principle it has been right to do so. The great disadvantage of televising any proceedings is that the process gives rise to play-acting. There are already occasions when speeches made in the House are designed mainly for the consumption of the general public, rather than to deal with the substance of the business in hand, for these speeches are reported in the press, on radio and on television. There is as yet, however, no necessity for members to indulge in unnecessary and irrelevant gestures and poses. Some speeches may seem to those in the public galleries to be dull, but this is mainly because there is no need for them to include any of those assumed effects to be found in theatrical performances or upon the hustings. To introduce the televising of debates would not only encourage the delivery of speeches in a false manner, but it would also encourage the delivery of far more speeches than at present which need not be made at all. Many members speak comparatively little in debate, though most are active in asking questions at Question Time. The reason is not the laziness which some may suspect, but the fact that their political activities are carried out 'behind the scenes', in committees of the House which usually sit in the mornings in private, in various party conclaves also held in private, and in constituency affairs which of necessity are only known to people actually in the constituencies. Some critics have argued that members in the House often look as if they are asleep, that some of them put their feet up on the Table of the House, or that others engage in conversations with each other during speeches, and all of these statements are true. But it is a traditional Parliamentary practice to *pretend* to sleep and to put one's feet up during an opponent's speech, while to indulge in individual conversations may often be the means of mobilising positive opinion among one's colleagues about the matter under discussion. It is also suggested that television would cause more members to spend more time in the chamber, but this criticism misses the point that much Parliamentary business is done outside the chamber. Every member of the governing body of a college at Oxford or Cambridge, every director of a company, and every member of a local authority knows that only a fairly small proportion of the actual work to be done is performed in the formal meetings of the bodies to which they belong. The same principle applies to Parliament. It is submitted that it will be unfortunate if Parliament and the Government ever accept the general suggestion that Parliamentary debates should be televised. But there may be no harm in allowing a limited period for the televising of proceedings in the two Houses. It should be very definitely limited, so that the work of the legislature may not be hindered, but there may even be some advantage in giving the people as a whole a chance to view our greatest constitutional institution, and to appreciate what goes on there.

Another suggestion has been made by no less a man than the Senior Clerk of the House of Commons itself. In an article in *The Times*, in April 1963, he suggested that the present select committees of the House, which deal with such problems as the scrutiny of Public Accounts, should be extended in their area of operation. Fact-finding would be the essential function of these committees. They would not normally examine ministers in person, but they would have the power to call for

149

oral and written evidence. This type of committee system has its most prominent example in actual practice in the United States, where the committees of both Houses of Congress have extensive powers to call for evidence, with the aim of discovering the facts about various situations connected with the national life. In America this type of committee is perhaps essential, because the members of the Government, from the President downwards, and with the single exception of the Vice-President, who presides over the Senate, are prohibited by the Constitution from having seats in either House of Congress. Thus Congress has no direct power, by means of such processes as Question Time or general debate, of ascertaining the identity or extent of Government activities. Such a system has frequently been opposed in the British Parliament, for the simple reason that ministers, as members of Parliament, are always open to the kind of challenge and questioning which cannot take place in America. The Senior Clerk of the Commons, however, believes that his idea, if put into practice, would have the merit of providing the Commons with the information which is essential to constructive criticism of Governmental administration in the later process of the debate or the Parliamentary question. It may well be doubted whether his suggestion will bear fruit, as busy ministers are unlikely to welcome anything which might make possible more effective criticism of departmental administration, and most ministers have always been of the opinion that the Parliamentary question alone is sufficient to provide the means of eliciting any information required. Again, it seems that the suggestion may never get any further than the pages of *The Times*, but it is no bad thing that we should be awake to the dangers which can arise from Government control of the Commons. It is this kind of alertness which keeps the constitutional machinery running in harness with democracy.

A problem which seems overdue for attention is the payment which M.P.s receive for their services. The present salary of a member of the Commons is £1,000 a year, plus a tax-free expenses allowance of up to £750 a year. Ministers receive higher salaries, and so does the Leader of the Opposition, but the ordinary back bench or Opposition M.P. must make do with the maximum of £1,750. According to present-day values this is a very small sum in comparison with most professional men, and it is highly inadequate for the remuneration of a man who has to spend money upon maintaining a residence in London and probably in his constituency as well, and who must pay a secretary for helping him with the great volume of mail which as an M.P. he will automatically receive, quite apart from all the more usual expenses attendant upon keeping alive and caring for one's family. It may be wondered why the salary of a member, which has remained at this level since 1946, should continue to be so low. Once more the reason is historical accident. Traditionally every M.P. is a part-timer. In past centuries he was invariably a rich merchant or a gentleman, in mediaeval times either a knight or a leading citizen or burgess, and it went without saying that he had means from his other more usual pursuits. Attendance of Parliament in the sixteenth century would often involve only two or three weeks a year, and in the days of Anthony Trollope, in the mid-nineteenth century, Parliament only met from February till August. The sittings have always been arranged to take place in the afternoons and evenings, with the most serious business taking place after six o'clock, and often considerably later. This was designed to allow the members to fulfil their day's duties as merchants or practising at the Bar before spending their evenings grappling with the nation's affairs.

There is probably no need to attempt any adjustment of the timing of debates, for in this turbulent age, with international crises constantly blowing up, and with Parliament and the Government ever dealing with social problems which were never considered to be the business of their predecessors of bygone ages, it is convenient to utilise the mornings with work in the Government departments or in the Cabinet for ministers, and with committee and constituency work for other members, not to mention the endless hours of preparation which go towards the making of speeches. But the personnel of the Commons has undergone a radical alteration. There are still some members with substantial private or business means, and with business duties to attend to, and there are still several successful barristers who go to the House after arguing in court, but there is also a large body of members, particularly within the Labour Party, who are mainly dependent upon their Parliamentary salary and allowances for their very existence. Our tradition is still one of the part-time M.P., but in reality we have been progressing more and more towards an age of full-time members. There is much to be said for maintaining a system which allows for part-timers, for they can keep the chamber in touch with the everyday affairs of the country, but this desirable state must not blind us to the needs of those members who are perforce full-timers. Some of these unfortunates have had to give up their seats because they cannot afford to remain in Parliament. Others have even gone bankrupt. The Government has for years been reluctant to take any effective steps to remedy the situation because such action could be interpreted outside as the feathering of the Parliamentary nest. In a recent sample survey of ordinary working class opinion upon members' salaries, a majority of those questioned thought that M.P.s were paid quite enough, and a substantial number even felt that they were paid too much! Little did those who answered know that it was the Labour M.P.s who, on the whole, were in the greatest financial difficulty. It is submitted that, however the move may be interpreted, the step must be taken very soon of providing all M.P.s with either a much greater salary, or else a much greater and more realistic expenses allowance. Perhaps the latter course might be better than the former, because the expenses would have to be justified, and the part-timers would therefore receive less than the full-timers. But the nettle must be grasped one way or another.

Before leaving the question of reform in the House of Commons, it may be noted that under present arrangements the Speaker of the House, who must act as an impartial chairman, is nevertheless still a member elected by the ordinary process of political party battle in a Parliamentary constituency. Once elected Speaker by his colleagues in the House he must, by convention, relinquish all political activities and cease to concern himself with constituency affairs. He remains

Speaker until he either dies or voluntarily retires (assuming, as is in practice always the case, that he is not removed by a vote of no confidence taken in the House itself). On retirement he traditionally receives a peerage and never sits again in the Commons. At a general election he may not take part in the usual political campaigning, and in fact he is often returned to Parliament unopposed. There has been growing criticism of a system which effectively results in the Speaker's constituency, whichever it may be, ceasing to be represented in the Commons, and both the Labour and Liberal parties have determined to put up candidates to oppose the present Speaker in the general election which is likely to be held in 1964. The time may not be far off when an M.P., on election by the Commons to the post of Speaker, will have to give up his elected seat, thus allowing a normal by-election to be held in his former constituency. The Speaker would then either hold office without a constituency at all or else represent some mythical constituency created for the purpose. Such a change in the law would certainly be more fair to the Speaker's original constituents than is the current position.

One of the most burning of all questions concerning Parliamentary reform has been that of the composition of the House of Lords. Until the last few months the nucleus of the House, unlike that of any other legislative chamber except a tribal assembly, has consisted of those men (but not women) who hold peerages of the realm, with the exception of those holding Irish peerages, who are entitled to be elected to the Commons, and those holding Scottish peerages, who have been entitled to elect sixteen from among their own number at the beginning of each Parliament to represent them in the Lords. To these have been added the Archbishops of Canterbury and York and the twenty-four senior diocesan bishops of the Church of England, the Lords of Appeal in Ordinary, or 'Law Lords', who are appointed to life peerages, primarily to sit as judges in legal cases coming on appeal to the House of Lords, and the other life peers (including women) who may now be appointed from time to time by the monarch on the advice of the Prime Minister, under the terms of the Life Peerages Act, 1958. Those currently qualified to sit in the Lords actually number only a little under a thousand, though it is unusual for more than some fifty or one hundred to be regular in their attendance, and the House has adopted a method of excluding those who do not usually sit from attending on special occasions by granting them 'leave of absence', lest they should bring the House into disrepute by voting mainly from prejudice rather than political experience. It should be added that the House of Lords, though technically the upper House, is in fact very much of a junior partner to the Commons. As a matter of law, if the Lords continue to oppose the passage of a public bill for more than one year, that bill will in any case become law by being presented for the Royal Assent without the Lords' approval; and financial bills, duly certified as such by the Speaker of the Commons, no longer need the Lords' approval at all before being presented for the Royal Assent.

It may be asked whether there is any point in maintaining the upper chamber any longer. Some countries, and in the Commonwealth notably New Zealand, have managed with a single chamber legislature. But, on balance, there is much to be said for a second chamber. In the first place it provides a forum for the expression of second thoughts upon legislation which may have been hastily concluded in the Commons, possibly because of the fire of party political controversy. During the Labour Government of 1945–50, well over 90 per cent of the detailed amendments provided by the Lords to the social legislation that had been passed in the Commons were later accepted by the Government and incorporated in the bills concerned, despite the fact that the Conservative party had a majority in the Lords. Secondly, less controversial bills, particularly upon purely legal reform, may be introduced in the Lords, and be debated there in detail, before going to the Commons, rather than *vice versa*. This saves the Commons some valuable time, as they are often able to accept most of the work already done in the Lords. Thirdly, the upper chamber is a suitable place for full-dress debates upon problems of importance which are nevertheless not of sufficient moment to warrant the setting aside of much time in the Commons. An example is the perpetual problem of the relief roads proposed for Oxford, which has been debated on more than one occasion in the Lords, while the Commons would probably regard the matter as too remote or too parochial to warrant more than the time taken up by the occasional Parliamentary question.

Yet, if there is a place for an upper chamber, is the House of Lords such a suitable body? The Liberal Government in 1910 had intended to abolish the House altogether, and to substitute for it some more representative second chamber. But since that time, with the diminished legislative power of the Lords, which had in fact been brought about during the period of the Liberal Government shortly before the First World War, the need to abolish the House has not been felt so strongly. Although the Conservatives have maintained a permanent party majority in the House, this has been hamstrung by the inability to oppose conclusively the legislation introduced by Governments formed from other parties. It may well have been this fettering of the power of the Lords which has resulted in a more constructive use of its time. There is no point in opposing a bill whole-heartedly if that bill is going to become law anyway: it is far better to try to put it into a more workable shape than it may possess at present. Oddly enough, it may well be the permanent Conservative majority in the Lords which has caused the Labour party to oppose consistently over a period of many years any substantial reform of the House, lest that reform should carry with it an increase in the power of the Lords, though this opposition has at least temporarily eased. On the whole such an increase in power seems unlikely for the future. The shackles which now bind the House have made it into a more responsible assembly, and its loss of legal power has led to an increase in its constructive activity. Recognition of this factor has led all but a small minority of M.P.s, who still hanker after abolition of the House, to lean in favour of reform of the composition of the House only, and a limited reform has very recently taken place.

The greatest spur to reform of the Lords' composition has been the fact that for centuries every man who has succeeded to an hereditary peerage has become automatically qualified to sit in the Lords, and equally disqualified from sitting in the Commons. Although this has usually caused no difficulty there have been at least three cases since the Second World War when active members of the Commons have, by the accident of their fathers' death, suddenly found themselves elevated to the Lords against their wishes. The most notable case was that of Mr. Wedgwood Benn in 1960, who despite succeeding to the peerage of his father, the first Viscount Stansgate, wished to remain as the member of Parliament for Bristol South East, and actually fought a by-election in the constituency after his succession to the title. Despite being returned by the electors with a large majority, his election was declared void. The direct result of this case was the formation of a Joint Committee of the two Houses to consider proposals for reform of the composition of the Lords, and this committee made its report late in 1962. A statute was then passed in the summer of 1963, with general all-party support. This provides principally that every peer may disclaim his peerage for the duration of his life, leaving his next heir to decide whether or not he also will surrender the peerage when the time comes for him to succeed to the title. Any M.P. who succeeds to a peerage will have one month, exclusive of any period of time when Parliament is not sitting, during which he must decide whether or not to surrender it. Peers who have already succeeded have one year from the date at which the Act takes effect (July 31st, 1963) to decide whether to surrender or not, while other peers who succeed to their titles in the future, unless they are M.P.s, are also given one year in which to make up their minds. Among other more minor provisions are sections for the first time giving peeresses and all Scottish, though not Irish, peers the equal right to sit in the Lords with other members of that chamber.

As a result of this reform reluctant peers like Mr. Wedgwood Benn may now return to the Commons, always provided of course that they are duly elected in constituencies. The present Prime Minister, Sir Alec Douglas-Home, formerly the Earl of Home, also returned to the Commons in 1963 under the terms of this Act. But it may well be questioned whether these changes are sufficient to cure the deficiencies of the second chamber. The present author is in favour of the retention of a system whereby membership of the upper House is not dependent upon election by any kind of voting upon party lines. Those second chambers in other countries which are elected upon such a system too often tend to mirror the wishes of the first chamber. Still worse are those second chambers which are composed of members elected or nominated either by the lower House, as in Northern Ireland, or by the Government, as in Canada. They tend to act as little more than Parliamentary rubber stamps. But the fact remains that, although there is a strong body of active members of the Lords, there are also far too many qualified members who do not usually sit, and who may indeed be prevented under the rules of the House from sitting for the duration of a particular Parliament. Law Lords and bishops clearly have something to contribute to the proceedings of the House, and the few life peers so far appointed have proved their value, particularly since the power to appoint life peers has so far been used partly to boost the Labour benches in the House, though there would be political dangers inherent in too wide an application of the powers given to the Prime Minister by the Life Peerages Act. But can it be regarded as satisfactory that the vast majority of the members of the House obtain their qualification merely by the accident of birth?

Few will question the wisdom of perpetuating the practice of granting honours to those who have served the community well in some way or other. It is human to wish to show appreciation for work well done, and it is equally human for those who have carried out their duties to be pleased by the honours they receive. But what justification can there be for regularly conferring at one and the same time, and inextricably bound up together, the right to sport a title with the right to take part in the legislative and other business of Parliament? This unique practice may have its roots in history, but it is not every old shrub which continues for ever to decorate the well-kept garden. It is submitted that the time has come for digging up these roots, and severing our modern Parliamentary composition from its mediaeval origins. There is no need to abolish the hereditary peerage, though the present author certainly thinks that there can be no point left in actually taking the step of conferring new hereditary titles. For the most usual kind of honour the Crown has at its disposal a large selection of orders and ribbons, medals and stars, together with knighthoods of varying kinds. Even the baronetcy is of little harm, since it confers no automatic right to a seat in either House of Parliament, though the author's prejudice is against the continued perpetuation of any honour to the descendants of the actual recipient, who alone has deserved it, and who has in any case probably only received it late in life. For the recipient to enjoy the fruits of his labours for, say, ten or twenty years at most, and then his possibly idle son to enjoy the same honour for perhaps fifty seems an odd result of the bestowal of a title for labours well accomplished. If the Prime Minister feels that a particular recipient is worthy of a place in Parliament, then he may make use of his power to appoint life peers.

Short of an actual abolition of the hereditary peerage system, which seems to be an unlikely step in the immediate future, it is suggested that no new hereditary peers should be created, and that the holders of those hereditary peerages which continue to exist should have the power to elect some, but comparatively few, of their number to represent them in the Lords. A suitable representative number might well be fifty, as this would amply cover the number of hereditary peers who currently are diligent in their attendance of the House. The bishops and Law Lords should remain as members, but some consideration should be given to providing for representatives of the Roman Catholic and Free Churches in the House, should those churches so desire. It is too complicated a topic for this book to consider the pros and cons of disestablishing the Church of England, but it may be that the admission of some limited representation of other churches in the upper House would not necessarily have to carry with it disestablishment (though there are several influential members of the Church of England who feel that it might benefit rather than lose from disestablishment). The University seats, which were abolished in the Commons some fifteen years ago, might also be recreated for the Lords, rather than the Commons. At the same time it may be that direct representation in the Lords of such bodies as the various professional associations and the trades unions might be considered.

It would seem to be inevitable that such a reconstituted second chamber would retain its quality of being what Sir Ivor Jennings has called a 'Conservative bulwark', as conservatism so often goes with the status of 'elder', and the basis of the scheme outlined above is that the Lords should be a more effective House of elders. Opposition to this scheme may therefore be expected from the Labour party, and also perhaps from the Liberal party. For this reason it may be that the plan will never achieve fruition, but it is submitted that the steps which have so far been taken in reforming the composition of the Lords (such as the introduction of Law Lords and other life peers, and the option to waive membership of the House) are all leading up to the time when a more radical and rational attack upon the problem must be made. When this attack is eventually made it will also be logical to provide for the first time a regular salary for members of the Lords. The current expenses allowance for members is three guineas for each day that a peer attends the chamber, and this can hardly be regarded as adequate. With a reformed House of Lords it is even possible that the Prime Minister, who under current practice must be a member of the Commons, and thus directly responsible to the elected representatives of the people, will eventually sit in the Lords, where he can have more leisure from his Parliamentary duties to discharge the ever-increasing burdens of his weighty office under the Crown. There is no reason why he should not be adequately represented by a deputy in the Commons, as was often the practice in the more leisured nineteenth century. It is significant that a year or two ago Mr. Butler was appointed as official Deputy Prime Minister, the first time such an office has existed since the war years in the 1940s, though this office has now been abolished again for the purposes of Sir Alec Douglas-Home's Government.

Finally, on the subject of Parliament, it may be noted that the members of both Houses possess a number of privileges by virtue of their membership. Notably, each member is protected from any legal proceedings (such as in defamation) which might otherwise result from any speech made in the House or from the contents of any document passing between members on Parliamentary business. This privilege is essential to enable members to discharge their constitutional functions of debating and questioning on any matters connected with the nation's affairs. But the extent of the privileges of members is perhaps rather greater than it need be, and a case of 1963 has brought attention to focus upon at least one unsatisfactory aspect of the present privileges. Among the privileges of the members of the two Houses which have been claimed for centuries, and which have been recognised by the courts as being part of the special law concerning Parliament, is the privilege of freedom from arrest. In past centuries, when there may well have been dangers of the arrest of members to prevent them from speaking or acting in Parliament, particularly when Parliament was in violent disagreement with the monarch, this privilege may well have been a necessary protection for members. But as time has gone by the need for its maintenance has evaporated, and by a gradual process the Houses have voluntarily relinquished the freedom of members from arrest on criminal charges. With the abolition in the nineteenth century of arrest and imprisonment for debt, except in very special cases, it was felt that the privilege had become a dead letter. Yet in 1963, when the wife of the Premier Baron of England, Lord Mowbray, sought to have her husband forced to comply with a decision of a court under which he had been ordered to give certain property to her, she was defeated in her claim. The only way in which her husband could be made to obey the order of the court was by arresting him and bringing him to the court to be punished unless he carried out his legal obligations, but Lord Mowbray claimed that he was privileged from arrest for what was a civil, and not a criminal, process.

The case was all the more unsatisfactory because although Lord Mowbray was entitled to sit in the House of Lords he was not in fact one of the more prominent attenders of that assembly. Members of both Houses were incensed at what they regarded as an unjustified claim of a privilege which, after all, in essence belongs to Parliament rather than to the individual member. It is likely, as a result of the notice caused by this case, that Parliament may take an early opportunity to abolish the privilege of freedom from arrest altogether. It cannot be expected that Parliament will take any steps to abolish some of the other controversial privileges, such as the power to punish both members and non-members for contempt of either House, or the right to control its own internal proceedings to the exclusion of any possible court challenge, as these privileges are of some practical use to Parliament, but at least some of the dead wood should be pruned away.

CIVIL LIBERTIES—EQUALITY BEFORE THE LAW, PRIVACY AND THE POLICE

It is a commonplace to say that England is a free country, by which is meant that the people are free to do and say what they please without fear of being penalised for their activities or their expressions of opinion. True there are obvious limitations to this kind of liberty, for the law has provided that citizens may only indulge in their freedoms provided they do not seriously infringe the interest of the state (as by the commission of treason, the passing of national security secrets to foreign powers, or the fostering of sedition) or the liberties of other individuals (as by defamation of character). But it is a curious fact that the civil liberties which remain after these exceptions have been syphoned off are in no way protected by actual law laid down. They exist by virtue of custom and convention. As has already been pointed out, it is always possible in law for Parliament to pass Acts dealing with any subject it pleases, and so statutes may well sometimes be designed to curb the freedom enjoyed by the individual. In wartime, for example, it has been common for Parliament to introduce compulsory food rationing, compulsory military service and exceptional powers of detention without trial against aliens or persons suspected of having enemy sympathies. And after the Second World War the institution of compulsory military service was even perpetuated for a period of some fifteen years before it was finally abolished.

It is clear that the legal authority of Parliament, exercised very largely as a result of the will of the Government in power, can be used where it is so wished to curb or even destroy the generally accepted liberties of the people. Powers assumed in wartime have had the general support of the nation, but there is no reason in law why those powers should not also be assumed in time of peace. We are accustomed to think of this country as a democracy, yet our legal system provides for a process which could quite easily transform the nation into a totalitarian state. It may therefore be questioned whether the law is satisfactory, and in particular whether it might not be more healthy if specific safeguards of civil liberties were to be included, by statute, in our laws. An Act dealing with civil liberties would at least provide a constant guide as to practice for future Governments.

If we look at the state of law to be found in most other countries, it will be seen that nearly all other systems make special provision for the protection of civil rights. The classic code of protection is to be found in the United States, where the first few amendments to the Constitution, added in 1791, and known as the Bill of Rights, make specific provision that, for example, a soldier may not be quartered in a private house in time of peace without the consent of the owner, that the people shall be protected from unreasonable searches and seizures, and that in criminal prosecutions the accused shall enjoy the right to a speedy and public trial according to specific basic rules of justice. Similar constitutional rights, with variations to suit local need, have been adopted in the legal systems of most of the newly created Commonwealth countries, while one of the older members of the Commonwealth, Canada, has recently amended its laws to incorporate a Bill of Rights. The Act of the Canadian Parliament which provides for this Bill of Rights is short and concise, and it is worth quoting its first section in full. It runs as follows:

It is hereby recognised and declared that in Canada there have existed and shall continue to exist without discrimination by reason of race, national origin, colour, religion or sex, the following human rights and fundamental freedoms, namely,

(a) the right of the individual to life, liberty, security of the person and enjoyment of property, and the right not to be deprived thereof except by due process of law;

(b) the right of the individual to equality before the law and the protection of the law;

(c) freedom of religion;

(d) freedom of speech;

(e) freedom of assembly and association; and

(f) freedom of the press.

Section 2 goes on to provide that every law of Canada shall, unless it is expressly declared in an Act of Parliament of Canada that it shall operate notwithstanding the Canadian Bill of Rights, be so construed and applied as not to abrogate, abridge or infringe any of these rights or freedoms. The section goes on to make special note of the kind of procedure in a criminal trial which must be followed in order to accord with the Bill of Rights.

Codes of civil liberties along the lines just indicated are clearly of some value in showing the kind of rights of each citizen which must usually be respected by the state and by other individuals. But it is worth remembering that even in the recent Canadian Act it is provided that Parliament may if it so wishes expressly declare some future statute to be passed notwithstanding the Bill of Rights. The Universal Declaration of Human Rights, adopted by the United Nations General Assembly in 1948, which supposedly binds all member nations, has hardly resulted in the kind of respect for civil liberties in all countries which one might regard as desirable. The truth is that no written document making provision for human rights is of much practical use unless the spirit of the nation is in general agreement with its provisions. Constitutional provisions safeguarding equality for all in the United States have not prevented race riots and bloodshed over the painful problem of desegregation in the southern states. Nor have civil liberty enactments been effective in many other countries to prevent detention without trial.

If this point is accepted, it follows that national traditions of equality and freedom for the individual are of more value in safeguarding democracy than any written provisions, which can be ignored by those in political power. The old-fashioned definition of democracy as 'government of the people by the people for the people' is in fact more nearly achieved in the United Kingdom than in most other countries in the world. In practice the Government has never taken any action to prevent freedom of activity and movement, or the free criticism of the institutions of 'the establishment', unless the exigencies of the times have made such a step seem necessary not only to the Government, but also to the people as a whole. Although some English lawyers have been considering the possible desirability of protecting civil liberties more effectively by the passage of some form of statutory Bill of Rights it may be submitted here that such an Act could have no more efficacy to protect the liberty of the individual than is already in existence, and it is therefore unlikely that such a step will ever need to be taken in England.

Yet there is one particular civil liberty which is practically unknown in England, and which may be becoming increasingly more necessary in the context of modern society. This is the right to privacy. It is well-known that film stars, sportsmen and politicians lead lives which are the subject of frequent comment in the press, on radio and on television. For the most part the very livelihoods of these people depend upon their constant presence before the public eye, and so there is usually little harm in the activities of reporters and commentators. But there are other people who may well find themselves the subjects of nationwide, or even worldwide, attention, for the mass media of the present day have made the world into a very small place. The wives and families of persons convicted of the most serious criminal offences may themselves be hounded by the press to tell their life stories, or they may find themselves the unwilling subjects of photographs which are displayed in the daily press and shown on television. Even those people who court publicity may well not be pleased to find that their private lives are treated by the press as being of equal news value as their public activities. The time has surely come for the law to recognise that provision should be made to protect citizens from invasions of privacy which are not desired by the individuals concerned.

In America the problem was seen far earlier than in this country. Two learned contributors to the *Harvard Law Review* in 1890 wrote:

> The press is overstepping in every direction the obvious bounds of propriety and decency. Gossip is no longer the resource of the idle and of the vicious, but has become a trade, which is pursued with industry as well as effrontery. To satisfy a prurient taste the details of sexual relations are spread broadcast in the columns of the daily papers. To occupy the indolent, column upon column is filled with idle gossip, which can only be procured by intrusion upon the domestic circle. The intensity and complexity of life, attendant upon advancing civilisation, have rendered necessary some retreat from the world, and man, under the refining influence of culture, has become more sensitive to publicity, so that solitude and privacy have become more essential to the individual; but modern enterprise and invention have, through invasions upon his privacy, subjected him to mental pain and distress, far greater than could be inflicted by mere bodily injury.

Following upon this view the courts of most of the states of the Union have been prepared to provide relief, mainly in the form of awards of damages, to a plaintiff whose privacy has been unjustifiably invaded by another. The rule has been derived from a development of the law as to defamation, invasion of property rights and breach of confidence or contract, and has been stated as providing that 'a person who unreasonably and seriously interferes with another's interest in not having his affairs known to others or his likeness exhibited to the public is liable to the other'. American courts have accordingly granted damages against, for example, a motion picture company which made a film depicting the earlier life of a prostitute, who had been the defendant in a sensational murder trial, but who had since changed her name and her habitat, gained new friends and lived a life free from the breath of scandal. The principle has even been extended to cover cases of eavesdropping.

It is curious that English law has made no such progress. There are isolated provisions in the criminal law whereby 'peeping toms' may be convicted of minor offences, but there are no known methods to prevent or remedy by awards of damages the persecution of innocent or reticent people by reporters or by the broadcasting of their private affairs, unless published statements should turn out to be untrue or objectively unfair, in which case an action for defamation may lie. A reporter who forces his way into a house would be guilty of trespass, but he is often guilty of no offence at all, civil or criminal, if he merely rings the front door bell or the telephone many times day after day, in the hope of persuading the occupant of the house to tell his or her story, providing he stops short of actual molestation. Lord Mancroft introduced a bill into the House of Lords a year or two ago with the object of making specific provision for offences against privacy, but it was later abandoned because of the difficulties involved in defining the distinction between invasions of privacy and mere exercise of the normal rights of free speech and comment, particularly in a free press. Yet this problem seems likely to be permanently with us until some effective step is taken. Reporters depend for their bread and butter upon their success in getting stories for their papers, magazines or television networks, and therefore it is not satisfactory to depend solely upon their own good taste in deciding when they ought not to press an individual further. It seems reasonable to expect that, as the problem becomes more acute as time goes by, legislation not dissimilar in content from the law currently prevailing in the United States will have to be enacted fairly soon. It is an essential element of a democracy that there should be a free press, and we should value the continuation of the present freedom enjoyed by the British press. But at the same time there is no doubt that in recent years the press has a sorry record as regards its taste concerning matters fit for publication, and to give the individual who is genuinely wronged by the press a private remedy in civil law would be a suitable way of providing a brake upon indiscriminate publication, while avoiding the dangers of wholesale censorship.

Although equality before the law, in the sense that the law of England applies to all its citizens, is rightly regarded as a cornerstone of our constitutional system, it is obvious that the law must itself make provision for exemption from the usual process of the law for certain categories of people. Earlier in this chapter it has been stated that members of Parliament are exempt from actions for defamation as regards anything they may say in Parliament, and it has been suggested that this privilege is necessary to enable members to discharge their duties efficiently. Similar privileges are accorded to judges and counsel in court cases, for it might well hamper the efficient conduct of, say, the defence in a case if the defence counsel were forever to have to bear in mind that he must avoid saying anything derogatory of a witness for the other side. These exceptions to the normal rules are well-recognised and accepted as reasonable. But there is one specially privileged group of people as regards whom it is less easy to justify the state of the law, namely the trades unions.

The present law provides that no action against a trade union, or against any of its members and officials on behalf of themselves and the other members, in respect of any tortious action alleged to have been committed by or on behalf of the union, may be entertained by any court. A tort, as has been seen in Chapter Four, is a civil wrong or injury for which the courts will normally provide relief. The effect of the law concerning trades unions, therefore, is to exempt these powerful bodies and their members, if acting on a union's behalf, from the provisions as to civil liability which affect other citizens, whether the usual action would have been for, say, negligence or trespass.

The historical reason for such an exemption from ordinary legal rules may well have been good in essence, for the trades unions went through a difficult period in the nineteenth century to gain legal recognition as bodies of workers which could engage in collective bargaining as to wages and conditions of work without being held to have committed any criminal offence. But today the trades unions form as powerful a group within the nation as any other. This being so, there can be no justification left for retaining a rule which exempts them from the rigours of a law applicable to all other people and groups of citizens in the land. The present Lord Chief Justice of Northern Ireland, in a series of public lectures delivered in 1957, severely criticised the present law, but the unfortunate fact is that it is unlikely that any Government will ever dare to take a step which would be so politically unpopular with what are usually referred to as 'the working classes' as the removal of a privilege attaching to the trades unions. The privilege was in fact once abolished, in 1927, after the General Strike of the previous year, but it was reintroduced by the Labour Government in 1946. Certainly no Conservative Government would have the temerity to antagonise the working class vote by repeating the step taken on a wave of popular emotion in 1927. It would seem, therefore, that the only real hope for a cleansing of the law in this sphere will lie with a responsible view of the situation to be taken by some future Labour Government. The need is great, as there have been several cases in recent years of trades unions victimising individual members or ex-members by means which would in all ordinary circumstances be held by the courts to be tortious. But hope of reform cannot be regarded at present as being bright.

One further inequality may be mentioned here. At common law the Crown (usually in fact the Home Secretary) has the power, within its own discretion, to deport an alien, if there is some genuine belief that expulsion from this country is in the public interest. This power must now be exercised according to certain statutory forms, but it remains in essence unfettered in scope, provided that the person deported is an alien. Accordingly the Home Secretary may well in some cases exercise his discretion by deciding not to issue a deportation order. Under certain Extradition Acts the Crown must also hand over to any foreign power with which this country maintains a reciprocal treaty any persons, whether aliens or British subjects, who have been found guilty of, or who have been charged with, committing any offence in that state covered by the Acts. The foreign state, in return, undertakes to surrender to the United Kingdom those who have committed extraditable offences in British territory. Extradition is narrower in scope than deportation in that it only covers cases where criminal offences have been committed or charged, and the element of discretion is absent, except for the one vitally important point that no one may be extradited for an offence described by the Extradition Act of 1870 as being 'of a political character'. So far there would seem to be little about the law with which one would wish to quarrel, though some critics distrust the wide discretion as to deportation vested in the Home Secretary. But grounds for disquiet become more apparent to all when the powers of deportation and extradition, which only concern *aliens* or offences committed in *foreign* countries, are compared with the provisions of the Fugitive Offenders Act, 1881.

The 1881 Act provides for the arrest and surrender of persons, accused of crimes in other Commonwealth countries, who have fled to the United Kingdom. Although the Act only applies to offences punishable with imprisonment for at least twelve months, it does not allow the authorities in this country to refuse to surrender a fugitive where his alleged offence was political. The only real discretion permitted is where it would be oppressive to allow the accused person to be surrendered. Accordingly, in 1963, when Chief Enahoro, who had fled to this country, was charged in Nigeria with offences in the nature of treason (the actual offences were called 'treason felony', somewhat less serious than treason), the Home Secretary, on receiving assurances from the Nigerian Attorney-General that the offences did not carry the death penalty, ordered his surrender to Nigeria. It is difficult to see how the Home Secretary's decision could have been otherwise, in view of the law binding him. But the fact remains that had Chief Enahoro been an alien rather than a Commonwealth citizen, a charge of treason felony in his homeland would have led to the granting of political asylum in the United Kingdom, under the terms of the Extradition Acts. The Fugitive Offenders Act was passed at a time when the Commonwealth was still an Empire, and the Empire courts were staffed by English lawyers. It was not unnatural then to regard them as more trustworthy in English eyes than the courts of foreign countries. Today this distinction between Commonwealth and foreign courts can hardly be supported if it results in the removal of privileges from Commonwealth citizens which are enjoyed by aliens. However unpopular such a move may be with some of the Commonwealth countries, it is clear that the Fugitive Offenders Act must be amended to make its provisions indistinguishable from those of the Extradition Acts.

It is perhaps necessary to say a word about the police. In 1962 the Report of the Royal Commission on the Police was published, and the Commission stated that on the whole the relationship between the public and the police was good. It is of course vital to the continued protection of civil liberties that this relationship should be generally harmonious, and that public confidence in the police should be maintained. Naturally the less law-abiding members of the community will always be antagonistic towards the police, but there is little reason to doubt the broad assertion by the Royal Commission. Yet some unpopularity or distrust of the police certainly does exist, and the reason, it may be suggested, has nothing to do with any habits of misconduct among policemen themselves. It is simply that in the twentieth century the police are forced to spend a large part of their time regulating motor traffic, and enforcing the multitude of traffic laws, mostly of a petty nature, which are necessary to keep the vehicles moving and the highways free of serious congestion or accidents. Those motorists who fall foul of the police are normally decent and law-abiding, and a sense of grievance tends to be built up against the body of men who have to perform the task of preferring charges against them.

Cases of actual unfair dealing by the police are rare, though there have been the odd occasions when policemen have committed perjury in attempting to gain convictions. Usually the officer concerned is convinced of the guilt of the accused, but cannot by other means provide the vital link in the evidence of the commission of the offence which he needs, and his mal-practice may well arise from over-work and extreme diligence in discharging what he conceives to be his duty. Both perjury and other offences, such as physical assaults upon suspected persons, committed by police officers must be condemned, but it is not wise to castigate the whole police force for the errors of the very few. It may be that the introduction of a national police force, rather than continuing to rely upon the present separate local forces (a matter upon which the Royal Commission was split in its opinion), would serve to increase the efficiency of a force which is in considerable difficulty in attempting to counter the wave of serious crime with which we are currently beset. A national force could, as Professor Goodhart, a member of the Royal Commission, argued, be organised into regional groups, thus helping it to maintain its present local connections which aid understanding between local inhabitants and the police. But the solutions to all these problems are at present still at the drawing-board stage, and it should be added that the majority of the members of the Royal Commission expressed themselves against the creation of a national police force.

One cause of the distrust of the police among some members of the community is the breadth of the discretion which police officers possess in discharging their functions of preventing crime. Few will quarrel with the existence of a power to arrest persons found in the act of committing offences, but there are more who criticise the power to arrest people on suspicion that an offence is about to take place. This latter power has mostly come into being by the agency of statutes designed to assist the police in preventing public meetings from giving rise to dis-order. There is statutory authority for any police officer to arrest without warrant a person who resists or wilfully obstructs a constable in the execution of his duty; and similar powers exist where a constable has reason to believe that there will be an obstruction of the highway. In a famous case of 1936, a Mrs. Duncan, who was about to make a speech in the street opposite a training centre for the unemployed, was told by a policeman that she must hold her meeting in another nearby street. When she persisted in attempting to hold the meeting where she had originally intended, she was arrested on a charge of obstructing a police officer in the course of his duty. As it was proved that the officer had in mind that a similar speech Mrs. Duncan had made in the same place about a year before had resulted in public disorder, it was held that he had acted reasonably, and Mrs. Duncan was convicted. More recently, these powers have been exercised by the police in dealing with members of the Committee of One Hundred and various fascist organisations, and although the main fears of those who criticise the very existence of these discretions stem from the fact that no magistrate's warrant has been issued on grounds duly stated, yet it is hard to see how the police could be effective in keeping public order without such discretions. To set against the criticisms of police discretion it may be mentioned that some other vociferous critics have recently complained that there ought to be new statutory provisions passed by Parliament to make criminal the incitement of people to racial hatred.

On the whole the present author is in favour of the *status quo*. The Public Order Act of 1936 already makes it an offence to use threatening, abusive or insulting words or behaviour in any public place or at any public meeting, with intent to provoke a breach of the peace or whereby a breach of the peace is likely to be caused, and a recent amending Act has increased the penalties to be levied for infringement of such provisions. It is submitted that this enactment adequately covers cases where fascist or other organisations openly preach racial hatred, and that to attempt to isolate further the specific offence of incitement to race hatred might take us dangerously near to an incursion upon the normal freedom of speech. Again the present discretions which the police are entitled to exercise seem on the whole to be reasonable. The actual cases where they have had to exercise their discretion in relation to offences against public order have usually resulted from political troubles of one sort or another, and, whatever the rights or wrongs of the political views expressed, it must always remain the first duty of peace officers to protect the general public from disorders. Anyone who has seen a child's face, when that child was in the proximity of a mob of angry people intent upon breaking up, say, a fascist meeting held in Trafalgar Square, will appreciate the need to confer discretionary power upon the police to take whatever action is required to restore order, or to prevent further disorder, regardless of the views held by those attending the meeting or opposing it. There is in any case the safeguard that any arrest must be proved to magistrates to have been objectively reasonable, and this should be enough to ensure that the police officers do not exercise their powers wantonly.

Perhaps, however, the public image of the police might be improved if they were relieved of the duty to prosecute accused persons in magistrates' courts—the courts in which all prosecutions for petty crime are conducted. It is not very long ago that the courts of the stipendiary magistrates in London were called Police Courts. This title has now been dropped, but, as with other magistrates' courts throughout the country, the police still retain the task of conducting the prosecution in the vast majority of cases heard. It seems not unreasonable to suggest that this job could with advantage be conducted by solicitors or by an extended version of the office of the Director of Public Prosecutions. Traffic wardens have already relieved the police of much of the routine donkey work as regards motor traffic in London and a few other cities. It may be that the need to channel the energies of the police into an efficient battle against the wave of really serious crime will in any case result in a reassessment of the time and energy spent upon prosecutions in unimportant cases, and that the police will cease to have to perform these duties. If this should take place, then it may be expected that such distrust of the police as there still is will be decreased. Even in cases of arrests without warrant for offences against public order, suspicion of doctored evidence and biased courts, however unsubstantial, will be bound to wane.

One further area for possible improvement of the law concerning the police is provided by the question of police examination of accused persons. Under present arrangements it is the function of the police to obtain all the information they can concerning crimes or offences which have been committed. The police have the right to question anyone regarding the commission of a crime, whether or not the person questioned is suspected of its commission. But they have no right to detain anyone against his will unless they make an arrest. Although there are certain statutory exceptions, as in the case of certain kinds of questions dealing with offences under the Official Secrets Acts, the broad rule is that no offence is committed merely by refusing to answer police questions, but it is not unnatural for most people being questioned to feel that they are obliged to answer. In 1912 the judges laid down a code of procedure which ought to be followed by police officers when questioning suspects, and although these rules, commonly known as the 'Judges' Rules', are not legal in the sense that any infringement of them amounts to an offence, yet they are regularly observed in practice. Thus, any police officer who has made up his mind to charge a person should caution that person before asking any questions or further questions, so that the person being questioned is sufficiently on his guard against making wrong or incriminating replies. Any statement then made by the person being questioned should, if possible, be taken down in writing and signed by the person making it after it has been read to him and he has been invited to make any corrections. The absence of a caution in the form prescribed by the 'Judges' Rules' does not necessarily render a statement inadmissible, but a court will be guarded in its attitude to any statement obtained in a more irregular fashion.

The rules of course provide a reasonable framework within which the necessary investigation of criminal offences can take place. But there is sometimes a difference between regularity or legality on the one hand and truth on the other. In recent years there has been an unfortunate number of cases in which the police have been proved either to produce false evidence or else to have extracted evidence by such undesirable means as physical assaults upon persons being questioned. In the latter type of case the police malpractice can be explained, if not excused, upon the grounds of over-zeal, for it must be very frustrating for a conscientious police officer who *knows* that he has found the criminal and yet has been unable to acquire the necessary evidence to obtain a conviction. If he is overworked and underpaid, as the police have regrettably been in recent years, he will occasionally succumb to the temptation to intimidate the suspect in the hope that he will break down and confess to his crime. All of which, of course, only helps to bring the police into disrepute. It is vital that the good name of the police should be retained, and it is no help to the maintenance of justice when there is suspicion of intimidation of witnesses or fabrication of evidence. It would appear, therefore, that there may be room for improvement of the English system of criminal investigation or examination of suspects or accused persons.

In France the problem is met by means of employing the services of a corps of stipendiary full-time magistrates who, after the apprehension of a suspect who is then charged with an offence, take over the whole business of interrogation. Indeed the police investigation itself, including the steps taken in the detection of the crime and its originators, is conducted under the supervision of these magistrates, who have the power to order the police to take certain courses of action in a field which, in England, is quite outside the judicial sphere. In England only the arrest need be approved by a magistrate, who signs the warrant presented to him by the police officer concerned. But in France the whole investigation is controlled by the magistrate, and this has the advantage of rendering the magistracy responsible for any irregularities which may then occur, and leaving the police, fortunately for them, not responsible to the public at large in the same way that they would be in England. When the interrogation is undertaken the advantages of the French system are again easy to see, for the police work has been completed and a heavy burden is thus taken off the shoulders of a hard-worked force. What is more, the magistrates, rather than being concerned with making out a good prosecution case for the later trial, as one might suspect a police officer may not unnaturally wish to do, will be exercised merely to discover the truth. At this stage of the investigation, therefore, 'Judges' Rules' become quite unnecessary, because a trained lawyer will be involved in the process of discovering what actually did happen, and why. It should be emphasised that this interrogation by the magistrate is not the trial of the accused, any more than the hearing before magistrates to decide whether an accused person should go forward for trial by jury for a serious criminal offence in England is a trial. The trial will only take place later if the magistrate decides that there is a case to answer, just as in England. But the process of deciding whether there is a case to answer is more likely to arrive at a true appraisal of the rights and wrongs of the case in France than it may sometimes be in England. This is not to say that the police in England are inefficient or in any way not usually *bona fide*. They most certainly usually do their job as well as possible. But they are only concerned with building up a prosecution case, and so often at the preliminary hearing before magistrates in England, although the prosecution case is put in full, the defence is reserved for the later trial, so that there is no necessity for the defence side of the case to have been seen by any judge until the whole issue comes on for trial itself. In France the examining magistrate will have full power in each case to question the accused in order to establish the facts, and very probably to obtain a more accurate picture of the likelihood or otherwise of an actual prosecution in open court being successful later on. We should, however, set against this possible advantage the fact that the court before which any later trial takes place in France may well be far more likely to convict the accused than would be its counterpart in England, as it may feel that the examining magistrate will himself have been satisfied of the guilt of the person sent for trial.

It is very difficult to weigh up accurately the advantages and disadvantages of the English and French systems respectively. On the one hand, in France the direct confrontation of an accused person with the skilled questions of the professional magistrate may be more likely to elicit the truth than the more one-sided type of interrogation to be found carried out by the police in England. The suspicion of malpractice by the police which sometimes exists today might also be averted by taking the duty to question suspects out of the hands of the police. But on the other hand the English jury may be more likely under our present system to maintain an open mind upon the question of the accused person's guilt when the case comes for trial. Furthermore, the jury is protected from the intrusion upon their minds of factors irrelevant to the trial of the offence actually charged, and the English rules of evidence have been designed to protect both sides from the use of any irrelevant evidence. It is not possible for the prosecution to acquaint the jury with the facts of any previous convictions obtained against the accused. In addition, the introduction of any system of criminal interrogation along the lines of that employed in France would necessarily involve the appointment of many more stipendiary magistrates than we have at present, and their functions would be altered considerably. Problems of finance and taxation are involved here, as well as a radical alteration in criminal pre-trial procedure.

All in all, it is submitted that there is unlikely to be any marked alteration in our system for interrogation of suspects, though there may well be more attention paid than in the past to the recruitment of police officers who have had a university education, particularly perhaps in law. The actual trial procedure of a criminal case is rightly weighted in favour of the accused in that no conviction may be obtained unless guilt has been proved beyond all reasonable doubt, and the report of a committee dealing with criminal law revision, issued in the autumn of 1963, recommends that even greater emphasis should be placed upon giving the defence a chance to refute the accusations made against the accused (primarily by means of allowing the defence always to have the last word in every trial before the summing up of the judge or the decision—a practice which at present only occurs in certain kinds of trial). Criticism of judges, courts and the police is a healthy thing in a democratic society, for it enables us to give our minds to the maintenance of vigorous public institutions. But it is most likely that the nearest we shall get to any alteration of the law concerning police examination of accused persons will be a general revision, mainly upon matters of detail, of the 'Judges' Rules', and even that will not in fact amount to an alteration of the law, as there is no legal sanction behind the present rules.

ADMINISTRATIVE JUSTICE

With the increase during the present century of Governmental power in the sphere of social problems, the need for adequate protection of the rights of individual citizens has been underlined. The award of pensions to old people and the disabled, national assistance grants for those out of work, and planning permission to those who wish to develop their land, all depend in the long run upon the gaining of the approval of some administrative authority. It goes without saying that the power of such an authority must be greater than that of any individual, and so it is vitally important in a democracy that there should be sufficient methods open to the citizen to obtain a fair hearing of his side of any question under consideration, and that he should be able to challenge any decision which is adverse to his interests. On the whole great steps have been taken to aid the individual in his struggles against bureaucracy. Tribunals have been set up before which his claims are considered and dealt with in a manner similar to that usual in the ordinary courts, but at relatively little cost. Anyone feeling himself aggrieved by a decision to grant or withhold planning permission has the right to require the holding of a public inquiry, at which his grievances may be aired—and the minister may be compelled to give his reasons for deciding one way or another. A Council on Tribunals has been formed to supervise the various tribunals which deal with problems of conflict between the citizen and the state, and to make recommendations as to their reform where it thinks fit. And there are several methods whereby administrative decisions can be challenged in the courts.

The story in this area of law has been one of constant revision and reform, and it is probably neither fruitful nor of interest here to harp further upon the likely progress in the detailed techniques of judicial control of administrative actions. But it will be appreciated that not all administrative rulings can be the subject of court or tribunal scrutiny. Just as we can hardly expect the law to provide that the courts may investigate the detailed conduct of foreign affairs by the Government, so it is possible to find many types of decisions in domestic matters which are protected by statute from the possibility of judicial challenge. In many cases the ordinary citizen would consider the position to be reasonable. Once an examination result or the award of a scholarship has been announced it would be intolerable to allow any kind of judicial revision of that result. Doubtless mistakes or errors of judgment occasionally occur, and it may very rarely be that, upon careful reconsideration, an honours degree candidate who has been placed in the second class ought to have been awarded a first. But the reverse might equally also be the case, and to allow even the *possibility* that someone placed in the first class or awarded a scholarship might later be divested of his apparent award would, by its injustice, far outweigh any good to be attained by the occasional upgrading of some other person.

But the need for maintaining a system where the citizen has no means of challenging decisions made is not always so clearly apparent as in the above type of case. Under the present law decisions of doctors concerning marginal benefits under the National Health Service, and of the Minister of Education upon the reasonableness of a local education authority in overruling parents' choice of school for their children, are made according to an unfettered discretion. The award of military pensions to retired officers or other ranks, and to their families in certain cases of disability, lies within the discretion of the Army Council or its equivalent in the other services (and it will presumably lie within the discretion of the new combined Ministry of Defence which is shortly to usurp the functions of the separate service councils and ministers). Many other examples might be quoted, but the above should be sufficient to show that there may yet be a need to judicialise some of the remaining discretions. In a recent Report made by a former Chief Justice of Singapore, under the auspices of an independent group of lawyers, called JUSTICE, it was recommended that, even in those cases where the actual exercise of administrative discretion ought to remain immune from judicial challenge, there was a case for allowing investigation by an independent official of any complaints of irregularity or 'maladministration' in the exercise of discretionary powers, such as by making a decision adverse to a citizen mainly because of personal dislike for him harboured by the official of the administration concerned. The basis for this recommendation was a study of the institution of the 'Ombudsman', a commissioner for the investigation of grievances who functions in Sweden, Denmark and, under very recent legislation, in Norway. The title suggested for the officer in the JUSTICE Report is that of Parliamentary Commissioner, and this title does indicate an essential aspect of his suggested function, which is that he would be responsible only to Parliament as a whole, and not to the Government. Among his more far-reaching powers would be that of access to Government departmental files. He would have no actual power to put things right where he found a grievance to be substantiated, but he would report to Parliament that action should be taken either by the legislature or by the Government. At the very least, the publicity which ensued would have a salutory effect upon the administration.

The JUSTICE Report suggests that the Office of the Parliamentary Commissioner would act as a significant help to citizens at present hamstrung by those statutory powers which preclude any form of judicial or other review, save for the Parliamentary question. Even the latter, it was suggested, is currently inadequate in many cases, because the M.P. asking the question must be content with the answer provided by the minister he is questioning: he has no means of going behind the minister to discover whether his answer was correct or justified by the circumstances of the case. Agitation for the creation of an Ombudsman in England has been fairly strong, though some people have doubted whether an institution which works in Scandinavian countries with populations of about four million or so would be equally efficacious in a nation of fifty millions: one of the main objects of the exercise is that the Ombudsman himself should deal personally with the complaints, and an English Parliamentary Commissioner might well be snowed under by a vast mass of complaints, most of which would almost certainly turn out to be unjustified, as they often do in Scandinavia. Even the institution of the first Parliamentary Commissioner in a Commonwealth country, New Zealand, in 1962, has done nothing to allay these fears, as the population of New Zealand is also small. On the other hand the fact that there may be a lot of complaints can hardly be regarded as a sound reason for taking no step at all to provide a means of meeting them.

At all events no immediate step in the direction of the creation of an Ombudsman can be expected in England. Late in 1962 the Government announced its rejection of the JUSTICE Report upon two grounds, that the work of a Parliamentary Commissioner would conflict with the direct responsibility of ministers to Parliament, and that the citizen already had adequate safeguards for his rights by means of his access to Members of Parliament. Neither of these reasons seems particularly convincing. It may be thought that, on reflection, most ministers might in fact welcome the work of an Ombudsman to assist them in discharging their responsibilities to Parliament, while the defect which we have just mentioned in relation to the Parliamentary question, admirable institution though it is, could have been cured by following the recommendation in the Report.

It is hard to forecast the future in this field. Certainly the citizen already has an impressive armoury on his side in his occasional battles with authority, but there could never be any harm to the administration in creating an Ombudsman, or perhaps, in view of the size of the population of England, even several Ombudsmen. The inquiry into and subsequent Report upon the security and other aspects of the Profumo affair in 1963, made by Lord Denning on an *ad hoc* basis, might perhaps have been better left to an Ombudsman, whose activities would not have attracted so much unnecessary publicity as beset Lord Denning. Possibly a start will one day be made by appointing regional Commissioners to concern themselves with complaints against local rather than central authorities. The present author does not believe that there is a great deal of maladministration either at the national or the local level, but there may be more risk of it in local government, where strong civil service traditions do not run. Perhaps it can at least be said that the cost of a few Commissioners would be well spent if only to remove the suspicions which some people currently harbour concerning maladministration. As with suspected physical illness, it is so often worth while to spend an hour or two of one's valuable time to attend the surgery and to learn that after all there is very little to worry about.

CHAPTER SEVEN

Planning Law

In the last chapter it was mentioned that anyone who wishes to develop his land, as by, for example, building further houses upon it, must obtain planning permission before he is entitled in law to proceed. There is no intention in this chapter to dwell upon the technical details of this procedure. Here we are concerned with the much wider problem of the whole future purpose of English planning law. England is the most densely populated country in the world, and there is every indication from statistics that the numbers of inhabitants will continue to increase. The reasons for this increase, such as improvements in medical science and the general continuation of economic prosperity, are no part of the subject of this book, but it is inevitable that population trends must affect the law of planning. Emigration and controlled immigration may together have some effect upon the number of inhabitants in this island, but they have never yet proved to be vital factors in curbing the relentless increase of the national population. If there are ever more people living in England it naturally follows that they must be housed, and that there must be adequate shops for them to buy the requisites of modern living, and industry to absorb the working members of the community. It is in the light of this general need that the law must be considered, and it will be seen that in the realm of planning we have a prime practical illustration of the need for law to mirror the requirements of society, and of the close affinity between law and policy.

The need for planned control of the development of land was first felt in England well over fifty years ago, but the growth of the law to fulfil it was gradual, and the rules provided were at times wholly inadequate to meet the demands of the situation. The motorist who passes along the A.40 road through High Wycombe will see a monument to the ineffective control of urban development which prevailed earlier in the century. A town which might have been built on a site perhaps one mile square was actually built in virtually one single street about five miles in length. Apart from the centre of the town, the remainder of High Wycombe still mainly consists of this one street which has effectively blocked off and spoilt an appreciable stretch of rural Buckinghamshire. This type of building precipitated legislation to prohibit what was called 'ribbon development'. But the most effective and comprehensive legislation came just after the Second World War with the passage of the New Towns Act, 1946, and the Town and Country Planning Act, 1947. These Acts have been amended from time to time, and the 1947 Act has in fact been entirely replaced by a codifying Act of 1962, but the present law is still substantially that which was enacted in 1946 and 1947.

The general law of planning has been provided by the Town and Country Planning Acts, while the New Towns Act deals with a more specialised problem. As far as general planning is concerned, the framework for healthy legal rules has now been created, but the restrictions upon private speculation are not yet sufficient for the needs of society at large, as will be argued presently. Although private landowners, builders and property companies may object to the law, the fact remains that we live in a very small country, and it cannot be tolerated that the good of the vast majority should be held to ransom by the requirements of private gain. The law now provides that no further building, or substantial alteration of the use of present buildings (which might well amount to the same thing if a dwelling-house in a residential area were to be turned into a factory!), may be embarked upon without the permission of the local planning authority, which is in fact usually the local civic authority, though an appeal from the local authority's decision will lie to the Minister of Housing and Local Government. Conversely, if the local authority should wish to develop land, either for building or for highway purposes, which it does not

own, then there are powers whereby it may compulsorily
acquire the land needed from the present owner, upon payment of the full value which the land would have had on the
market if the owner had voluntarily sold it for the development planned. In this way those responsible for the conduct of
local public affairs may decide upon the way in which the
future development of their area shall be planned and carried
out, always subject to the final decision, in cases of dispute, of
the minister. The only substantial change in this general
provision which the present author foresees is that the day may
come when it might prove desirable to remove some of the
control currently exercised by the local authorities, and to
place it instead in the hands of the minister and his assistants.
The reason is that many members of local authorities are
successful local businessmen and merchants who may be
suspected upon occasion of favouring schemes for development
which fit in with their plans for personal profit, or which would
aid financially fellow businessmen who might reasonably be
expected to do them a good turn in some other way later on.
It is not suggested here that such a suspicion is often well-
founded, but it has been voiced, and even if it should turn out
to be untrue its very existence may be enough to make it
desirable to place the matter in the hands of those who cannot
be suspected of local bias. The available land of England is too
precious to be put in jeopardy by even a suspicion of this kind.
Once built upon, the countryside is lost for ever.

This brings us to the central point of planning policy and law.
Anyone motoring out of London, or in industrial Lancashire,
must drive through a continuous built-up area which would
appear to be all part of the same town. It comes as something of
a surprise to realise that the journey has in fact been made
through several different towns before the countryside is
reached. It may not be too fanciful to imagine that if the process
of extending the boundaries of towns were to continue unchecked there would in due course be an unbroken urban area
from London to Glasgow, by way of Birmingham and Lancashire, and from London to South Wales, by way of Oxford and
Swindon. When this point is grasped the urgency of effective

planning law becomes apparent, and the reason for the New Towns Act is uncovered.

Briefly this latter Act provided the machinery to remove portions of the population, together with their accompanying industry and shopping centres, from already congested urban areas to other parts of the country, not by means of compulsion, but by attraction. Under the Act various pieces of land have been earmarked for the development of completely new towns, about a dozen of which have been substantially completed. Far from being dormitory towns, they are complete entities in themselves, and thus they do not have the effect of swelling the masses of the working population who commute to and from the older towns at rush hour. Each designation order for a new town must be made by the minister, though he must always consult all local authorities which appear to him to be concerned by his proposal.

The only real trouble with the working of the New Towns Act, from the point of view of purely objective planning, is that it has not prevented the continued expansion of some of the older towns, which have continued their relentless encroachment on the countryside. This is not for any reasons of incompetence upon the part of local planning authorities, but rather because the continued pressure upon them by those requiring houses in which to live forces them to agree to the planning of new housing estates. Indeed it is conscious Government policy that more and more houses must be built to cater for the needs of the people. Before discussing the possible remedies, some or all of which will have to be considered for the future if the country is to avoid the chaos of complete urbanisation, it may be well to give one example of a particular pitfall which has often faced both local planning authorities and the minister equally, however well-intentioned their planning efforts have been.

A basic difficulty in planning policy has been to relate the requirements of urban development to those of relief of traffic congestion. For many years in England it has been a favourite policy of planners to solve traffic congestion within a town by building a series of by-passes to take 'through' traffic round it.

But instead of constructing these roads a long way away from the town they have usually planned them to fall just outside each town concerned, so that there is just a thin strip of country-side between a by-pass and the town it serves. This has often been done in order not to eat too far into the rural surrounds of a town, but once the road has been made and is being used by quite a lot of traffic it is then soon appreciated that the particular stretch of land between the by-pass and the town, and even immediately on the outer side of the by-pass, has been spoilt as far as true rural amenities are concerned. It is then thought that the spoilt area might just as well be used for building new houses to relieve the housing problem which doubtless exists in the town anyway. Thus in the space of a few years a town will have expanded appreciably by incorporating a strip of land all round its previous boundaries. In a few cases the cycle has been completed by the internal traffic from the newly created urban area around the by-pass causing serious congestion upon the by-pass itself, so that an additional or substitute by-pass is then planned to pass through the rural area just beyond the fringe of the new urban area. The stage is then set for further urbanisation of the country round the outer by-pass.

The ordinary householder's desire to live in the suburbia of existing towns instead of moving into newly built towns is natural, for a variety of reasons. The innate conservatism which is in nearly every Englishman will often make him feel that it is safer and more comfortable to live in an old-established community than to move to a new and untried area. Again, although many people like the idea of living in or near the countryside, most still like to be within easy reach of the traditional shopping centres, theatres, cinemas, clubs and other comforts of modern urban living. It therefore comes as a fairly natural compromise for a large number of ordinary people to wish to live on the edge of older towns, so that they can drive into the centre of the town for business or pleasure, but also gain some of the advantages of rural England. There are other pressures at work too. In this advanced age of the internal combustion engine, the centres of towns are not ideal places in which to live: they are noisy and dirty, and, during day-time at any rate, the streets are choked with crowds of people. This makes them excellent places for the conduct of retail businesses and for the siting of offices, but hardly for the peace and quiet which most people require for their private houses. Furthermore, the large houses which families occupied as a matter of course in former days have become inconvenient now that most people expect more efficient methods of general heating in winter than our predecessors did, and in an age when the servant problem makes large dwellings difficult to run with ease.

Many of the older houses near the centres of towns have been converted into office blocks, and their popularity for this purpose has led to a great increase in their market value. Who would not be tempted to sell his large city house to a business concern, or a development company, for £30,000 or £40,000, and then escape from the noise and bustle to a pleasantly situated house on the fringe of the town, which will only cost £6,000 or £8,000, and which will in any case be modern and of a more moderate size, and equipped with all the contrivances and gadgets which make for twentieth-century comfort?

During the past dozen years a very large number of people have ceased to live in or near the centres of towns, and the expression of their need to build dwelling-houses upon the fringes of the existing urban areas has acted as a constant pressure upon planning authorities to grant the permissions asked. At the same time the clamour for business premises inside the cities, where customers and business rivals will all be in close proximity, has produced another pressure leading to the granting of permission for the change of use of many existing buildings in the centres of towns. Yet, as has already been indicated, the trend of multiplication of business interests inside the towns has had the effect also of sharply increasing the values of land and houses in the towns. This has meant that when older buildings have ceased to be economic, permission has often been granted for their destruction so that new buildings may be erected. Accordingly it has now become the practice for those who wish to develop the sites of older buildings inside towns to build 'high'. Except in London and in one or two of the other big cities planning authorities have so far been reluctant to grant permission for the building of 'sky-scrapers', but they have nevertheless usually been prepared to allow the construction of blocks up to eight or ten stories in height. Now that this practice has become established it has become economic for property companies to purchase old houses at more or less any price asked, to pull them down regardless of their present efficiency or beauty, and to build blocks of offices (or, nearer to the outskirts of towns, flats) which can be let off to tenants at rents which will adequately make up for the capital outlay and also produce a handsome profit.

It is beyond our present purpose to speculate upon the effects of these trends on the general economy of the country and upon inflation, though they must be considerable. But pausing at this juncture it is possible to assess the results which can be seen today in the field of planning. Over the space of perhaps twenty-five years the whole nature of English towns has altered. Shops, factories and offices now occupy all the central positions, either through the conversion of the use of existing buildings, or else by their demolition and the substitution of new blocks. The residential population has now nearly all moved out of the centres of the towns to the fringes, and thus we have seen the steady spread of urban development, ever pushing out and gradually destroying the rural scenery and amenities. The construction of new towns has eased some of the pressure upon planning authorities to grant permission for development within or near existing urban areas, but the fact that the New Towns Act contains no actual legal machinery for preventing the spreading of existing towns as a complement to the completely new development which it authorises means that there has been little incentive for planners and developers to concentrate upon sensible mixed development within, and only within, the boundaries of existing towns. It is this lack of mixed development within the present urban areas which is perhaps the crux of the whole cumulative problem of planning today.

To take the example of the city best known to the author, Oxford, industrial, commercial, and, in this case, university expansion has resulted in the disappearance of practically all residential accommodation (not counting that within the colleges themselves which is mostly for undergraduates), other than that of the most squalid type, within about one mile of the centre of the city. Certainly nearly all the private houses of any character have either become offices or else have been pulled down. This destruction has not been limited to the central part of the city, for within the last two or three years two beautiful houses (one of which was a Georgian house in near perfect condition, with a walled garden) have been pulled down about two miles north of the city centre in order to make way for a block containing a supermarket and several shops, with offices above it, and a large block of flats and maisonettes respectively. The need for planning permission provided by the Town and Country Planning Acts should have made it impossible to commit such acts of vandalism, but unfortunately it is all too easy to obtain planning permission in a society where the population *must* move out of the town centres, and where the people must therefore be accommodated and served by shops as satisfactorily as possible outside the central area. Needless to say, the boundaries of the city have also been progressively extended, and housing estates have now sprung up on the outer edges of the various by-passes which had originally run through open country.

Linked to the problem of destruction of the countryside, and the acts of vandalism brought about by speculative building, the problems of road traffic and parking have become intense. The more business premises that are concentrated into a single small area, the more cars and lorries there are which must travel there and back every day. When almost everyone lives outside the central area of a town, but works inside it, the problem of road congestion is bound to become acute, particularly at 'rush hours'. A strike of workers on the underground trains in London in 1961 had the effect of bringing nearly all traffic to a standstill for several hours, and the problem is just as acute, though over a smaller area, in many other towns. Newspaper articles have from time to time criticised the present trend in the building of vast new office blocks in London, on the ground that they can only serve to increase the daily road traffic in and out of the city, and thus render congestion

on the roads even worse than it is at present. It may have been
the effect of those articles, combined with the results of public
transport workers' strikes, which brought home to the Government in 1961 that the problem may be in danger of slipping
beyond control. In January 1962 the Minister of Housing and
Local Government indicated in a public speech that the
Government had become concerned at the unmixed nature of
modern planning. For the future he thought that the accent in
planning should be upon mixed development, so that in most
places business premises should only be built if private dwelling
accommodation is also provided in the same area. He hinted
that, unless the trends of modern planning were to conform
with his ideas on this subject, the Town and Country Planning
legislation might have to be amended to enable planning
authorities to exercise a proper control upon proposed new
developments. In the view of the present author, these indications are more encouraging than those presented by the
recent history of actual development that has taken place, but
the minister's statement is still too vague to offer any prospect
of concrete hope that the faults in modern development of
existing urban areas will be satisfactorily cured. Some may
think that the rot has gone too far for different and effective
Government policies to be introduced, but, as with all law, we
can but do our imperfect best to put right what is currently
wrong. There is still quite a lot of countryside to be saved, and
there are still many undesecrated houses of architectural
significance to be preserved.

The basic trouble is that society today is so materialistic. Few
people are immune to the aesthetic values, but far too many are
prepared to sacrifice them if they conflict with the profit motive.
It is for this reason that it is hard to blame businessmen and
property dealers for the current ills of planning policy, for they
are the products of the age, and it just so happens that profit
from property deals provides their way of making a living for
themselves and their families, just as other pursuits provide the
means of existence for the rest of us. But the fact that they
cannot really be blamed for their current practices is no reason
for the law to permit them to perpetuate their present habits,

which can only end, if unchecked, in the destruction of a portion of the priceless heritage to which we are all entitled. We all regard it as proper that the Tower of London should be preserved in its historic form, and that National Parks should be protected from urban development. It is now time for us to realise that the *whole* of England, and indeed the United Kingdom, should be scrutinised to see what is worthy of preservation and what is not. A balance must be found between the needs of accommodating the mass of the population in decent homes, of providing for good road communications, and of protecting rural and architectural beauty. All three of these requirements are vital, and it is submitted that all three can be satisfied. Commercial desires and personal profit must be subordinated to the proper planning for all three of the primary needs, and in providing laws which can achieve this subordination will lie the success of planning for the future.

Turning, therefore, to positive suggestions, the New Towns Act, 1946, probably requires amendment to give planning authorities the power to prevent totally the extension of existing urban boundaries. One result of the success of commercial interest in urban development has been that much unpromising land within existing town boundaries has remained undeveloped. It is possible to walk round any town and come across quite large areas where places formerly used for refuse dumping, scrap metal yards and many old and squalid buildings are left untouched. In the very towns where houses of architectural value are pulled down and replaced by office blocks it is common to find acres of what might still be termed slum property untouched. Slum clearance and replacement has been constantly and earnestly carried out by many local authorities, but private developers have on the whole not been very interested in this type of work, as it is less immediately remunerative than their present practices, and also because many local authorities have been short-sighted enough not to permit anyone but themselves to engage in the development of the sites. Within Oxford there is still an area of several acres near the centre of the city which is mostly covered by slum property, punctuated by quite big stretches of waste land. This area is nearly all owned by the city council, yet its modern development has made very little progress over a space of twenty or thirty years. Many thousands of people, together with various offices and small factories, could be accommodated there, thus relieving the pressure upon the outer fringes of the city, but at present the population of the area is small compared with what it might be, and the amenities are practically nil. It is fair to add that progress has been hampered in this case by continued uncertainty about the route of an inner relief road which will probably run through the area, but the untapped possibilities of the site have been enormous for too long.

If local authorities cannot with success be made to operate new and more strict powers conferred upon them, then perhaps the Ministry of Housing and Local Government itself will have to take over the present work of the planning authorities. But whichever way it is done, it is submitted that the law must make some provision for the positive prevention of further expansion of the area of cities and towns, and turn the attention of developers to the task of planning their existing areas more effectively, and with proper mixed building. If the need to plan each town with the correct proportions of dwellings, offices, shops, factories and green spaces is made imperative by the requirements of the law, the pressure upon the countryside at present exerted by urban spread will be relieved. A resolution passed by the House of Commons on February 21st, 1962, may be worth quoting here in full. It ran as follows:

This House, recognising the commendable progress that has been made in housing and slum clearance in recent years, and the shortage of suitable sites for all kinds of building in a country as small as Great Britain, urges Her Majesty's Government to hasten the process of designating Green Belts in order to prevent sporadic development, and to take measures to stimulate in-filling in urban areas and the development of building sites which may not be entirely economic from the builder's point of view, in order to preserve agricultural land on the outskirts of towns and villages without slowing the pace of building.

This resolution, of course, has no direct effect upon the law, as it is not part of an Act of Parliament, but it is at least indicative of the fact that many M.P.s are at last aware of the dangers which beset us, and the time has come for the planning of the whole country to be organised more consistently than in the past. One fruit of this resolution has been the recent decision of the Government to resist the pressure from builders and speculators to allow the Green Belt around London to be scrapped. The present policy here is to allow more building within present urban districts which project into the Green Belt, but to prevent the actual countryside from being further punctured.

It is a corollary of such a policy that adequate provision must be made for building in other places if towns become full to saturation, and it is here that the powers to designate new towns become vital. Over the past couple of years several new town areas have been designated in England and Scotland. This is a healthy sign, for, providing the sites are carefully chosen, as for the most part they are, the towns can be built so as not to destroy any significantly beautiful stretches of country. Furthermore, the prevention of further expansion of older towns will have the effect of providing greater encouragement than there is at present for people to move to the new towns. The excess urban population cannot be 'deported' to new towns, but the attraction will be all the more urgent if planning law is made more strict. And the countryside, instead of being blotted out and inaccessible for the inhabitants of vast conurbations, will be reasonably accessible to all.

Finally, the trunk roads of the future must be built to connect the great urban areas with each other, and not to serve directly a host of smaller towns as well. The M.1 was the first example of a well-planned trunk road in England, for it connects London and Birmingham, and is built primarily to take fast traffic. Several other such roads are under construction, and a few are largely completed, and it is important that urban development along these roads should be prevented. For the most part the old by-passes have proved a failure, for they often serve to make traffic congestion worse, particularly where traffic 'islands' are placed at all junctions, and they tend also to cause the artificial extension of the boundaries of many towns. The roads of the future must be planned to be quite distinct from urban development.

It may be that, in order to facilitate the laws outlined above, it will prove necessary also to control strictly the market value of land. It is already a part of the policy of the Labour party to exert itself towards curbing profiteering in land values. It is possible that if the restriction upon urban extension proposed in this chapter is enforced (and it is hard to see how any Government can fail to realise the urgency of its need before long), the natural market price of land for development within towns will continue to rise. If so, then it will be necessary for the law to provide protection for the ordinary man by price controls, or even by some form of municipalisation of land. In the welfare state it should no longer be possible for the price of a house, which is after all one of the most basic necessities of life today, to be kept outside the financial range of the ordinary prudent family man merely to provide substantial profits for the few.

CHAPTER EIGHT

The Courts and the Legal Profession

THE COURTS

IN the first chapter of this book it was thought unnecessary to burden the reader with a detailed list of the various courts which currently exist in England, and there is no intention here to repair this omission. When attempting to evaluate the law and the judicial system in a general work of this kind it is hardly relevant to insist upon placing the exact name to each court. It is enough that we should realise that some courts are civil courts, while others conduct criminal trials, that some hear appeals and others do not. Granted that the work of administering the law has been parcelled out to appropriate courts, all that is intended here is to criticise some of the less happy aspects of the court system as it is at present organised, and to make suggestions about likely future changes which will be made to meet these criticisms, by no means all of which are entirely original.

Taking criminal courts first, it may be remembered from the first chapter that the trials of the most serious criminal offences usually take place at Assizes or in Quarter Sessions. Dealing with Assizes for the moment, it may be noted that these courts are held locally in certain specified Assize towns, usually three or four times a year. Actually these courts also have a jurisdiction over a number of ordinary civil cases, though this work is generally regarded as being less important than the jurisdiction over criminal cases. The history of the Assizes goes back many centuries to the times when the Assize judges were sent round the country to see that the 'king's peace' was kept, and that criminal justice was brought to all local areas. Somehow the tradition that criminal offenders should be tried reasonably near to the places where their offences were committed has stuck in a way that has never prevailed as regards civil trials. Apart from the limited jurisdiction of Assize courts over certain civil cases, a jurisdiction which has had a chequered life that need hardly concern us here, no general provision for the trial of civil cases locally was made, after the decease, during the middle ages, of most of the old local courts which had administered the law that existed before the coming of the royal common law, until 1846. In that year there was established a system of county courts for the trial locally of civil cases in which only small sums of money were involved. But nearly all criminal trials, whether for petty offences before justices of the peace, or for more serious offences, have been held locally since the early middle ages.

Again, as will be remembered from Chapter One, the other courts for the trial of serious criminal offences are the Central Criminal Court and the Crown Courts, which will be discussed again presently, and the Quarter Sessions. These latter courts also date from mediaeval times, and they sit in each county and in each of the larger towns. Quarter Sessions have as a primary function the task of trying all persons accused of what might be termed the less serious or less technically complicated of the serious offences. Thus those defendants who are not tried summarily in petty sessions will normally be tried either at Quarter Sessions (held usually, as one would imagine, quarterly) or at Assizes, in either case before a jury. The judge of each Assize court is either a High Court judge or else, more rarely, an eminent practising barrister specially commissioned for that Assize. In the Quarter Sessions for towns the judge is called a Recorder, and is normally a practising barrister who takes on the post on a part-time basis, while in county Quarter Sessions the position of judge is filled by a bench of magistrates, though recent Acts of Parliament have made it necessary for each bench to have a qualified (and paid) chairman or deputy chairman. It may be surmised that the lay magistrates are playing less and less of an active role in Quarter Sessions, and that they will, before long, be rendered quite otiose. Already many chairmen or deputy chairmen of county Quarter Sessions are actually also the Recorders of nearby town Quarter Sessions, and the time cannot be far off when the lay justices will, by statute, be prevented from sitting at all.

At present the Assize towns of England and Wales are grouped into seven circuits, and one or more judges of the High Court, together sometimes with eminent members of the Bar, are sent out from London to 'go on circuit' each time the Assizes fall due. There is a certain amount of pomp and circumstance attached to the occasion in each Assize town, and though this has been criticised as a waste of time and money, there is probably little harm done by it, and it may even foster a not unwholesome respect for the judge. Points of criticism may, however, be more serious when it is found that if a particular trial has taken longer than was estimated beforehand it may become necessary for the judge to move on to the next town on the circuit before finishing his list of cases at a town which has been busy so far as criminal work is concerned. This means that those cases not heard at the first town must be heard either at the next town, or sometimes even at an Assize town on another nearby circuit, in any case with a great deal of consequent inconvenience to the accused, the witnesses, and the counsel and solicitors on each side. With the increase in crime throughout the country, this type of delay and inconvenience is most undesirable, for it not only tends to become cumulative as the circuit progresses, but it also offends against a principle of criminal justice that the trial of all accused persons should be expeditious. At the same time it should not be so expeditious as to be hasty, and there are times when there must be a pressure upon the judge to speed up the conduct of trials, if at all possible, in order to reach the end of the list before him.

In the most densely populated conurbations of all, London and Liverpool-Manchester, the problems have been tackled by the setting up of permanent courts. The Central Criminal Court at the Old Bailey in London acts as the Assize court for London, Middlesex and parts of Essex, Kent and Surrey, and it was established as early as 1834. For all practical purposes it is in almost constant session, so that there is no need for a trial to await the next holding of an Assize, which may be weeks or even months off: the case can come on for hearing as soon as all parties are ready for it. Two Crown Courts were set up, one in Liverpool and one in Manchester, by a statute of 1956, and these courts now conduct the trials of nearly all serious criminal cases in those areas, for they have jurisdiction to try all cases which would otherwise have gone to the Assizes *or* to Quarter Sessions (though there is provision for the Assize court in each town, which still sits at the usual times for the hearing of civil cases, to try any criminal cases of especial difficulty). Again, these courts may be in almost continuous session, for it is provided that they must hold at least eleven sessions a year, which means in effect one a month, each lasting until the list is finished. For some time it was thought by many lawyers that these Crown Courts were prototypes of courts all over the country which would replace the old Assize system, and when the Home Secretary in 1958 set up a Committee under the chairmanship of Mr. Justice Streatfeild, to make recommendations upon the Business of the Criminal Courts it was confidently expected by many that the Committee would suggest, among other things, the extension of the Crown Courts experiment.

This Committee reported in February 1961, and, much to the surprise of many, it reported against the setting-up of more full-time criminal courts dealing with serious offenders throughout the country, and staffed by full-time criminal judges. It seems that one of the difficulties encountered in practice in the Crown Courts is that, although the judges who are entitled to sit there are all the High Court judges together with the Recorders of Manchester and Liverpool respectively, in fact it is not usual for anyone other than the two Recorders to sit. The Streatfeild Committee considered that, with the best will in the world, such permanent judges must be in danger of becoming stale, of developing local antipathies, and of becoming prosecution-minded in that they will be accustomed to trusting the evidence, judgment and integrity of the police in all cases of doubt. The Central Criminal Court is not quite in the same position, as it is so busy that several different judges have to sit together in different court rooms in order to dispose of the business. Indeed the Recorder and Common Sergeant of London and the Judge of the City of London Court, who regularly sit at the Old Bailey are frequently supplemented in their efforts by High Court judges, so that there is a degree of change of identity among the judges sitting on the bench in London.

There is much force in the arguments raised by the Streatfeild Report against permanent courts and judges in criminal cases, but it may be doubted whether they are entirely convincing. Is it, for example, necessary that a permanent court should always have the same judge? Could not a fixed court still have peripatetic judges? In other words, could not a number of fixed courts be created, holding regular sittings much more frequently than the present Assizes, indeed perhaps eleven sessions a year, as in the Crown Courts, while the judges should still be the High Court judges going out from time to time, and on the kind of rota system which currently prevails for Assizes, though probably for not more than one session in one new court at a time. In this way the number of Assize towns could be reduced drastically to some eight, ten or twelve fixed courts instead. There would be no need for cases to be put off to other towns, all parties would be able to know definitely where the case would be heard, and more or less exactly when, while the judge would never be in danger of falling into those pitfalls of local antipathy and prosecution-mindedness which had worried the Streatfeild Committee. At the same time the number of 'judges' lodgings' currently added to the expense of the ratepayers in all Assize towns would be reduced, and much needless expense saved. It would be too bold to suggest that such a development is likely in the near future, in view of the Streatfeild Report, but if the methods of speeding up delays in trial which are now being tried out, such as the holding of extra Assizes and Quarter Sessions where necessary, prove to be no real answer to the criticisms of the Assize system which have been voiced, it may be that something along the lines just mentioned could be subjected to experiment.

An additional advantage of a new system of fixed local

'superior' criminal courts would be that it may become feasible to abolish courts of Quarter Sessions along with the Assizes. It is difficult to estimate whether the transfer of all Quarter Sessions' jurisdiction to the new permanent courts might not mean an overburdening of the new courts; it might even necessitate the creation of too many fixed courts to make the experiment worthwhile (particularly since Quarter Sessions, though not Assizes, also at present hear appeals from decisions of magistrates at petty sessions—though when discharging this function no juries sit). But this is a matter for detailed study. Certainly the addition of Quarter Sessions work to the business of the new courts would liberate many barristers, who under present conditions discharge the duties of Recorders and chairmen or deputy chairmen of Quarter Sessions, to ease the burdens of the High Court judges by being appointed periodically, though not permanently, as special commissioners for the new courts.

Turning to civil cases, there can be no doubt that the innovation of county courts in 1846 has been an unqualified success, in that cheaper and speedier justice has been available for all. By successive Acts of Parliament the jurisdiction of these courts has been increased, so that now nearly all civil disputes may be tried locally, rather than in the High Court in London, provided that the sum in dispute does not exceed £400—and this sum may be exceeded in certain special types of case, such as claims for salvage of boats wrecked or sunk at sea (county courts near the coast having jurisdiction to hear such claims). But although the ordinary monetary jurisdiction of the courts has been increased from a mere £20 in 1846 to the modern limit of £400, this rise is partly explained by the decline in the value of money, and it seems reasonable therefore to suppose that the financial limits will continue to mount progressively as time passes.

There is one type of civil case, the suit for divorce, that has never been within the jurisdiction of county courts, and it is submitted that this is an unfortunate gap in an otherwise sound system. Provision has been made for the hearing of some divorce petitions, particularly those which are undefended, in local courts, but these courts are quite separate both from the county courts and from the various local criminal courts. In fact the county court judges, who are full-time appointees from among the ranks of the practising Bar, frequently sit as special commissioners to hear these local divorce petitions, but the hearings do not take place in the ordinary county courts. One reason which has been put forward is that solicitors, as well as barristers, have the right of audience in the county courts—an aspect of county court practice which has always aided the purpose of keeping down expense for litigants. As divorce involves a serious matter of status it can be argued that the senior branch of the legal profession, as the Bar is sometimes called, should provide the only lawyers entitled to represent their clients in open court in these cases. But this view deserves scant respect, as the vast majority of divorce cases are undefended and very simple in essence. There is certainly something to be said for providing that defended divorce suits should be tried with the greatest of care, and with adequate representation by members of the Bar, but there is no reason to believe that the kind of care required cannot be provided by solicitors in undefended cases with simple fact situations, under the guidance of a professional judge. It may be added that the current usual all-in cost of an undefended divorce is no less than £100, taking into account counsel's fees, solicitor's fees and court costs. A busy barrister may well today present the petitions in ten or twelve undefended divorces in a morning, and be entirely free to do his paper work in chambers in the afternoon. He adequately discharges the care which is required, but no barrister would pretend that very much work or difficulty was involved. If undefended divorce cases, at the very least, were brought within the jurisdiction of the county courts expense could be saved, and there is no reason to believe that justice, within the framework of the present law concerning matrimonial causes, would not be done.

The High Court of Justice maintains an unfettered jurisdiction over all civil disputes, and in practice it hears all civil cases which do not come within the more limited jurisdiction of the county courts. The High Court sits in London, in The Law Courts in the Strand, and it is divided into three parts, the

Chancery Division, the Queen's Bench Division, and the Probate, Divorce and Admiralty Division. The purpose of dividing the court up into these three Divisions is primarily practical, in that each Division deals with a certain specific portion of the whole wide range of possible civil actions. Broadly, the business of the Probate, Divorce and Admiralty Division is apparent from its name, while the Chancery Division is mainly concerned with disputes concerning land and trusts. The Queen's Bench Division is then left with a variety of litigation embracing, among other things, 'running down' cases, defamation, breach of contract and all sorts of actions for personal injuries.

Few will find any cause for complaint about the general organisation of the business of the High Court, save on matters of detail. But one criticism which has frequently been raised is that the Probate, Divorce and Admiralty Division could be abolished, and its jurisdiction over three such ill-assorted subjects with advantage transferred to the other two Divisions. Problems concerned with the proving of wills could be dealt with in the Chancery Division, while divorce and Admiralty disputes would go to the Queen's Bench Division. There is no good reason why the Chancery Division, suitably bolstered by the assignment to it of one or two of the present Probate, Divorce and Admiralty judges, should not absorb probate litigation without difficulty, as the matters at issue are often similar to those it currently deals with in connection with trusts and the administration of estates. Similarly, despite arguments to the contrary by Admiralty specialists, it appears that most Admiralty cases, which are in any case rather rare, do not involve principles or procedure very far removed from those in operation in the Queen's Bench Division when dealing with commercial matters. At present one judge in the Probate, Divorce and Admiralty Division is by tradition appointed for his expertise and experience in Admiralty matters, and this judge could be transferred to the Queen's Bench Division. The divorce jurisdiction of the present Probate, Divorce and Admiralty Division occupies most of its time, yet the problems involved are rarely very complex, and even when they are they are not very different from the types of problems, of evidence and legal distinctions, which are sometimes encountered in the Queen's Bench Division. To transfer this jurisdiction and the remainder of the Probate, Divorce and Admiralty judges to the Queen's Bench Division would simplify matters for litigants, and also make the allocation of judges for particular hearings within the Division or upon Assize (or the successors of the Assize courts, as discussed above) more flexible. The solitary Admiralty judge, when no Admiralty business is pending, may even find it more congenial to hear ordinary commercial actions, rather than the probate and divorce cases which, under present conditions, are his only alternative fare.

To the layman, one of the oddest features of the judicial system in this country is the Judicial Committee of the Privy Council, which is strictly not a court at all, but merely a committee of Her Majesty's Privy Council specially charged with the task of advising the monarch upon the law at issue in cases appealed to Her from the highest courts of the various countries within the Commonwealth. In fact the Judicial Committee operates in very much the same way as a court, and its function is therefore to act as ultimate court of appeal in Commonwealth cases (certain other much rarer functions in connection with English courts will be ignored for our present purposes), its 'advice' to Her Majesty having the practical effect in each case of a judgment in any other court, and not requiring any further action on the part of the monarch. Unfortunately the Judicial Committee has been criticised in many quarters in the past, though there is little reason to believe that its decisions have departed from the high standards of integrity and impartiality expected from judges in this country. The main points of criticism have arisen from the staffing of the Judicial Committee almost entirely by British judges, with only the leavening of this composition by a few Commonwealth judges, so that the finer points of Commonwealth laws may be in danger of not being appreciated, and also from the fact that the Committee sits only in London, thus enforcing travel and a great deal of expense upon litigants and their lawyers from other Commonwealth countries. These criticisms have only been heeded belatedly, and although a much greater number of Commonwealth judges than hitherto have now been made Privy Councillors, so that they may be eligible to sit in the Judicial Committee, the change of policy only came in 1962, by which time many of the independent Commonwealth countries had already abolished the right of appeal from courts of their countries to the Privy Council. Although appeals still lie from the British dependencies, and from Australia, New Zealand, Ceylon, Malaysia, Sierra Leone, Uganda, Kenya, Zanzibar, Jamaica, and Trinidad and Tobago, it may be expected that others among the African and Asian countries particularly will take the step of abolishing the right of appeal to the Privy Council.

The remedy to this trend would seem to be to spread the location of hearings before the Judicial Committee to other Commonwealth countries, or, in other words, to send the Committee out on circuit through the various Commonwealth countries. In this way it would become a true Commonwealth ultimate court of appeal, and it would be easier for those Commonwealth judges qualified to sit in the Privy Council to take their places in the Committee in cases appealed from courts of their own countries. It may even be that, in this way, certain of the Commonwealth countries which have so far abolished the right to appeal to the Committee would reintroduce this right, for the Judicial Committee would then have a real chance to help towards a unification of the different laws of all the countries concerned, most of which are in any case based upon a common law system. The opportunity for legal development through comparative methods is clear, and it is hoped that not many more years will pass before a step of the kind suggested is taken.

Reverting to municipal law, the ultimate court of appeal for both civil and criminal cases is, as was mentioned in Chapter One, the House of Lords. In most types of legal dispute it is possible for either party who is dissatisfied with the decision of the trial court to appeal to an appeal court, after which either party may again appeal from the decision of the appeal court to the House of Lords. This rule holds true for both civil and criminal cases, save that in criminal cases the prosecution may only appeal at the second stage and not at the first. Technically, therefore, only the accused may appeal from the decision of his trial court in a criminal cause, though either side may appeal thereafter to the House of Lords. Under the Judicature Act of 1873, which established most of the modern superior courts, the jurisdiction of the House of Lords to hear appeals was abolished, though this jurisdiction was re-established by a statute of the following year before the 1873 Act had come into force, largely because the House had up till then heard appeals in Irish and Scottish as well as English cases, and there was a need to provide or retain some kind of appeal court to hear the Irish and Scottish cases. In the event, the present two-tier appeal system for England remained, though appeals in the House of Lords are only heard by the Lords of Appeal in Ordinary (together with the Lord Chancellor and certain peers who have held high judicial office, such as ex-Lord Chancellors and ex-Lord Chief Justices) specially appointed to sit in the House for the purpose, so that there is a clear division between the House sitting as a legislative chamber and as a court. The two-tier appellate system has survived continuous criticism, and in fact the jurisdiction of the House over criminal appeals, which was originally limited to cases involving points of law of exceptional public importance, was extended in 1960 to cover appeals in cases where points of law of only general public importance are involved.

On the whole, it is submitted that the two-tier system of appeals is no bad thing. It is certainly far from unique, for it exists in different forms in many other countries, including the United States of America. It has been suggested in some quarters that some rearrangement of the regulations of the ordinary appeal courts might be made, so that the usual three judges sitting for an appeal might adjourn when appropriate into a division of five judges having the authority of the present House of Lords (which is also normally composed of five judges or Law Lords when hearing an appeal). But the advantage of such a system is hard to see. It might not become apparent until the arguments of counsel before the appeal court were well advanced that it was desirable for two extra judges to be called in, and then the arguments would have to be started all over again—and no man is at his best in repeating to a group of people an argument which he has already just made to some members of that group. Repetition before a completely fresh panel of judges in the House of Lords is quite a different thing. Again, the present 'first instance' appeal courts are very hard-worked, and most of their judgments are given orally, only the most important and difficult cases being reserved for written judgments. The great advantage of the House of Lords is that, although very far from being an idle court, it only hears a very small number of appeals compared with the other appeal courts, criminal and civil. Consequently time and trouble are no obstacles to a full and careful consideration of the issues involved in each case. The fact that the members of the House sometimes disagree on their decisions, and arrive at a result by a majority, is more of a commentary upon the difficult nature of the points of law which require decision by the highest tribunal than a criticism of the House of Lords itself. When these points of law are so disputed there will always be lawyers who will criticise the actual decision reached in the end in the Lords, but providing the most distinguished of the available judges are appointed to the Lords, as for the most part they almost certainly are, there can be little ground for complaint about the care taken in arriving at the decision.

Accordingly it is submitted that the House of Lords will continue to function as at present, and where its decisions give rise to general dissatisfaction with the state of the law then the Government and Parliament must be persuaded to set in motion the normal machinery of law reform. The fact that legal decisions of the House of Lords automatically become binding precedent makes this reform all the more urgent, but it is not an argument against the existence of the Lords as a court or against the doctrine of binding precedent, which at least aids certainty of the law, as was explained in Chapter One.

There is no current dissatisfaction with the arrangements for civil appeals at the lower level from the House of Lords. These appeals lie mostly to the Court of Appeal, whereas criminal appeals lie from the court of trial to an entirely different court. So far as the more serious criminal cases are concerned the relevant appeal court is called the Court of Criminal Appeal, which was first set up by an Act of 1907, and a few words should be said here about this court, as it has come in for some criticism in recent months.

In essence there is little doubt that the Court of Criminal Appeal provides a useful safeguard to the liberties of the individual. Unlike appeals to the House of Lords, appeals to the Court of Criminal Appeal may only be brought at the instance of the accused person, and never at the suit of the prosecution. As a matter of right any accused person may appeal upon a point of law against his conviction, and, provided in this case he obtains the leave of either the Court of Criminal Appeal or of the trial judge, he may also appeal on a question of fact, or of mixed fact and law. He may also appeal, with the leave of the Court of Criminal Appeal, against any sentence passed upon him, even though he does not appeal against the actual conviction. On the hearing of the appeal, the Court of Criminal Appeal may, broadly, either allow the appeal and quash the conviction, or dismiss the appeal and thus uphold the conviction, or vary the sentence without disturbing the conviction, or sometimes, and within strict limits, substitute for a conviction for one offence a conviction for another, or very occasionally order a proper trial to be held at first instance. This last power can only be rarely exercised, in circumstances where the appeal court is satisfied that the original trial was so defective that in fact no trial had taken place at all. If, for example, a Recorder of Quarter Sessions had been unable to sit on a particular day, and he had appointed a deputy to sit in his place (as he is empowered to do), but the deputy turned out in fact not to be a barrister, then it seems clear that the Court of Criminal Appeal would be bound to order that a proper trial should take place in the future. But it is equally clear that the irregularity at the original trial must be extreme and serious before the appeal court may consider that it was a nullity. Apart from this rare power to order a new trial, therefore, it can be seen that the Court of Criminal Appeal has no power in ordinary circumstances to order a new trial to take place. This is a controversial matter, and many people have felt that it is unfortunate that the court has no power to order a new trial to take place when the ground for an appeal turns out, as it not infrequently does in view of the complicated state of the criminal law, to be nothing more than a legal technicality. There have been many cases in which convicted persons who have clearly committed offences have nevertheless had their convictions quashed because they were charged with the wrong offence, or because there was some technical defect in the indictment upon which they were tried. Both the present and the immediate past Lord Chief Justices are known to feel that this represents a serious loophole in our law, but the justification for the present position is that it preserves the generally desirable principle that no man should be put in peril of trial for the same offence on more than one occasion.

There are of course a great many appeals to the Court of Criminal Appeal, and the procedure which currently must be followed in the court is largely designed to enable it to deal as efficiently as possible with such a volume of business. The judge of Assize or Recorder or chairman of Quarter Sessions before whom the prisoner was convicted must supply his notes of the trial and a report on the case, and these are considered by the judges of the Court of Criminal Appeal, together with the grounds for the appeal, as supplied by the defence, and such other papers as may be relevant, before the hearing in the Court of Criminal Appeal itself. Thus the arguments on both sides will have been for the most part put to the court before it even sits, a practice which is contrary to that of most other courts in England, and more akin to the procedure in some American courts. Most appeals are dealt with in court, therefore, in a very short time, a mere matter of a few minutes, and oral argument is often extremely brief, and sometimes non-existent. The court has power to admit fresh evidence, but this power is usually only exercised when such evidence was not available at the original trial, and in any case the Court of Criminal Appeal is reluctant to hear the new evidence unless it is tested at the appeal in the usual way by cross-examination by counsel for the prosecution. It is upon this latter matter that the recent criticism of the court has arisen.

In the summer of 1963 the Court of Criminal Appeal quashed a conviction for wounding a Miss Christine Keeler which had been obtained against a Mr. Gordon, a West Indian. The case attracted a most unusual notoriety because it was a small part of a chain of events which together amounted to one of the greatest scandals in British public life that has ever taken place. A Secretary of State, whose mistress Miss Keeler had been at one time, had resigned from office and left Parliament after admitting that he had lied to the House of Commons in a statement previously made about his relations with Miss Keeler. Gordon was only one of two West Indians, both former lovers of Miss Keeler, who had quite separately been convicted of attacks upon her, and Gordon's appeal against his conviction had come before the Court of Criminal Appeal at a time when a Dr. Ward was still on trial on charges which involved the criminal offences of living on the immoral earnings of Miss Keeler and other women, a trial which achieved enormous publicity at the time, and which revealed considerable sexual depravity involving many people. It was generally known before Gordon's appeal came on for hearing that Miss Keeler had made a long tape-recording which had later been made available to other people, and which it was understood revealed that much of the case against Gordon had been fabricated. It was also known that certain other men, who had not given evidence at Gordon's trial, had since been interviewed and had made statements to the police. It was therefore popularly expected that the hearing of the appeal would reveal the contents of this tape-recording and these statements, and the salacious appetite of the public was unusually whetted. But the appeal itself actually took only about nine minutes. The Court of Criminal Appeal quashed Gordon's conviction on the ground that there was new evidence, not available at the time of the trial, which threw reasonable doubt upon whether, had that evidence been available at the trial, the conviction would have been obtained. Counsel for the prosecution said in court that he entirely agreed with this view

of the judges, and counsel for Gordon was also satisfied with this
method of dealing with the case.

The subsequent furore in the press and in the country
generally was doubtless partly prompted by a disappointed
appetite for more scandal, but there was also a more responsible
feeling that the case had the ugly look about it of having been
hushed up; and secrecy is a fertile soil for rumour and suspicion.
Some of the wilder comments upon the affair alleged a number
of improbable, and certainly, so far as the information available
was concerned, entirely unsubstantiated things. The police
were accused of duplicity, in particular by favouring Miss
Keeler and possibly suppressing evidence which might have
aided the defence at Gordon's trial. The Government was
vaguely accused of interfering with the judiciary, though no
reasonable thinking person can seriously suspect either that the
British Government would attempt to do so or that the judges
would countenance such a proceeding. Very few people were
prepared to try to investigate the normal practice and powers of
the Court of Criminal Appeal to see whether what had taken
place was really out of the ordinary. Had they done so, they
would have found very little in the court's behaviour in the
Gordon appeal to suggest that the judges had in any way departed from their strict impartiality and high professional
ethics. The kernel of all criticism of the court was that it had
not allowed the new evidence to be given in open court, yet, as
has already been pointed out above, the Court of Criminal
Appeal (which in any case has a great pressure of business upon
it) does not like to hear actual evidence before it, and it prefers
to exercise its discretion by giving the accused the benefit of the
doubt in such a case. To allow the new evidence to be given
would have meant that it would have had to be tested by cross-
examination to justify any court accepting it as truth, and
counsel for the Crown had already conceded to the court that
the evidence threw a reasonable doubt upon whether the conviction should have been obtained in the first place. In every
trial for a crime the prosecution must prove guilt beyond all
reasonable doubt, a heavy burden of proof, so that the prosecution counsel at the appeal was in effect admitting that it would

be a waste of time, and of course money on both sides, for the Crown to go on presenting the case for a conviction. To this should be added the fact that the Ward trial was still in progress at the time, and the case against Dr. Ward depended in part upon the veracity or otherwise of Miss Keeler, who was one of the witnesses for the prosecution in that case. For the Court of Criminal Appeal to allow new evidence in the Gordon case to be given in open court, and of course to be tested by cross-examination, would inevitably have had the effect of providing a comment one way or another upon Miss Keeler's truthfulness. By taking the course it did the Court of Criminal Appeal very carefully avoided prejudicing in any way the trial of Dr. Ward.

Clearly the whole trouble could have been avoided if the court had had the power to order a fresh trial of Mr. Gordon to take place, for at that trial all the evidence, including the new evidence, could be given. Lord Parker, the present Lord Chief Justice, has long favoured the acquisition by the court of a power to order a new trial in cases of doubt, or where there is no more than a technical defect in the conviction, and it is not without interest that Lord Parker was himself presiding over the Court of Criminal Appeal in the Gordon appeal. To grant this power to the court would mean an infringement of the principle that no man should be put in peril of more than one trial, and conviction, for the same offence or charge, but the infringement would be small, and it would be a comparatively trifling price to pay to allay the general feeling of suspicion of the courts and of the judiciary which has, most unfairly, been aroused by the present limitation of the court's powers. At the time of writing the Government has announced its intention to introduce a bill which will, if enacted, give the Court of Criminal Appeal the power to order a new trial, though only where new evidence has become available. It is regrettable that there is still no intention to give the court a similar power where there is a mere technical defect in the indictment or conviction.

Although the jury is often thought of as a basic feature of the English legal system, its employment has in fact been progressively decreased over the past half century. Today a jury must sit to decide the facts in all defended criminal cases tried at Assizes or Quarter Sessions, or at the Central Criminal Court or the Crown Courts, but it is not used for the trial of petty criminal cases summarily before magistrates. On the civil side, however, although rules of court make it possible for a jury to be empanelled for the hearing of almost any defended case, as a matter of practice the jury has been abandoned in all civil causes except for a few cases involving fraud, and five other types of action commonly regarded as containing more factual than legal problems: defamation, malicious prosecution, false imprisonment, seduction and breach of promise of marriage, of which only the first is at all commonly litigated, while the last two are ripe for abolition anyway, as has been pointed out earlier in this book.

Perhaps the main value of a jury is that it is composed of twelve ordinary people who may be more reliable in arriving at a true assessment of facts than a single professional judge, particularly since the members of the jury are required to be unanimous in their decision. But unfortunately the jury, under present conditions, must decide not only the facts in issue, but also the law which results from those facts once determined. As an example, in a criminal trial for murder, the jury must not only determine whether the accused committed the act of shooting or stabbing, or whatever has been alleged, but it must also then decide whether, in the light of their opinion of the facts, the accused was guilty of murder or manslaughter, or alternatively not guilty of any homicide at all. Naturally the judge is under a duty to instruct them carefully as to the kinds of decisions open to them, but once their verdict has been reached he is then only empowered to pass sentence, if the accused has been convicted of an offence, or to discharge him if he has been acquitted by the jury. Similarly, in a civil action for, say, defamation, the jury must not only decide whether the alleged statements were made, but also whether they were in law defamatory. Furthermore, if they should find in favour of the plaintiff, it is then also their duty to assess the damages which must be paid by the defendant.

213

There are perhaps two respects in which the jury system is unsatisfactory. First, there is always the danger that a jury may fail to reach agreement, and in such a case there must be a complete rehearing of the whole case before a different jury at a later date. This involves not only greater expense, but, in the case of criminal trials at least, considerable mental hardship for the accused. Some years ago, Lord Goddard, while Lord Chief Justice, suggested that it might be worthwhile to reduce the numbers sitting on the jury from twelve to seven, and to permit each jury to arrive at a verdict by a majority, provided no more than two members of the jury disagreed with the view of the majority. The objection to this scheme is that it would reduce the protection which the present system provides for the accused, for it would become possible for a man being tried to be convicted despite the firm opinion of two jury members that he was innocent. Although Lord Goddard's suggestion has the merit that it would avoid waste of time and expense in the holding of second trials, and that it would enable the accused to know his fate for certain with the minimum delay, it is significant that no substantial support has been gained for his idea. Where the liberty, and even under the present law the life, of an accused person is at stake, it seems best to maintain the very considerable protection from unjust conviction which the law provides for him under present circumstances. Yet there may well be something to be said for Lord Goddard's plan in the case of civil jury trials, where the liberty of the individual is not at stake.

The second objection to the jury system is solely concerned with civil trials. Although the types of civil cases which are still tried by jury involve the kind of factual problems which ordinary laymen are quite competent to assess, it seems quite wrong that jurymen should have the task of determining the actual amount of damages to be awarded to a successful plaintiff. Judges are constantly making awards of damages, and they are acquainted with the principles and practice involved in arriving at a suitable sum. But jurymen are not so experienced. Indeed most of them will be sitting on the jury for their first time. It seems that at the very least the function of the jury in a

professional judge can, and thus may be less likely in some cases
to lose sight of reasonable objective standards when assessing
matters which are almost entirely factual

Apart from the J.P.s, who only sit in petty sessions (together
with certain other special sittings in connection with such
matters as licensing, matrimonial disputes other than divorce
cases, and the trial of juvenile offenders) or, in the counties, in
Quarter Sessions, as has been mentioned earlier in this chapter,
all judges are paid and have a legal training. In fact these
judges, in all courts, are appointed from among the practising
lawyers, and a judgeship is regarded as a just reward or pro-
motion for lawyers who have proved themselves to be of
judicial calibre, though some practitioners have been known to
turn down invitations to become judges because they prefer to
continue in practice and, if they are at the top of their profession, to earn considerably more in fees than the £8,000 or
£9,000 that a superior judge receives by way of stipend (the
figures are well under £5,000 for other professional judges).
The difference between the two branches of the legal profession,
the barristers and the solicitors, will be adverted to later in this
chapter, but it is sufficient here to mention that barristers may
be appointed to any judicial post, while solicitors may only be
appointed as stipendiary magistrates. This seems an odd distinction. There may be no very great point in arguing for the
admission of solicitors as judges in the superior courts, such as
the High Court, the appeal courts and the House of Lords,
because barristers are the advocates who alone, except for
litigants in person, have the right to argue in these courts, and
who are therefore most suited to preside over the business of the
courts when their time comes. But in several of the lower courts
solicitors are permitted the right of audience, and the able and
experienced solicitor would seem to be just as suited to judicial
work as any other lawyer. To the knowledge of the present
author, only one of the many stipendiary magistrates so far
appointed has been a solicitor at the date of his appointment
(though some solicitors who have later changed over to the
barristers' branch of the profession have gone on to be appointed
to the bench even in the superior courts). It would seem that, in

fairness to the solicitors' profession, more use of the power to appoint solicitors as stipendiary magistrates should be made. It is also submitted that no harm could be done by opening the county court bench to solicitors. Solicitors have the right to practice in the county courts, and the civil litigation normally heard in these courts involves only comparatively small sums of money: indeed it is often the case that the issues tried in the county courts involve more commonsense than difficult law. Who better to administer a court of commonsense than a solicitor who, while in practice, has had to advise clients personally, mixing legal principles with objective fairness and an understanding of human nature?

Finally, on the subject of courts, it may be worthwhile to mention an interesting recent development in connection with the undertaking of prosecutions by the police in petty cases. It may be remembered from Chapter Six that we have already suggested that the task of prosecuting should be removed from the police, but if such a reform does not come about a public statement made by the Chief Constable of Southend in March 1963 may be indicative of a possible lightening of the heavy burdens which currently beset the police. The Chief Constable stated that his police force would in future adopt a new policy towards cases of shoplifting reported to it. Whilst every case would be considered on its merits, the Southend police would also consider the previous record of the alleged offender, the value of the property taken, and the likelihood of the offence recurring, and they would not prosecute where they thought the circumstances did not justify it, particularly where the value of the property taken was small.

Sir Carleton Allen, a distinguished jurist, has described this statement, being made by a responsible guardian of the law, as 'startling, unprecedented and contrary to public policy'. But the Chief Constable's view is not dissimilar from that voiced in 1951 by a former Attorney-General, Sir Hartley (later Lord) Shawcross, when discussing the relevant principles as to prosecution and non-prosecution. Sir Hartley stated in the House of Commons that the duty of the Attorney-General in deciding whether or not to authorise a prosecution in those serious cases over which he has in fact authority to decide upon the future course, as, for instance, in cases involving suspected espionage, was not limited to deciding whether the evidence was sufficient to justify a prosecution, and that wider considerations had to be taken into account. It would seem that the duty of prosecutors in less serious cases should be much the same. The likely success or failure of a prosecution should never be the only criterion by which the course of the police should be judged. It is surely only in accord with reasonable twentieth century attitudes that a man who has offended for the first time in some trifling way should be given a chance to show that there is no need for a prosecution to bring home to him the error of his ways. Many motorists have experienced the dreadful feeling of being caught for the first time exceeding the speed limit, or driving up a one-way street in the wrong direction, and they have usually been so chastened by the experience and so thankful that the police have taken no legal action that they have made very sure that they do not err again. It is only right that a similar kind of discretion should be exercised in relation to very minor offences committed by housewives who may, for example, have literally given way in a supermarket to the mass advertising campaigns which urge them to 'get it now'. It is probably in accord with modern ideas of punishment, discussed in Chapter Three, that prosecutions should not be entirely automatic, for the culprit is often reformed by the mere fact of being apprehended. In any case, as English law permits *anyone* to prosecute for a criminal offence, it is always open to the shopkeeper or self-service store manager to start proceedings himself if he really feels sufficiently strongly about the offence.

COSTS AND LEGAL AID

In the first section of this chapter we have given one example, that of an undefended divorce case, of the high level of the present-day costs of legal proceedings. The great expense of litigation has been a constant feature of the English legal system since mediaeval times, when the salaries of judges and court officials were little more than nominal, so that a living wage had to be acquired through the medium of court fees paid by the litigants. Today the stipends of all judges and court officers are realistic, but the cost of paying them and of maintaining the courts and keeping the wheels of the machinery going have to be borne very largely out of the fees paid for their services. It is too difficult a financial problem for the purpose of this book to raise the question whether, despite the obvious expense of keeping the administration of the law efficient, court costs generally could be lowered. A step in this direction was taken when the county courts were created in 1846, for the costs charged by these courts are very much lower than in the High Court. But even if we cannot here question the general scheme of things, there are some obvious economies which might be made in the future. Under present requirements all the documents of a case which goes on appeal to the House of Lords have to be specially bound in volume form, while the statement of a case for appeal to the Judicial Committee of the Privy Council actually has to be printed rather than typed. It is surely time that unnecessary extravagances of this kind were eliminated.

Oddly enough, one of the great advances of recent years for the benefit of the poor litigant, free legal aid, paid out of central funds, has probably contributed to the continued rise in court costs, and also in fees payable to solicitors and barristers. If the state, an impersonal and wealthy creature, is to pay, an attitude that the fees might as well be as large as possible is not an unnatural result. Certainly the rises in court costs and lawyers' fees during the past fifteen years since the legal aid scheme came into being have been quite high, though a substantial part of these rises is of course due to the inflation which has affected us all in every way anyhow. Perhaps this is a disadvantage of the legal aid scheme which must just be accepted, for the general advantages of the scheme, which far outweigh its faults, can hardly be disputed. People who previously were not wealthy enough to be able to risk embarking upon litigation, in case they should lose, need no longer hold back because of this fear. It is not surprising, therefore, that there are more law cases brought today than before legal aid became effective. Yet this very increase in litigation makes the problem of costs more acute, for only those who cannot themselves afford to pay the costs of litigation will be legally aided, and there are still many individuals, and more corporations and companies, who will have to bring or defend actions entirely at their own risk as to costs.

The main difficulty for the unassisted litigant is that it is usual in civil cases (though not a strict rule, for the court retains a discretion) for costs to 'follow the event'. That is, the party who loses the action, whether he is the plaintiff or the defendant, normally finds that he is ordered by the court to pay all the court costs of the action, together with the reasonable expenses incurred by the other party in opposing him, as well, of course, as his own expenses. This does not mean that the successful party has to pay nothing at all, as the court official who vets the claims for his reimbursement does not often allow everything claimed. But the usual fees of his solicitor and counsel, together with the cost of obtaining evidence necessary to the suit, will be allowed. In principle this system may seem fair, for the party who is in the right ought not to have to pay for the privilege of showing that he was in the right. But the defects of the arrangement become plain when it is appreciated that the same rule as to costs following the event is usually applied when a case is appealed to a higher court, and furthermore the appeal court usually orders whichever party loses the appeal to pay the costs of both parties before the appeal court *and* before the court or courts below, regardless of which party had been successful below. This means, therefore, that a party who loses the suit at the appellate level may find himself having to pay heavily for having persuaded the court below to make the mistake of giving judgment in his favour, a fact which adds a certain terror to making an effort to win a case!

A striking example of this defect in the English legal system, and indeed in practically the whole of the common law world, was a case which arose in Australia, and then went on appeal to the Judicial Committee of the Privy Council in 1961. The defendants were charterers of an oil-burning ship called 'The Wagon Mound'. While she was being bunkered in Sydney Harbour, some furnace oil was spilt into the sea by the negligence of some of the defendants' employees. This oil was carried on the water towards a wharf owned by the plaintiffs, a firm of shipbuilders and repairers. At the material time some of the plaintiffs' employees were refitting another vessel, in the course of which they were using electric and oxyacetylene welding equipment. During this work, some molten metal fell from the wharf into the sea, a not unusual or unnatural occurrence when welding operations were in progress. But unfortunately the molten metal set fire to a piece of cotton waste which was floating on the oil. Had the oil not been there, the cotton waste would probably have been too wet to catch light, but even had it caught light no damage would have been likely to result, as the flame would soon have been put out by the sea. On this occasion, however, the burning waste set fire to the oil, and the plaintiffs' wharf was seriously burned. The plaintiffs therefore sued the defendants for the loss they had suffered, basing their claim on negligence. The negligence was clear, and in ordinary circumstances the plaintiffs' success in the action would have been a foregone conclusion, but in this instance the defendants claimed that the damage done was too remote from their actual negligent act, and that for this reason they ought not to be held liable.

The trial judge rejected the defendants' argument because he held that a decision of the English Court of Appeal, given in a case in 1921, which had been to the effect that a negligent party would be responsible for all damage that was the direct consequence of the negligence, was also applicable in similar Australian cases, in the absence of any Australian authority to the contrary; and on appeal the Supreme Court of New South Wales agreed. But when the defendants appealed further to the Privy Council the Judicial Committee held that the 1921 decision had been misconceived, and that the true test of remoteness of damage was that a defendant should only be held liable for injuries which a reasonable man should have foreseen as reasonably likely to occur as a result of the negligence. As the burning of the oil was a circumstance no such reasonable man should have foreseen as likely to occur (and expert witnesses had been called at the original trial to testify as to the extreme improbability of such a thing happening in the fact-situation presented), the damage suffered by the plaintiffs was too remote, and so the judgments of the lower courts were reversed. The Judicial Committee also ordered the plaintiffs to pay the costs of the hearing in all three courts. In the result, therefore, the plaintiffs lost their wharf, their action, and the court costs and legal expenses on both sides at all stages of the action.

The implications of this decision so far as costs are concerned are clear. If a rule of law has not been settled by the highest court of all, the House of Lords in the United Kingdom or the Privy Council for several other Commonwealth countries, there must remain an element of risk in relying upon legal principles settled lower down the hierarchy of courts, for these rules *might* be upset on appeal to the highest court. The injustice of this is all the more plain when it is realised that the appeal in the case of 'The Wagon Mound' was upon pure law, so that any reversal of the lower courts' decisions could only be upon the ground that the Court of Appeal in 1921 had been wrong in its idea of the state of the law upon remoteness of damage. By no standard could the state of the law be regarded as the fault of either party to the suit.

Sooner or later the injustice of cases of this kind must be more generally recognised. Three solutions seem possible. First, appeals upon pure points of law might be made to lie from the court of trial direct to the highest possible court, though the disadvantage of this might be that the House of Lords and Judicial Committee of the Privy Council might become flooded with appeals upon relatively minor matters of law, so that they lose their present virtue of being able to consider the points in issue at leisure and without the need to hurry through the hearing of the appeal. Secondly, the costs of any appeal upon pure law might be apportioned between the parties, regardless of the actual result of the case, the apportionment in each case usually being upon the fifty-fifty basis. We have met apportionment before in Chapter Four, and here the principle which is becoming more and more popular as a solution to many of the problems of substantive law could be adapted without difficulty to the award of costs. It cannot be pretended that such a solution would provide absolute justice for the parties, for in true justice perhaps they ought not to have to pay anything at all for the accident of 'law' as opposed to 'facts'. But at least it would be fairer all round than at present. Thirdly, the costs of all the appeals upon law might be borne by public funds. It is hard to say which of these solutions will be chosen, and it is even possible that either the second or third might be combined with the first, or that some proportion of the costs should be borne by public funds, and the rest apportioned between the parties. Naturally the interests of the taxpayer must be taken into account, but at least these suggestions may provide a basis upon which the detailed working out of a fairer system as to costs could be evolved.

Another unsatisfactory aspect of the present provisions as to costs has till now been provided by the kind of case in which a legally aided plaintiff has brought an action against an unassisted defendant. If the action is unsuccessful, the legal aid scheme makes provision for the payment of the costs of the plaintiff, but not for the costs of the defendant. A successful defence might in such a case be hollow, for the defendant would have to pay out quite a lot of money anyway, to cover the cost of defending the suit. In some cases it could even prove cheaper for the defendant to settle the unjust claim out of court, instead of defeating it inside the court! The Legal Aid Bill, published in 1963, is intended to provide for payment of a successful defendant's costs out of the Legal Aid Fund where the defendant would otherwise suffer financial hardship. It is perhaps a little odd to make the criterion for this payment a type of means test, which is, very properly, the basis of legal aid itself. It is hard to see why an injustice to a defendant ceases to be an injustice if it is not severe, but at least the Bill is a step in the right direction, and its enactment as a statute may be hoped for in the very near future.

One final aspect of legal aid may be mentioned here, though it is not proposed to discuss it in detail. The present rules whereby a person convicted of a criminal offence may obtain legal aid to cover the costs of an appeal have been shown in a Report published by JUSTICE in 1963 to be complex and hard to understand. Legal aid is equally applicable to civil and criminal cases, though for obvious reasons only the accused is able to obtain such financial assistance in criminal cases. But it seems that a number of prisoners in the past have not taken the step of appealing, because of the difficulty of applying for legal aid within the very short space of time at present allowed. Lord Shawcross, who has been mentioned already in this chapter, and who is now Chairman of the Council of JUSTICE, has said that: 'The lack of legal help with appeals can easily mean, and in some cases may well have meant, that men have served long sentences for crimes which they did not commit: and there can be no worse blot on a system of justice than that'. A different and departmental Working Party reporting upon legal aid in criminal proceedings generally in the same year came to rather similar conclusions, and so it may be assumed that faults of this kind in the otherwise generally beneficial and just arrangements for legal aid will be tackled before long.

THE LEGAL PROFESSION

As has been mentioned in Chapter One, the legal profession is split into two quite separate groups, the barristers and the solicitors. One result of the distinction is that it is not proper for any member of the public to consult a barrister direct, so that each barrister depends for his livelihood upon being consulted for opinions or briefed to appear in cases by solicitors. In most countries, even within the common law world, there is no such division within the legal profession, and all qualified lawyers are entitled to do the work which is undertaken in England by either side of the profession. It is sometimes asked, therefore, whether the English division, which is strict (so that no man may be both a solicitor and a barrister at the same time, although he is permitted to change from one branch of the legal profession to the other, if he wishes, by an expensive and time-consuming procedure), is really necessary. Would it not be more flexible, and therefore more beneficial all round, to lawyers and to clients, if the two branches were fused?

It is difficult to answer this question with confidence, for there are both advantages and disadvantages in the English system.

On the debit side, the split in the profession means that every litigant, at least in the superior courts, must retain for his case two lawyers, a solicitor and a barrister, unless he decides to dispense with lawyers altogether. A lawyer in England who finds that he has chosen the wrong side of his profession for his own abilities also finds it is a difficult and costly process to change over to the other side. But on the other hand the English system is at least plain. Even in those countries where the profession is a single fused entity, most practitioners in fact specialise upon one side or the other; certainly the advocate usually gives up much of the routine office work, and the man who interviews clients when they first come to the office rarely goes into court. So that in other countries the expense of two lawyers may have to be borne anyway by the litigant. In the absence of a really convincing reason for fusing the two branches of the profession, it would seem that the critics can be answered with a 'not proven' verdict, though the virtual monopoly of the judicial offices by the Bar is a defect in the system, at least as regards the strict exclusion of solicitors from the county court bench, as has been mentioned earlier in this chapter.

But if we assume that there is no compelling reason for the fusing of the legal profession in the near future, there are still certain aspects of the two professions, for in fact they are two quite distinct professions, which demand criticism. The most notable problem is presented by the fact that although firms or partnerships of solicitors are a normal feature of that profession, barristers are not permitted by the rules of their profession to associate themselves together in this way. Each barrister practises entirely on his own, though it is usual for several barristers to share a set of chambers, together with the services of a shared clerk. The prime disadvantage of this system within the Bar can be seen when it is remembered that barristers are wholly dependant for their livelihood upon the work which is sent to them by solicitors. A young, newly qualified barrister has often in the past found that he simply cannot get started in his practice because no one sends him any work to do. Solicitors will from time to time be prepared to try out a new barrister by sending him some fairly simple opinion to write, or a not too complicated case to argue in perhaps a county court or at Quarter Sessions. And the clerk of a set of chambers, who arranges the appointments and engagements of the barristers who make use of his services, may well urge a solicitor to give some piece of work to a young man in the chambers when one of the more senior barristers is too busy to take on the brief or opinion. Nevertheless most solicitors most of the time will obviously wish to play safe on their own account and on that of their clients by engaging the services of a tried counsel, if he is available. At the present time, partly as a result of the legal aid scheme, the courts are so fully engaged with both civil and criminal business that many young barristers are finding it fairly easy to start up their practices, for if the older members of the profession cannot take on the work solicitors must brief the younger ones, but it is difficult to say whether this present trend will continue indefinitely. A lot may depend upon whether the recent increase in litigious business will mean an expansion of the practising Bar, which over the past ten years has remained more or less constant at about two thousand, though there has been a small increase in the numbers during the past two years. If the practising Bar expands even by as much as one or two hundred, and then there is a falling off in litigation, it will probably mean that some of the younger or less able members of the Bar will find it impossible for economic reasons to continue in practice.

The present system may be supported on the ground that it leads to a very high standard among the barristers in practice. If every man must fend for himself, with no advertising permitted (a rule which applies equally to both barristers and solicitors), and a barrister's continuation of work depending entirely upon the reputation he gains among other lawyers practising in solicitors' offices, it is clearly hard for anyone who cannot measure up to the highest common standard to hold his own and earn a sufficient living for himself and his family. It is also possibly worth noting here that quite a large number of barristers have either never married or else have married fairly late in life compared with people who earn their livings in other ways. Perhaps it is that the truly dedicated professional man, whatever may be his profession, will often be prepared to make a sacrifice of normal family life in this way, but fewer and fewer young barristers seem to be content that they should have to do so. Though the maintenance of a high standard of professional competence and etiquette within the profession is essential, it seems unnecessary that people who would measure up to these standards should have to turn away from the barrister's life merely because they also want to marry and found a family with a reasonable sense of security.

The dilemmas of the young barrister have been eased considerably in this century, not only by the increase of work available, but also by a system of scholarships and grants which the Inns of Court make readily available to serious intending practitioners. These grants are often made without any prior written examination and purely upon the record of past accomplishments as university students or at school, taken with the impressions of the selection committees after personal interviews, and they are often given to those who are in genuine need of financial assistance even if they are not of the highest intellectual calibre. This at least ensures that each intending barrister has a chance to prove whether or not he has the right kind of ability for practice at the Bar, although the sums granted, generous by the usual standards of scholarships, are hardly sufficient to support a young family as well as the actual barrister himself. Furthermore, the etiquette of the Bar permits and encourages a busy barrister who finds that he has two conflicting engagements, such as where two separate cases in which he has been briefed happen to come on for hearing in different courts on the same day, to hand over his brief to another counsel who will represent him, usually with a financial return for the service. The barrister who steps into the breach in this way is said to be acting as a 'devil' for the other. Older established barristers are very willing to lend a helping hand to younger men, and the able man need not today fear that he will be given no chance at all to prove his worth. But he will still have to be prepared to receive a very uncertain income for his first years of practice, and there is, as has already been mentioned, no guarantee that the present spate of litigation will continue.

One other unsatisfactory aspect of the system whereby each barrister practises on his own account is that it occasionally happens that a barrister who has accepted a brief later returns it to the solicitor because he finds that he just cannot fit in the work with his other commitments, and he cannot find another barrister in his own chambers who is able to take on the brief for him at short notice. In March 1963 in the Court of Appeal an appellant appeared in person and asked for an adjournment of his appeal because his counsel, who had only received his brief the day before, had had to return it. It is not unusual for a barrister to receive a brief at short notice, particularly in an appeal, which may come on for hearing in an urgent case with very little delay, but it is always regrettable when he has to return it after accepting the case, because it means that the litigant has not been given an adequate opportunity to be represented. The present author has long felt that the time must come when partnerships will be permitted at the Bar. Up to now the Bar as a whole has always been set against such a change, but then the members of the practising Bar are mostly men who have already made their mark, and who see no need to alter a system which now favours their prosperity. The few younger men who are still struggling are too concerned with their vital efforts to succeed to worry about changing the system until they have also joined the ranks of the successful, or else have left the profession. But if partnerships were permitted, then there need never be returned briefs, for the partnership as a whole would be responsible for the conduct of a case which had been accepted. Furthermore, the practice of 'devilling' could be more systematically organised within each partnership. The general standard of competence and integrity at the Bar could very likely be even more closely maintained, for each firm of barristers would be collectively interested in the quality of a new recruit, while the firms would themselves remain subject to the disciplinary authority of the Inns of Court and of the General Council of the Bar (a body elected by and from among the practitioners to represent their practical interest), which currently applies to all individual barristers.

It has often seemed to the author that practising barristers are mostly divided into two groups, those who are struggling for a living and crying out for more work to do (and who, incidentally, must leave their chambers as little as possible in case the vital briefs or opinions should arrive for them when they are out), and those who are now earning a good living, but working very hard for it. In this latter group, which under the present favourable conditions of litigation is predominant, it is unusual to find barristers who are content to ease off a little, because this might result in work going elsewhere. As each barrister alone works for himself, he can hardly ever afford to give the impression that he is unlikely to be available if wanted, and he can scarcely afford to be ill. The happy mean between the two groups is rarely found. The members of the first group need more money, those of the second have plenty, but little time to enjoy it. This dilemma would be ended by the introduction of partnerships, which would enable the busy barrister to ease off at times without fearing that his regular solicitor clients will decide to take their custom to some other independent barrister instead for the future.

Of course the saving of some of the busiest barristers' lives has sometimes been the call to the bench. Judges have security of tenure and salary, and the man whose health might have been about to break up may be saved by ceasing to have to compete with his colleagues at the Bar. Judges work hard, but there are regular periods of rest which they need not fill with more work (such as writing or the chairmanship of various committees of inquiry) if they do not wish to do so. It may be worth mentioning here that the suggestion has been made from time to time that academic teachers of law, as well as practising barristers, ought to be eligible for the bench, at least in the appellate courts, where their ability to think about the principles of law involved would be a useful supplement to the more practical approach of the ex-practitioners. It is possible that sometime in the future we may see an occasional academic lawyer made an appellate judge, as has happened in the United States of America, but the argument against it is mostly that academic lawyers in England have no experience of procedure, and so they would be lost in the intricacies of much that goes on in court. This is certainly an objection to their appointment, but it ought not to be insuperable. With a careful introduction to the proceedings of the court and perhaps some instruction, at the instance of the Lord Chancellor's office, in the procedure of lower courts (knowledge of which would be necessary in order to understand many of the matters discussed on appeal), a distinguished academic lawyer ought to be able to take his place on the appellate bench with advantage to himself and his colleagues among the judiciary. It cannot be anticipated that an appointment of this kind is likely for many years, for there is still, regrettably, a considerable prejudice among the members of the practising Bar and on the bench against academic lawyers, and the Lord Chancellor, who would be responsible for any such appointment, is of course also an ex-practitioner. But this prejudice is receding gradually. As was mentioned in Chapter One, the members of the practising Bar and of the bench in the twentieth century are taking more notice of the writings of academic lawyers than their predecessors did, and it is becoming appreciated that, despite his deficiencies in knowledge of procedure, the jurist has much more opportunity to think about 'law in the round', and about the many pressures bearing upon it, than has the practitioner, who is inevitably hampered by the necessity to do the best for his client on the facts of the particular case before him. There is more and more likelihood of a real co-operation between teachers and practitioners in the future, and the appointment of an academic appellate judge may be an eventual result of this happier relationship.

Legal Education

The general provision of legal education for future lawyers has been referred to in Chapter One, where it was pointed out that the two branches of the profession maintain their own examinations which every intending practitioner is required to pass before he becomes qualified. Furthermore the student must serve a period as an articled clerk to a solicitor, if he wishes to become a solicitor, or as pupil to a barrister, if he wishes to practise at the Bar, though the requirement of pupillage for intending barristers has in the past been more of a practical necessity than an actual legal obligation. University law degrees, though they are accepted by the professional bodies as providing exemption for students from a portion of the professional examinations, still are very far from providing a coverage of even a majority of the practical subjects with which a lawyer in practice must be familiar. Civil and criminal procedure, tax law, conveyancing of land, local government law and accounts, to mention but a few subjects, rarely come within university law degree syllabi, while company law, though taught in several Law Faculties, has not penetrated to them all. On the other hand, the study of the more basic common law subjects of contracts and torts, together with aspects of land law and family law, is taken very much more deeply in the universities than in the preparation for professional examinations; while legal history, jurisprudence (which might be described as a study of the science of law, and the purpose of legal principles), comparative law and the principles of Roman law are virtually a monopoly of the universities, though a very moderate coverage of Roman law and of legal history forms a part of the Part I examination for the Bar.

The question arises whether the differences between the coverage and methods adopted by the professional law schools, such as the College of Law and the Council of Legal Education, and by the university Law Faculties should be erased. An advantage of minimising the differences in the approach of the two different kinds of institution to the teaching of law would be that in the course of time their efforts could be fused, and students would be able to cover the necessary book-work for their professional examinations in universities. This would reduce the number of institutions required for the training of lawyers, economise in effort as far as teaching is concerned, and also make possible a requirement that all practising lawyers should have been to one or other of the various universities as part of their training. The articles with a solicitor or pupillage with a barrister could then follow upon the taking of professional examinations, which would themselves follow soon after the end of an undergraduate's career at his university. It is even possible that some arrangement might be made whereby the university and professional examinations themselves might be fused, though it is at present hard to visualise the possibility of the Inns of Court and the Law Society, which so jealously and justifiably watch over the standards demanded from the members of the respective professions, being prepared to surrender any substantial part of their responsibility for determining the competence of students in professional examination papers. It is, however, fair to point out that already the Council of Legal Education employs the services of a number of university teachers of law to give instruction at the Council in London, and to assist the Council in setting and marking some of the papers in the Bar examinations, particularly of course the papers in Roman law and legal history.

Despite the advantages just outlined, the bias of the present author is against any fusion of the legal education provided by the professional law schools on the one hand and by the universities on the other. Though it is submitted that it would be a desirable thing that every practitioner should have had the advantage of a university education, it must not be forgotten that the purpose of a university is not to prepare a man in the practical subjects which he needs to master in order to be able to embark upon his vocation. University education is primarily intended to broaden the mind and to encourage the student to think for himself. When an undergraduate is faced with a legal problem set for him by his tutor he will often be told that it is a matter of little consequence what he thinks about it provided that he does think about it. In a university examination upon a legal subject no good examiner should penalise a student for arguing in favour of a point of view which may not strictly be supported by the legal authorities relevant, or for arguing in favour of reform of the law, provided that the student is aware of the relevant authorities and has been able to display an ability to think about them logically and without folly. A practitioner must be sure he is right, and a professional examination must of necessity be designed to test the ability of a student to give sound advice to his client and to master the actual law as

233

it stands. This requirement is not demanded of an under-graduate, and so there is time to indulge in real thought about the underlying characteristics of law, and its purpose: hence the concentration upon basic subjects within the law, and upon legal history and jurisprudence. There is plenty of time for the assimilation of the vital subjects of practical interest later on in his professional training, and the student who has mastered the art of thinking, which is by no means easy, for real creative thought is a painful process, will be all the more able to discern the vital issues and exact problems at stake in the law in practice.

In the author's view, therefore, the purpose of a university law course is quite different from that of the course in a pro-fessional law school. In a sense, the fact that a student chooses to read law in a university can be regarded as accidental, for any subject will do as the basis for thought. The intricate problems of law, and the wealth of case and statute law, provide excellent ground upon which to exercise the mind, and it is of course necessary that the teacher of law should be well acquainted with the details of his subject so that he may provide the type of accurate guidance needed by his pupils. But the student could just as well choose history, English, politics, philo-sophy, or even some branch of mathematics or science as the subject upon which to train his mental processes. Several highly successful practitioners and judges read other subjects than law at their universities, though most students today who wish to practise law in the long run will naturally deem it more profitable to start work upon some aspects of the subject which is going to concern them for the rest of their lives.

In some subjects it is inevitable that university training should be fairly near to vocational training. Medicine and the sciences are clear examples here. But it is not necessary, or even in any way desirable, that law should follow suit. No university can provide the practical training which the student must gain in chambers or in the solicitor's office, and for university law teachers to feel bound to attempt the teaching of essentially practical subjects like conveyancing or taxation would probably be a waste of their time and talents. The university Law Schools in the United States have already become largely vocational, and graduates of these Law Schools are usually able to take their professional examinations and embark upon actual practice within a very few months of leaving the university. Some of the provincial universities in England are also in danger of becoming too practical in their approach to the law, and there are some law teachers, happily a small minority still, who are beginning to take the attitude in their teaching that certain principles and rules are right and that all other possible interpretations of the authorities are wrong, so that any student who argues in favour of an 'incorrect' rule in an examination paper or in a tutorial gets short shrift. This is a tendency to be deplored, for it militates against the proper training of an undergraduate's mind, and will be likely to hamper him in the practice of his profession in later life. Lawyers should never be narrow-minded, lest they should fail to see the possible implications of a case or rule of law which has not been fully considered before.

The most likely future developments in legal education would seem to be that, while the university Law Faculties will retain their present function and purpose, the two different professional examinations may be fused. With recent reorganisations of the syllabi of both the Bar and the Law Society examinations it has become clear that there is much in common between them. Many of the papers cover similar subjects, and both the Council of Legal Education and the Law Society insist upon a high standard of competence from the candidates. It would seem to be a reasonable economy of effort, therefore, to combine the examinations, and the book-work training required for them. The way may become clear for this development when in a few years' time most of the Commonwealth law students, a majority of whom have been from Africa, cease to come to London for their professional training. In the past these Commonwealth students have formed a large proportion of the audiences at the lectures given at the Council of Legal Education, and of the candidates in the Bar examinations. At present there are still many Africans coming to London to read for the Bar, because in East Africa particularly there are still very few locally qualified native lawyers. But with the independence of the former African and other dependencies within the Commonwealth, there has come the foundation of a number of new universities in these countries, together with their Law Faculties. The present need is to provide active help for these Faculties by the secondment of English law teachers, but when the Faculties are fully established and there have been a few years of graduates turned out by the home law schools, there will no longer be any need for future African law students to come to London for the necessary legal education. This drying up of the flow of Commonwealth law students to London will be gradual, but it is inevitable.

Already the members of the Council of Legal Education, the Inns of Court and the Law Society have been actively considering a fusion of professional law examining, and there have even been suggestions that an intending barrister ought to have to undergo a short period in articles with a *solicitor*, so that he may become acquainted with the processes of the offices of the people who will later, he hopes, feed him with work. The streamlining of the legal profession and its concomitant training requirements will take years, but it is confidently forecast.

INDEX

Index

Index

240